10699213

STRAND PRICE
5 00

BY THE SAME AUTHOR

Wild Justice: The Evolution of Revenge

The Possible She

Inside Soviet Schools

Moscow Conversations

HALF-JEW

A Daughter's Search

for Her

Family's Buried Past

Susan Jacoby

SCRIBNER

New York   London   Toronto   Sydney   Singapore

SCRIBNER

1230 Avenue of the Americas
New York, NY 10020

Copyright © 2000 by Susan Jacoby

All rights reserved, including the right of reproduction
in whole or in part in any form.

SCRIBNER and design are trademarks of Macmillan Library
Reference, USA, Inc., used under license by Simon & Schuster,
the publisher of this work.

Designed by Brooke Koven
Set in Van Dijck MT

Manufactured in the United States of America

1   3   5   7   9   10   8   6   4   2

Library of Congress Cataloging-in-Publication Data

Jacoby, Susan.
Half-Jew: a daughter's search for her family's buried past/Susan Jacoby.
p. cm.
1. Jacoby, Susan—Family. 2. Jacoby family.
3. Jews—United States—Biography.
4. Children of interfaith marriage—United States—Biography.
I. Title.
E184.37.J33A3 2000
929'.2'08992407471—dc21
99-086271

ISBN 0-684-83250-X

"The Place Where I Have Not Been," from *The Early Books of Tehuda Amichai*, © 1968, by Yehuda Amichai. Reprinted by permission of The Sheep Meadow Press, Riverdale-on-Hudson, New York.

Excerpt from "Letter of Recommendation" from *Amen*, © 1977, by Yehuda Amichai. Reprinted by permission of HarperCollins Publishers, Inc.

Excerpts from Dartmouth College administrative and alumni correspondence used in Chapter VI reprinted by permission of Dartmouth College.

For the next generation:

Alexandra Sara Jacoby
Anna Sofia Broderick Jacoby
James Gorman Jacoby
Katherine Louise Jacoby
Jon Maximilian Jacoby Simpson

Jacoby Family Tree

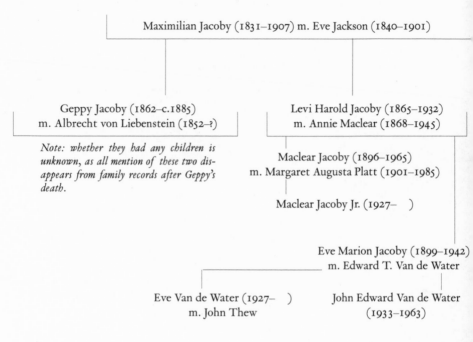

Maximilian Jacoby (1831–1907) m. Eve Jackson (1840–1901)

Geppy Jacoby (1862–c.1885)
m. Albrecht von Liebenstein (1852–?)

Note: whether they had any children is unknown, as all mention of these two disappears from family records after Geppy's death.

Levi Harold Jacoby (1865–1932)
m. Annie Maclear (1868–1945)

Maclear Jacoby (1896–1965)
m. Margaret Augusta Platt (1901–1985)

Maclear Jacoby Jr. (1927–   )

Eve Marion Jacoby (1899–1942)
m. Edward T. Van de Water

Eve Van de Water (1927–   )
m. John Thew

John Edward Van de Water
(1933–1963)

Oswald Nathaniel Jacoby (1870–1931)
m. Edith Sondheim (1878–1966)

Oswald (Ozzie) Nathaniel Jacoby Jr. (1902–1984)
m. Mary Zita McHale (1909–1987)

Edith G. Jacoby (1907–1995)
m. Theodore S. Faller (1900?–1982)

James O. Jacoby (1933–1991)
m. Judy Mudd (1936–   )

James Jacoby (1962–   )

Jon Jacoby (1938–   )
m. Caroline All (1940–   )

Mary Barstow Jacoby (1966–   )
Elizabeth Banpfield Jacoby (1968–   )
Susannah Swinton Jacoby (1970–   )

Robert Jacoby (1914–1986)
m. Irma Broderick (1921–   )

Susan Jacoby (1945–   )
m. Anthony M. Astrachan (1932–1992)

divorced, no children

Robert James Jacoby (1948–   )
m. Eve Moscicki (1948–   )

Alexandra Sara Jacoby (1982–   )
Anna Sofia Broderick Jacoby (1990–   )

Everybody knows there is no fineness or accuracy of suppression;
if you hold down one thing you hold down the adjoining.
     —SAUL BELLOW, *The Adventures of Augie March*

CONTENTS

ACKNOWLEDGMENTS

THIS HISTORY OF THE Jacoby family would have been extremely difficult to reconstruct without the many photographs supplied by Judy Mudd Jacoby, Jon and Caroline Jacoby, and Maclear (Mac) Jacoby Jr. The photos, dating from the early 1860s, provided essential documentation of private life in a family that saved almost none of its personal correspondence. Jon, Mac, and another cousin, Eve Van de Water Thew, were generous in sharing memories of what they learned—and did not learn—about the family history from their parents.

I am grateful to Walter Austerer, a true craftsman, for his meticulous restoration of the old, originally tattered, family snapshots.

Anne Ostendarp, archivist of the Rauner Special Collections Library at Dartmouth College, helped me locate correspondence from the 1920s and 1930s on the subject of "the Jewish problem" at Dartmouth and made me realize how much Dartmouth has changed for the better since my father was a student there nearly seventy years ago. All of the excerpts from administrative correspondence, quoted in Chapter VI, are reprinted by permission of Dartmouth

College. They include letters from the President's Office Records and the Ford Whelden Papers. I am particularly indebted to Alexandra J. Shepard, whose senior history honors thesis, "Seeking a Sense of Place: Jewish Students in the Dartmouth Community, 1920–1940," first drew my attention to the existence of these revealing letters.

The Columbiana Collection at Columbia University's Butler Memorial Library; the New-York Historical Society; and the Polytechnical Preparatory Country Day School provided invaluable information about the lives of the Jacoby men in New York.

Angeline Goreau, Alex Levin, and Jack Schwartz read the manuscript at various stages and made important editorial suggestions.

As always, Georges and Anne Borchardt, my literary agents, gave me their full support. Denise Shannon, who worked at the Borchardt agency for many years, always seemed to come up with a new magazine commission for me when I needed it most during the long period of research on this book.

Aaron Asher, my longtime editor before his retirement from publishing, scrutinized the penultimate draft with the invaluable combination of a friend's empathy and a merciless professional's critical eye.

Jane Rosenman, my editor at Scribner, gave me and my book the meticulous attention that every writer wants and needs but doesn't always get.

Robert James Jacoby, my brother, confirmed the memories we share.

Alexandra Sara Jacoby, my niece, was one of my first readers for portions of the manuscript. She gave me a special form of encouragement that I truly needed at that stage of the work.

Irma Broderick Jacoby, my mother, gave me unstinting support—something not to be taken for granted by a daughter writing a book about her father—and scoured her memory to correct factual errors.

PREFACE

THERE ARE MANY WAYS to measure large expanses of time—by light-years, geological eras, evolutionary stages, millennia, centuries, calendar years. All of these standards—even the fleeting year—tend to distance the past from the present. Devotees of the forgive-and-forget school of history (usually members of groups with little to forgive) frequently admonish minorities to stop bearing a grudge for what are, if viewed from a strictly chronological perspective, old and moldy grievances. Why should African-Americans expect an apology for slavery when, after all, there have been no slaves in America for more than 135 years? Why are American Jews still so touchy about anti-Semitism when, after all, it has been more than forty years since Jewish opportunities were significantly affected by quotas in academia and restrictive covenants in desirable neighborhoods?

But when generations replace years as the standard of measurement, time is telescoped rather than expanded: events that have a "once upon a time" quality when consigned to a hundred-year-old dustbin acquire an immediacy when viewed through the eyes of "my grandparents" or even "my great-grandparents." A black American born in 1920, for instance, might easily have heard searing firsthand accounts of slavery from a beloved grandparent born in 1850. To put it another way, only one generation lies between those born into slavery and millions of Americans who are alive today.

I did not begin to appreciate the telescoping effect of a generational approach to time until 1969, when I was twenty-four, newly married, and enjoying a honeymoon in Florence. In one of those serendipitous encounters that occur more frequently in detective novels than in life, an old woman fainted in my arms in the courtyard of the Uffizi. After I helped the weary but still imperious lady to a chair in a café overlooking the Piazza della Signoria, we exchanged names and discovered a connection.

She turned out to be Estelle Frankfurter, the only sister of Supreme Court Justice Felix Frankfurter (as she informed me without my asking). When I told her my name, her exhausted expression was replaced by a look of sharp interest. "Jacoby . . . you aren't by any chance related to the famous bridge player Oswald Jacoby?" I informed her that I was the daughter of Robert Jacoby and that the bridge champion was his elder brother—Uncle Ozzie to me.

"I didn't know there was a younger son," Miss Frankfurter said dismissively, "but I always hoped I'd meet your uncle one day. I was personally acquainted with your grandfather—a most charming man. Of course, you know that he was named Oswald too." In fact, I did not know my grandfather's first name—or much of anything else about his life—because his children, including my own father, almost never talked about him. When I told Miss Frankfurter I would be indebted to her for any information she might be able to give me about the Jacoby family, her eyes lit up with a glee that contained a hint of malice.

"Why, my dear, there was a time when people thought your grandfather might become the first Jewish justice to sit on the Supreme Court. He went to school with Justice Cardozo—they were quite good friends at one time, I believe—and he was one of the more talented trial lawyers of his generation in New York. That was in your grandfather's youth, of course. But there were certain—shall we call them *weaknesses?*—that prevented him from realizing his potential." (In 1916, Louis Brandeis became the first Jew to serve on the Court. Benjamin Cardozo was appointed by Herbert Hoover in 1932 and Felix Frankfurter by Franklin Roosevelt in 1939.)

In four sentences, the redoubtable Miss Frankfurter—whose store of gossip concerning the New York (especially the New York Jewish) legal community seemed inexhaustible—had told me more about my grandfather, who died in 1931, than my father, aunt, uncle, and grandmother had revealed since I was old enough to begin asking questions. Miss Frankfurter was an emissary from the not-so-distant past—a past in which the question of when, and whether, a Jew might be elevated to the Supreme Court was a matter of more than passing concern to the Frankfurter family and its most brilliant son. What really struck me, though, was the casual reference to the Jacoby family's Jewish origins. Brought up as a Roman Catholic in a small Midwestern town, far from New York City, where my father was born and raised, I had only recently figured out, and elicited the admission from my dad, that the Jacobys were Jews. Or, as my father corrected me, that they had been "born Jewish."

At that moment, I was too entranced by my own future to focus on the past. My new husband and I, both reporters for *The Washington Post*, were on our way to the Soviet Union, where he would take up his duties as the paper's Moscow bureau chief and I would gather material for a book on everyday Russian life. Nevertheless, that night I took careful notes on my conversation with Miss Frankfurter, whom I intended to write as soon as I arrived in Moscow. Predictably, Russia and my new marriage would absorb all of my energies for the next few years. Inquiring into "everyday" life, in an era when the secret police did everything they could to impede foreign journalists, proved to be an arduous round-the-clock effort that left no time or emotional space for anything else. My notes from Florence gathered dust in a yellowing file marked "FAMILY," and nearly two decades would pass before I felt free—in large measure as a result of my father's death in 1986—to fully explore a past that had caused him so much pain.

Happy or unhappy, nearly all families have their secrets. The difference between a happy and an unhappy family lies not so much in the objective repugnance or the scandalous nature of whatever is being hidden but in the degree of energy and organization that a profoundly unhappy family invests in preserving the secret—regardless of how innocuous it might seem to others. My father grew up in such a family, dedicated not only to hiding its Jewish past but to maintaining many other small and large deceptions ranged around the primary fiction. These secrets defined and distorted the lives of my Jacoby grandparents, deeply wounded my father and his siblings, and left my generation with a legacy composed of a surface *tabula rasa* with layers of pain underneath.

At the time I met Miss Frankfurter, I knew only that my father, his older brother, and his sister had all married Irish Catholics, converted to their spouses' religion, and done everything possible to prevent their children from learning anything about the family's real history. It would take me years to sift through the fictions created by the three generations before me, beginning at the midpoint of the nineteenth century with the arrival in New York of my great-grandfather, Maximilian Jacoby.

An acculturated, German-speaking Jew from Breslau (ceded to Poland, and renamed Wroclaw, after World War II), Maximilian was one of many refugees who left their homelands in central and eastern Europe after the unsuccessful democratic movements of 1848. In the United States, he would shorten his Teutonic name to Max and build a successful art importing business.

Max's sons, including my grandfather with the mysterious "weaknesses," had attained enough success by the turn of the century to be considered worthy subjects of personal profiles in various New York publications. In these articles, Max was always described as a political refugee "of German origin." Of course, this locution could hardly have fooled anyone in New York. My conversation with

Miss Frankfurter forcefully impressed one fact upon me: had my father remained where he was, he could not have escaped who and what he was. Only by leaving New York, and settling far from any centers of Jewish population, could he hope to transform himself into someone other than a New York Jew.

Until I began to think in generations rather than years, I could not begin to comprehend why my father's family felt that the transformation was necessary. I was born in 1945, my father in 1914, my grandfather in 1870, and my great-grandfather in 1831. Now it seems to me that nothing has been more important than these dates—the earliest separated from the latest by 114 years but only two generations—in my effort to understand why my father, and his father, made the choices they did. My grandfather came of age in New York at a time when his alma mater, Columbia University, held entrance exams on the High Holidays in order to discourage religious Jews from applying. And my father grew up in a country where only yesterday—not "once upon a time"—he was called kike on the school playground.

In my father's and grandfather's generations, there were of course many ways for a Jew to respond to the tantalizing American combination of unprecedented opportunities for Jewish advancement with anti-Semitic barriers that could not always be anticipated. The Jacobys' long, concerted effort to transform themselves into gentiles was one such response. This book is my attempt to understand what was gained and what was lost in that incomplete transformation.

I

Always Say Jewish

MY PATERNAL GRANDFATHER died in 1931, when my father was only seventeen, and Dad always claimed that every photograph of his dimly remembered parent had been lost in a fire. That, like much of what my father chose to say about his childhood family, was untrue. In 1986, after Dad's funeral, my aunt Edith unexpectedly handed me an eighty-year-old snapshot of the elusive paterfamilias, Oswald Nathaniel Jacoby. At forty, I looked for the first time into the eyes of the man my father claimed not to remember but remembered all too well.

The 1906 image, captured at a time when families were just beginning to chronicle their lives in candid photos, has retained a surprising clarity. A robust man, clearly in the prime of life, stretches out in a hammock with an equally robust, curly-haired boy—his four-year-old son, Ozzie—and a small terrier. This is my grandfather at thirty-six—a provocatively handsome and seductive figure, staring into the camera with a sensual, worldly smile that suggests a wide variety of possibilities . . . anything, really, except the contented Edwardian domesticity implicit in the trio of father, first son, and family dog. I recognize Oswald Jacoby as the sort of man I could fall in love with instantly—a more dangerous, less reliable version of my father. Beneath the superficial resemblances—the same lavish dark hair just beginning to gray, the same coiled, barely concealed restlessness that makes the hammock, surrounded by greenery on the porch of a summer house, look more like a stage prop than a resting place—is a cynical expression I never saw on my father's face.

Looking at my grandfather for the first time, I can easily believe that this was a man who let his children down badly, so badly that they never displayed a picture of him in their homes. Perhaps I think this only because I am gazing with hindsight at the appealingly arranged domestic scene. I know that the sunny little boy will be forced to grow up too fast by the fecklessness of the man in the hammock. I know that his daughter, his favorite child, will be scarred forever by discovering him with another woman in the bed he usually shared with his wife. I know that by the time he dies, in mysterious circumstances, he will have gambled away the money that should have taken care of his widow and sent the neglected baby of the family—the young man who will become my father—to college. I know that this charmer in the picture is a man who cannot be trusted.

MY FATHER, by contrast, was a man who made every effort not to let his children down—but he too was a man with secrets. Known for his unfailing optimism, gregariousness, and a childlike inability to conceal his emotions, he grew taciturn only when the subject of his family was raised. "What was your daddy like?" I would ask when I was seven or eight. "Why, I hardly knew Father," he would answer. (For my dad and his siblings, their long-dead father was always, in the Victorian manner, Father with a capital *F*, and their living mother was Mother with a capital *M*.) For much of my childhood, I assumed that my dad had been a baby, rather than a young man about to enter college, at the time of the death of the distant Father he hardly seemed to remember.

From an early age, then, I sensed the existence of painful secrets somehow connected to my grandfather. I knew that my father, Aunt Edith, and Uncle Ozzie had married Catholics and converted to the Faith; I did not know that they had also invented a Protestant pre-conversion past and lied, by omission or commission, whenever they were asked a question that might reveal their true origins. "What were you before you were a Catholic, Daddy?" "An Episcopalian." The baffling storehouse of inconsistencies that made up my father's version of his own and his family's past remained closed to me until, in 1965, I left the small Michigan town where I had spent most of my childhood for the more cosmopolitan environment of Washington, D.C. There, at age twenty-one, I managed to put some of the pieces together—mainly the Jacoby name and my dad's "Jewish" appearance—and to penetrate the outer layers of avoidance and omission in the family narrative. I finally understood that all of my father's evasions had been designed to conceal the fact that he was born a Jew.

"A Jewish parent is hardly a skeleton in the closet in this day and age," a friend of mine remarked when the Jewish lineage of Secretary of State Madeleine Albright became a major news story in 1997. True. But Albright's evident distress at the revelation, and her initial resistance when reporters, as was quite natural in view of her prominence, began looking into her background, demonstrated that there are people—only some of them Jews—for whom Jewish origins remain a highly charged subject. Albright's parents, Czech Jews of considerable prominence who fled to safety in London on the eve of World War II, had determinedly attempted to conceal their Jewishness after the war. They never told their daughter that they were Jews or that most of the family had perished in concentration camps. While it is not surprising that Madeleine the girl believed what her parents told her, it is difficult to credit her assertion that as an adult—and a diplomat with wide-ranging international contacts—she never suspected what was well known to many of her contemporaries, including surviving Czech Jewish relatives of whose existence she was fully aware (and whom she stonewalled when they attempted to contact her after she was appointed U.S. Ambassador to the United Nations). Even in this day and age, there are still Jews—some with positions in society that would seem to render them impregnable—who fear that a clear-eyed glance backward can only consign them to the fate of Lot's wife.

For my own father, his Jewish lineage definitely was a skeleton in the closet, a source of shame that shadowed his entire life and required him to construct a false identity in an effort to shield his children. Long before I had any idea that my father was a Jew, I sensed a reservoir of self-doubt at the core of his nature. It expressed itself in many ways, but nowhere was it more evident than in his life-long tendency to deprecate the personal and professional achievements that represented a real triumph over his own sense of unworthiness.

As an adult, I felt considerable guilt about asking my father questions that evoked his old sense of shame, but my need to know was stronger than my desire to protect him. "Why do you gnaw at this?" Dad would ask, over and over, until his death. "Didn't your mother and I give you a good foundation? Don't you have a wonderful job? Why can't you just let this Jewish business alone?" He was the reason—he and the religion in which he and my mother had tried to raise me. I just never could accept it, even in the stage of childhood when it is natural to accept what everyone around you believes. Yet such was the power of the Roman Catholic Church of that era—"it was the only *The* Church," a Catholic wit once said—that I invested a great deal of my emotional energy, at a time when most teenagers' minds are filled with dreams of the opposite sex (not that there wasn't room for those too), in a struggle to escape the prediction of the nuns: "Once a Catholic, always a Catholic." The discovery that my father was a Jew—just as I embarked upon adult life—seemed to offer one explanation for the smoldering *no* that had shaped my girlhood.

When I say I had no idea that my father was a Jew, I mean I had no idea on a conscious level. Until I began writing this book, I had

forgotten one of the recurrent dreams of my adolescence—a nightmare in which I was a prisoner in a concentration camp. My head
was shaved, but I wasn't wearing a striped uniform; the yellow star
was attached to my everyday clothes. "I haven't done anything, I
don't belong here," I would say. Adolf Hitler himself would reply,
"That's what every prisoner says. And we've even let you keep your
clothes. But they won't last long. You're no better than anyone else
here." Concentration camp dreams, I learned as an adult, were in no
way unusual among my contemporaries—children born shortly
before, during, or soon after World War II. But while I have many
friends who remember similar dreams, every one of them is Jewish,
brought up in a Jewish home where the murder of the six million was
treated (and this was sometimes literally the case) as a death in the
family.

As teenagers, some of my Jewish friends were exasperated at
their parents' "harping" on the Holocaust—and they were angry
that they could not escape the camps even in their dreams. It never
occurred to me, as an adolescent, that either of my parents had any
connection with the nightmares that left me in a cold sweat. Hitler's
attempt to exterminate the Jews was discussed in my home—and
this was unusual in Okemos, Michigan, a small suburban community, with few Jewish residents, where we lived throughout my
teenage years. My parents talked about the Holocaust (though they,
like most Americans at the time, did not call it that) in the same
informative tone that they talked about the Depression, the dropping of the atomic bomb on Hiroshima, and the Cold War. If we
watched large portions of the trial of Adolf Eichmann on television
in 1961, this merely reflected my parents' customary interest in history and current events. Neither my mother nor my father said anything to indicate that our family had any extra reason (indignation at
injustice and suffering being a given) to worry about what had been
done to the Jews of Europe. But my vivid nightmares suggest that I
was receiving another, unarticulated message: *You're no better than
anyone else here.*

I stopped having that dream in my early twenties, not long after I figured out, and my father acknowledged, that he was a Jew.

WHEN CERTAIN subjects are routinely suppressed rather than explicitly and dramatically forbidden, they impinge upon the consciousness of a child intermittently, as minor discordances that cause a momentary sense of unease before being dismissed. One day, when I was in the sixth grade at St. Thomas Aquinas School—one of the thousands of parochial schools built by upwardly mobile American Catholics who moved to the suburbs after the war—I proudly read my composition about a girl trying to concentrate on her homework while a spider concentrated on spinning a web underneath her dress. Everyone in the class laughed out loud—everyone, that is, except Sister Misericordia. She called me up to her desk after school and said sharply, "That composition was in very poor taste." Mortified, I blinked back tears as I made my way to the cloakroom to put on my boots. Sister was whispering to another nun, "Of course, there may be *certain influences* within the family. The father, you know, is a convert. I believe he was born in *New York*." Later that night, I repeated Sister's comments to my mother. "Just forget it," she advised, ignoring my question about the meaning of those "certain influences" and reminding me that no nun would have been pleased with a story alluding to undergarments or bare legs. After kissing me good night, Mom added with a studied casualness, "Don't bother your father about this."

I never forgot the incident and my teacher's tone, with its faint but unmistakably derogatory implications. I could summon up the sound of Sister's voice a decade later in Washington, where most of my colleagues at the *Post* assumed, because of my last name, that I was Jewish—and where I finally realized that a man named Jacoby, with a mother whose maiden name was Sondheim, must have been born a Jew. Which made me a half-Jew—whatever that might mean. As a reporter in the racially charged atmosphere of Washington in the mid-sixties, I was much more interested in how it felt to be black in white America than in what it meant to be a half-Jew raised as a Catholic.

At that point, I simply could not understand why my father had tried so hard, throughout my childhood and even after I was old enough to figure out the secret for myself, to conceal his true background. I was still measuring time by years, not by generations. I knew that he knew that I knew, but I never brought up the subject until I blurted out my knowledge of my father's Jewish origins in a manner calculated to establish his misguidedness and the superiority of my own "moral compass" (a term that turns up with embarrassing frequency in my writings from that era). In the kitchen of the house where I grew up on Greenwood Drive, Dad was making blueberry muffins—cooking (but not cleaning up after himself) being one of the many pursuits that set him apart from my friends' more conventional Father-Knows-Best fathers. At fifty-two, a bundle of nervous energy who would never develop a paunch, my dad usually jumped out of bed around five o'clock and was deeply involved in something—cooking, gardening, cleaning out the basement—by the time the rest of the family woke up. On this particular morning, he had been looking forward to nothing more complicated than sharing a hot buttered muffin with his little girl. Home for a brief break from my dream job at the *Post*—I was in that transitional stage when fledgling adults still refer to their parents' house as "home"—I disrupted the morning peace and ended the silence between us by informing my father that it was no longer necessary for him to "go on pretending" that he hadn't been born into a Jewish family. I announced my absolute delight at the certainty that "at least one" of my parents was a Jew. The only thing that could make me happier, I added, would be to learn there was also a Negro in the family tree.

Choking on the flour that coated his nostrils and lips, Dad turned toward me, lit a cigarette, and cursed under his breath as an ash fell into the batter. His eyes filled with tears as he said, "I never wanted you and your brother to feel that if you didn't get something you wanted in life, it was because you were Jewish. I never wanted you to blame me for this . . . this burden, this *cross*. And by the way, always say *Jewish*. *Jew* is rude and disrespectful."

My father refused to explain himself any further, and though I experienced a belated sense of shame at my outburst, I was incapable of understanding the sources of his raw emotion. Not only had my father told me almost nothing about his past, but his suggestion that being a Jew, or a half-Jew, might prevent me from getting anything I wanted seemed preposterous in 1966. By then it had become chic to be Jewish—in the journalistic world I already inhabited in Washington and in the broader cultural world to which I aspired. Because I had been raised as a Catholic and educated in parochial elementary schools, and spent most of my childhood in a relatively small town with few Jews (though I was born in Chicago), I did not really think about the meaning of my father's name and appearance until I started meeting a great many Jews as an adult. Only then did it become apparent to me—with the obviousness of a lightbulb flashing over a cartoon character's head—that my father, born and raised in New York City, must be a Jew. *New York Jew*. With his lavish, curly black hair and his moderately but unmistakably hooked nose, my father *looked* so very Jewish—or so very much like what Jews are thought to look like.

In Washington, friends often asked about my background because they had trouble putting my last name together with the blond shiksa looks I had inherited from my mother's Irish-German side of the family. The truth was that my shiksa image would have been much less striking without the assistance of Lady Clairol. When I began sifting through childhood pictures for this book, I was quite surprised to see snapshots of a little girl with light-to-medium-brown hair. I have thought of myself as a blonde since my mom began applying peroxide to my tresses in ninth grade. Most of my friends' mothers, at a time when artificial hair coloring still conveyed a whiff of moral turpitude (hence the success of the advertising campaign with the sly question, "Does she or doesn't she?," and the immortal answer, "Only her hairdresser knows for sure . . ."), would have grounded their daughters for pursuing blondness in a bottle. "You mean it was your *mom's* idea?" an envious friend asked. I now wonder whether my mother's alteration of my hair color at such an early age was an attempt, on a conscious or unconscious level, to make me look more like her family and less like a Jacoby. I do know that when I recently tried on a brown-haired wig over my blond "highlights"—just to see what sort of a brunette I would make—the face in the mirror looked like no one in my mother's family but instead bore a startling resemblance to a nineteenth-century portrait of my Jacoby great-grandmother. How easily I discarded the memory of the brown-haired girl—even though I am perfectly aware that my blondness as an adult is attributable not to nature but to the efforts of professional hair colorists who took up, at considerable expense to me, where my mother left off.

At any rate, I looked like an archetypal shiksa to people who met me in the mid-sixties in Washington. When my name prompted them to ask if I was Jewish, I always answered "half"—and wished that I didn't have to qualify my reply. Interestingly, black acquaintances asked the question more readily than whites—and I interpreted the inquiry as a compliment in an era when Jews and blacks, at least in my world, were linked by a commitment to the civil rights movement and were more than willing to give each other the benefit of the doubt. For this and many other reasons, I longed to identify myself with Jews as deeply as my father had once longed to deny his origins. How could I understand a man who would not use the word *Jew* as a noun because he viewed it as an epithet? Until the end of his life in 1986, I never heard my father call himself, or anyone else, a Jew. Jewish was as Jewish as he got.

I WAS SEVEN when Dad converted to Catholicism—from the Episcopal Church, I was led to believe. There was no shame attached to being a convert in the American Catholic world of the fifties. Quite the contrary. The nuns and priests always emphasized that converts were far more deserving of praise than "born" Catholics, because a convert had voluntarily chosen to assume the obligations imposed by the Church. That was why I didn't know what to make of the unfamiliar edge in Sister Misericordia's voice when she linked conversion with "certain influences."

My mother and her parents knew the truth about my father's origins, and they acceded to his request that the facts be concealed from my brother Rob and me. My maternal grandmother, who was still vibrant and clearheaded before she died in 1999 at the age of ninety-nine, told me not long before her death that she vividly remembered the day my father revealed his "secret." "Bob told us he wanted us to know 'the whole truth' about him before we gave our blessing to the marriage," Granny recalled. "Of course, he also told us he and your mother were going to get married whether we gave our blessing or not. . . . When it was all out in the open, your gramps said, 'Well, that's a relief. I thought we were going to find out you'd been in jail.' I felt bad for Bob that he felt so bad—there were tears in his eyes— but those were different times and I understand his not wanting you kids to know when you came along. Later, when the war was over, and we knew about the concentration camps . . . well, it's not something you'd want to pass on to your children, if you could avoid it. Of course, that was probably a wrong way of thinking, an old-fashioned way of thinking. But it was how your dad felt. And to be honest, it was how we felt too. I feel a little ashamed of that today."

Don't ask, don't tell. At the time of our kitchen confrontation in the summer of 1966, my father's closed-off attitude toward his own and his family's past had not changed appreciably since the 1940s. But he began to open up that same year when his mother, Edith Sondheim Jacoby, died in New York at the age of eighty-eight.

We buried her on a raw November day, surrounded by driving sleet that undermined the footing of the mourners at the grave site, in St. Peter's Roman Catholic Cemetery on Staten Island. My mother was recovering from an illness and could not make the trip from Michigan, so my father phoned me in Washington and asked me to fly up to New York to meet him for the funeral—an extraordinary request in view of his usual impulse to keep his children far removed from the family into which he was born. His desire to have me near him, in spite of (or perhaps because of) the expected presence of his brother and sister at the funeral, spoke eloquently of his unwillingness to deal with the family of his childhood without support and comfort from the family he had created, and drawn solace from, as an adult.

When Dad was born in 1914—the youngest of three siblings— his mother was thirty-six. A chilly woman of Victorian demeanor, Granny Jacoby frequently referred to my father as her "accident." When my brother and I wrote to thank her for a birthday present (usually something, like a bookmark, that no child wants for a gift), we would open with "Dear Granny Jacoby"—never just "Granny"— because, as far as we were concerned, our real granny was our mom's softhearted mother. Granny Jacoby once suggested that I call her Nana, but I never did. On our annual visits, I addressed her as nothing but "you"—an omission she was too perceptive to miss. To my "Would you please pass the potatoes," she would reply, "Whom are you addressing? A ewe is a female sheep."

One of the least pleasant experiences of my girlhood was my family's annual thousand-mile drive from our home in Michigan to the quiet Staten Island street where my father's mother and sister lived. Equally oppressed by the discomfort of car travel before the age of air-conditioning and by the prospect of seeing Granny Jacoby again, I suffered from severe nausea during those days on the road. My usually cheerful father grew more snappish as we approached New York. Somewhere in the Bronx, he always managed to lose his way and miss the turnoff for Brooklyn and the Bay Ridge terminal of the Staten Island ferry.

As we passed through Brooklyn, Dad never stopped to show us his old school or the house where he spent most of his childhood. Nor did I ask to visit any of the scenes of my father's youth. Even though the declared purpose of these trips to New York was to enable my brother and me to become acquainted with our Jacoby relatives, I surely sensed that on some level, my father didn't want to be there at all.

After we found the ferry entrance and made our way to Granny Jacoby's apartment—always several hours late—she would say something like, "Robert, it's fortunate that we planned a cold supper so that supper couldn't get cold." "Mother," my dad would reply, "it's wonderful to see you too." I developed a real antipathy toward my aging grandmother during those brief visits. She belittled my father's job as an accountant and compared him negatively (as she had when he was a boy) to his elder brother and her favorite child, Ozzie. Ozzie—the little boy in the 1906 snapshot—was born in 1902 and named after his father. He would grow up to become the family star—one of the two most famous tournament bridge players (the other was Charles Goren) of his generation; a syndicated newspaper columnist; and a prolific author of books on bridge, canasta, and backgammon. A calculating professional at the card games, requiring immense skill, that made his reputation, Ozzie was also a compulsive gambler who would come out on top in a lucrative bridge or backgammon tournament and promptly lose his winnings in after-hours games and gambling establishments. There the odds always favored the house (as Ozzie himself wrote in many newspaper articles intended to discourage novices who thought they had figured out a way to beat the system). But my uncle didn't take his own advice. In the absence of formalized gambling, he would bet on anything from the length of time it would take room service to arrive to the number of steps in the staircase of an apartment building. My father shared this "gambling gene" (as he called it many years later), but I didn't know that until I was in my teens and Dad's gambling was only a bad memory for my parents, who always conducted their arguments about money behind closed doors. The gambling of the Jacoby men, although it was a pattern formed over generations, was a subject the family rarely discussed openly; *reckless* and *profligate* were words the Jacoby wives applied to their husbands when they thought the children were asleep.

At those rare Jacoby family gatherings in New York, there was talk of a moneyed past, but no one explained how or why the money had disappeared. Nostalgic references were made to the early part of the century—before my father came along—when the Jacobys had owned a summer home near Saratoga in upstate New York and lived in a splendid apartment on Manhattan's Riverside Drive. Granny Jacoby almost never mentioned her long-deceased husband, and I was not even sure of his birth and death dates until I looked up his name in *The New York Times Index* in 1990. To my surprise (for I had never placed much credence in the occasional allusions to my grandfather's brilliance), he turned out to have merited a substantial collection of clippings in the *Times* morgue—especially substantial in view of the fact that most of the articles appeared when he was still under thirty-five.

The man whose family tried to erase him from its collective memory was born on December 24, 1870, and entered Columbia University in the fall of 1886. Oswald Jacoby had passed the Columbia entrance examination at fourteen but could not begin his studies until the following year because fifteen was the mandatory minimum age for entering freshmen. He would graduate as the youngest member of the Class of 1890. Benjamin Cardozo, who graduated in 1889, was also the youngest in his class—a social liability that may have brought the precocious teenagers together at Columbia. After graduation, the nineteen-year-old Oswald bowed to his father's wish that he join him in the family import business. Soon afterward, though, Max gave in to his son's desire to enter law school. By the early 1900s, Oswald was an up-and-coming Manhattan lawyer, often mentioned in the press as a brilliant trial attorney, and had started his own family with Edith Sondheim, the daughter of a Brooklyn classics teacher.

By the time my father was born, just before the outbreak of World War I, something had gone terribly wrong with Oswald's career. The family had moved from Manhattan to Brooklyn—a definite step down from Riverside Drive. While Uncle Ozzie and Aunt

Edith had attended private schools, my father had to make do with a public elementary school. In the homes of my grandmother and aunt, there were pictures on display of Ozzie, Edith, and Bobbie as children—always with their mother or aunts but not with their father. My father, aunt, and uncle were unable or unwilling (probably both) to provide a context for these snapshots. The one unfailing topic of conversation on our family visits to Staten Island—always introduced by Edith—was the remarkable coincidence, if that is what it was, of the Jacoby siblings all having met, fallen in love with, and married Catholics, thereby placing themselves directly in the beam of God's grace.

Edith, born in 1907, had married and divorced in her wild youth—but by the time I met her, she had become a truly devout Catholic convert and a devoted wife to Uncle Ted. Ted—Theodore S. Faller—was a Macy's executive and a millionaire landowner on Staten Island, where real estate values had skyrocketed in anticipation of the opening of the Verrazano Bridge. Uncle Ted was also a Papal Knight, an honor conferred for extraordinary services (and contributions) to the Church. Edith's status as a divorcee, as divorced women of her generation were customarily called, had posed a grave problem when she and Ted fell in love in the late thirties. Then (as now), divorced Catholics were prohibited from remarrying within the Church unless their original marriages had been ecclesiastically annulled; the same prohibition applied to a marriage between a Catholic like Ted, who had never been married, and any divorced person—Catholic or non-Catholic. Edith and Ted had originally applied for an arcane ecclesiastical exemption, called the Pauline Privilege, which might have allowed them to marry within the Church because Edith had not been baptized in any faith at the time of her first marriage. But it turned out that the Privilege applied only when *both* partners in the original marriage were unbaptized. Edith's first husband, whom she and her mother always called "that wretch, Feeney," had been a Catholic himself. Just when it seemed that Edith and Ted would have to give each other up or live in sin, the wretched

Feeney died (a victim, it was said, of liver failure brought on by chronic alcoholism)—a fortuitous event that Edith considered nothing less than miraculous. She had become a widow in the eyes of the Church, and she and Ted were free to marry.

In view of Ted's piety, it is highly unlikely that he would have married Edith had he not been able to make her his wife within the Church. If they had been wed in a civil ceremony, he would have had to resign himself to living in what the Church declared to be a state of mortal sin. That hadn't bothered Feeney, but it would have proved an insupportable burden to Ted, who, in spite of a demanding executive schedule, made time to attend Mass and receive communion several times a week. Edith herself attended daily Mass and constantly prayed for the souls of her less pious brothers; she considered it a sign of God's special grace that Uncle Ozzie, who had avoided (or evaded) the embrace of the Church throughout many years of marriage, finally agreed to be baptized after he broke his back in an automobile accident and his survival seemed to be in doubt. Ozzie did recover, and his wife took great pleasure in reminding him that baptism wasn't something you could undo. Of all the Jacobys, only my obdurate grandmother continued to resist her daughter's pleas that she convert to Catholicism. From time to time, Aunt Edith would declare, "We must always remember that Our Lord was born a Jew"—an admonition that struck me as an utterly mad *non sequitur* when I was a child. Why should I care that Our Lord was born a Jew?

In my father's family, two and two never made four—whether the subject was something as complicated as religion or as straightforward as a cause and date of death. Dad believed his father had died of a stroke. When I was in my twenties, Aunt Edith told me her father had expired of a heart attack after being run over by a car—the first of her many versions of the end of the paterfamilias. Still later, she told me he had died of syphilis as well as of a failing heart (something Ozzie agreed was a distinct possibility, if not a certainty).

• • •

MY GRANDMOTHER'S funeral was one of the few occasions that brought my father, aunt, and uncle together—at least for a half hour at the grave site. And Aunt Edith got her wish: my grandmother died a nominal Catholic, though she was already suffering from senile dementia when she agreed (or so it was said) to be baptized in the nursing home where she spent her last years. Her funeral Mass was held in St. Christopher's Church, where the Faller family had long been parishioners, and her eulogy was delivered by a priest who obviously never knew her. "Mrs. Jacoby was a woman of great charity and culture," he declared. "Culture, yes," whispered Ozzie, who had announced his arrival, en route from his home in Dallas to a bridge tournament in Paris, by propping his portable typewriter directly in front of the coffin in a manner suggestive of a pharaonic offering intended to accompany Mother into the afterworld. "Don't you think Mother would rather have a lock of your hair?" asked my father. Ozzie explained that he needed to turn out one of his newspaper columns before taking off for Paris, and he didn't want to forget the typewriter. "Take that thing out to the vestibule," Aunt Edith hissed. "You know how Mother hated lateness." *Dies irae.*

In the cemetery, Edith Sondheim Jacoby was laid to rest in Uncle Ted's family plot, where she became the lone Jacoby under a headstone inscribed with the names and dates of countless Fallers, Doughertys, and Keegans. As we drove away after the burial ceremony, my father turned to me and said in a bleak and unfamiliar voice, "She never really loved me, and now she never will." I asked him whether he would mind if I tried to discover more about his family's shuttered past. "Even if I did, I couldn't stop you," he replied, neatly sidestepping the question. As he put me on the plane for Washington, his last words were, "I hope you're not going to become too obsessed with this Jewish business."

II

Conversions

And as he journeyed, he came near Damascus: and suddenly there
shined round about him a light from heaven: And he fell to the earth,
and heard a voice saying unto him, Saul, Saul, why persecutest thou
me?

—*The Acts of the Apostles, 9:3–4*

IN THE RELIGION CLASSES of my childhood, Paul was always
described as "the first Jewish convert." That Jesus himself was a Jew
was never mentioned explicitly until high school, when the apparent
paradox would presumably be less puzzling to the students. Saul's
transformation into Paul was presented as a metaphor for the miracle
of newfound faith: blinded by error, a man regains his sight through
the inexplicable grace of God. "Conversions of convenience"—
sometimes called "social conversions"—were discouraged by the
Church. Before baptism, a non-Catholic married to a Catholic was
questioned at great length about the sincerity of his intentions, in
an effort to ascertain whether he was converting out of a true belief
in Roman Catholic teachings or simply to please his spouse. I have

no idea how my father answered these questions, because his was surely a social conversion—if social motivation is understood not only as the need to fit in and please others but as the desire to slough off a past identity in order to escape external persecution or self-laceration. Saul would doubtless have understood my dad's motivation perfectly, but the priest who baptized Robert Jacoby in 1952 did not know that he was welcoming yet another Jew into the Catholic fold. Only my mother and her parents were privy to that secret.

MY PARENTS met, as so many couples did during the war, over drinks at an officers' club. Thirty years old and deemed unfit for combat because he was blind in one eye as a result of a teenage accident with a stick, my father was stationed in Chicago as a first lieutenant in the Quartermaster Corps. Irma Broderick, nicknamed Stevie, was working in the personnel department of a large company and living, at age twenty-three, in her own apartment in downtown Chicago. Her parents, who lived just south of the city in the blue-collar town of Harvey, regarded their daughter's living arrangements with an unease perfectly understandable for members of a generation born in an era when girls, whatever their economic circumstances, lived at home with their parents until they married. They took an immediate liking to Bob Jacoby because he was intelligent, witty, handsome (with the infectious smile and thick, wavy black hair inherited from his father), and—above all—obviously and overwhelmingly in love with my mother. My Broderick grandmother, who bore scars of a childhood in a home dominated by the rages of her alcoholic father, regarded my dad's Jewishness as something of a plus. She had never really known any Jews, but, like many gentiles, she was convinced that Jewish men didn't drink and doted on their wives. For my father, the child of a cold and critical mother and a largely absent father, my mother's parents were more than a plus: they gave him the unwavering affection and approval (which would, in time, be sorely tested by his own actions) so conspicuously lacking in his upbringing.

Although my grandparents definitely wanted their grandchildren to be raised in the Church, they would never have pressured my father to become a Catholic. Even so, I find it slightly surprising that Dad did not even think about conversion until he and my mother had been married for eight years. Although conversions were somewhat more unusual (even from one Christian denomination to another) in the forties and early fifties than they are today, they were already a familiar phenomenon, extending back several generations, in both the Broderick and Jacoby families.

Aunt Edith, the first Jacoby convert in my father's generation, had already become the kind of Catholic who made pilgrimages to Lourdes, prayed for the conversion of Russia, and regarded the anticommunist crusades of the fifties as the work of the Lord. Her brothers, even after their own conversions, regarded her views as bizarre. "Sis, couldn't you just be content with reading G. K. Chesterton?" Uncle Ozzie once asked her. Edith's extremism probably rendered conversion a less appealing prospect than it would otherwise have been to her two brothers. But my dad had another, more agreeable example of what it meant to be a Catholic convert (albeit from Protestantism) in the person of my Broderick grandmother.

To the former Minnie Rothenhoefer, who had been a Lutheran but became a Catholic when she married Jim Broderick in 1919, conversion had nothing to do with theology and everything to do with pleasing her husband's family. "It's the same God, no matter what church you go to," she would say. My grandfather concurred. Granny had converted, he explained, in order to make his mother happy. My mother's parents would have been mystified by the pejorative meaning attached by the Church hierarchy to "social conversion"; as far as Granny and Gramps were concerned, it made perfect sense to change religions in order to attend church services with the rest of one's family.

When my father finally decided to take instruction in the Faith, he was drawn in not only by his marriage to a Catholic but by that greatest of socializing instruments, television, and by the first

American televangelist, Bishop Fulton J. Sheen. When I was seven and he was thirty-eight, Dad began to watch Bishop Sheen's weekly show, *Life Is Worth Living*, on our nine-inch black-and-white screen. I remember being pleased about my father's interest in Bishop Sheen's message, because it meant extra television-watching time for me. In the first half of the fifties, when television was still a novelty (at least in our house) rather than the metronome of daily life, any program—even one filled with sober homilies—was a treat. Dad decided to begin instruction only a few weeks after he began watching the show. I remember this period very well, because I used to drill Dad on the Baltimore Catechism (our parish priest used the same book for adults that he did for parochial elementary school students). "Who is God?" "God is the Supreme Being." "Why did God make us?" "God made us to know, love, and serve Him in this world and to be happy with Him forever in the next."

While it seemed perfectly natural to me that my father would, as my grandmother suggested, want to go to Mass and take Holy Communion with his family, I was nevertheless slightly mystified by his willingness to take on all of the spiritual obligations incumbent upon Catholics at that time—abstaining from meat on Fridays, fasting after midnight if you intended to take communion the next morning, waiting in line for confession if you had a serious sin on your conscience. I already knew that Protestants did not need a priest to register their contrition with God and wondered why my dad would abandon a direct pipeline to the Almighty in favor of an intermediary. He told me he had been raised as a Protestant—specifically, as an Episcopalian.

Thus, my father's baptism, which could have provided an opportunity for a discussion of his real origins, instead served to promote an elaborate fictitious version of his past. Catholicism was a truer religion, Dad explained, because there would never have been an Episcopal Church in the first place if an English king had not wanted to divorce his wife in defiance of the Pope. Had it not been for Henry VIII's break with Rome, the American descendants of the English colonists—my dad presumably among them—would all have been Catholics instead of Protestants. This overly elaborate, and slightly wacky, explanation of his embrace of the Church can have had only one purpose—to suggest that my father, like my Broderick grandmother, was simply shifting from one branch of Christianity to another.

My father's construction of an Episcopal boyhood was entirely consistent with the behavior of the many German Jews who chose, in his father's and grandfather's generation, to bury their "Hebrew" backgrounds. In 1848—the year before Maximilian Jacoby left Germany for America—John Jacob Astor (who had inserted John in front of his first name in order to sound less Jewish) died and was buried in a service conducted by six of New York's most prominent Episcopal clergymen. The same year saw the wedding of the financier August Belmont to the daughter of Commodore Matthew Perry. The son of a German Jewish merchant named Simon Schönburg, Belmont had obscured his origins by translating his name (meaning "beautiful mountain") into French. His Episcopal marriage service was conducted in Grace Church, with a socially impeccable congregation that included members of the wealthiest old Dutch and English families in the city.

Since Episcopalianism and (for freethinkers) Unitarianism were the preferred escape routes for German-descended Jews who did not wish to be thought of as Jews in America, it is not surprising that my father would claim the Church of England as his original ecclesiastical home. Much later, I would learn that while my father's family did not take part in any form of religious observance, the children were sent to prep schools where Protestant chapel was compulsory. Aunt Edith told me that she had presented herself to grade school classmates as an Episcopalian and to high school friends as a Lutheran. (At Smith College, where she was identified as a Jew by being assigned a Jewish roommate, she abandoned the attempt to obscure her origins and stopped claiming membership in any church.)

The mixed marriages and conversions in the Jacoby family began
not in the twentieth but in the nineteenth century. Two of Max
Jacoby's three children—my grandfather's sister, Geppy, and his older
brother, Harold—married gentiles. In 1881, Geppy was married at
New York's City Hall to a German baron named Albrecht von Liebenstein. Harold and Annie Maclear, a granddaughter of Sir Thomas
Maclear, the Astronomer Royal in Capetown, South Africa, were married in 1895 by an Episcopal priest. I had heard about Great-Uncle
Harold from my father and uncle. He was a mythical figure in the family—a scientist who became a full professor of astronomy at Columbia, the older son who succeeded where his younger brother, my
grandfather, did not.

What my father and his siblings did not know was that Uncle
Harold's real first name was Levi. But that is not surprising: as I
found when I finally tracked down Harold's grandchildren, neither
had heard the name Levi attached to their eminent grandfather—
and they were quite sure that their parents, Harold's children, were
equally ignorant of the fact that there had ever been a Levi in a family boasting several Episcopal bishops and priests.

Whether or not Harold formally converted (the nineteenth-
century Episcopal Church having been somewhat more relaxed than
the Roman Catholic Church about mixed marriages), his children
were raised as Episcopalians and were married in the early 1920s in
High Church ceremonies noted in the society pages of *The New York
Times*. Both of these weddings took place in New York, but no one
from my grandfather's branch of the Jacoby family was in either wedding party—an omission that suggests a good deal about the degree
of estrangement between my grandfather and his prominent brother.

For Jews who were ashamed of being Jews, the marriages of
Uncle Harold and his children unquestionably represented a step up
on the social ladder. But unions with Irish Catholics represented no
more than a lateral move (if that) in the American class-social hierarchy during the first half of the twentieth century—a realization
that galled my Jacoby grandmother. With the hauteur of an Our

Crowd Jew (in her case, Our Crowd manqué) Granny Jacoby used to make tart remarks about Uncle Ted's position as a vice-president of Macy's. She had taken music lessons (or so she said) from the same teacher as the granddaughters of Isidor Straus, the owner of Macy's, who went down with his wife on the *Titanic*. When all was said and done, Granny Jacoby would remind Ted, he was a mere *employee* of the Straus family. I could not grasp the social implications of these remarks at the time, and I disliked my father's mother so much that I never followed up and asked what she meant. Whenever Granny Jacoby began to drop names like Straus, Guggenheim, and Schiff, my father and Aunt Edith would yawn and change the subject.

As one after the other of her children married into Irish Catholic families, Granny Jacoby must have been appalled by the evidence of her failure to transmit her particular brand of snobbery to the next generation. By the time my father converted in 1952, Catholicism was no longer the social debit it had once been (and would cease to be, once and for all, with the 1960 election of John Fitzgerald Kennedy as president). In any event, my father's desire to leave the past behind and begin again with a clean slate had little to do with conventional social climbing and even less to do with theology. Nevertheless, it is still difficult for me to understand how an American Jew, even one as detached from and ashamed of his origins as my father, could turn to the Church of Rome shortly after World War II. In the 1950s—before the ecumenical era ushered in by that great soul, Pope John XXIII—conversion to Catholicism meant accepting a religious tradition (at least insofar as it was translated by many parish priests) that held the Jews responsible for crucifying Jesus. I asked my father, when he was well into his sixties, whether he was ever bothered by the crucifixion story when he was taking instruction. Since Dad did not reveal his Jewish origins, his catechism instructor never raised the subject directly. Nevertheless, Dad remembered that the priest had brought up the culpability of the Jews in the death of Christ. "He said that the Jewish people, also the Romans, did have a special responsibility for crucifying Jesus," my father recalled with a laugh, "but only the ones who happened to be there in Jerusalem at the time. If Christ had been born in America, he said, the Indians would be to blame."

A minority of Jewish converts to Catholicism—like the father of novelist Mary Gordon—became devotees of the reactionary right wing of American Catholicism exemplified in the 1930s by the xenophobic, anti-Semitic radio priest Father Charles Coughlin. Gordon, who describes her search for her father's past in her 1996 memoir *The Shadow Man*, grew up with secrets that were an inverted version of those in my family. Unlike me, she knew that her father was a Jew by birth but knew nothing at all about the details of his conversion, which took place long before her birth. Growing up in a working-class urban neighborhood in the New York City borough of Queens, surrounded by anti-Semitic neighbors fully aware of who did and didn't look like a Jew (and with a father far more stereotypically Jewish in appearance than mine), Gordon would surely have figured out at an early age that her father had been born a Jew even if he had tried to lie about his origins. Perhaps that explains why, by her own account, she never questioned the teachings of the Church during her childhood: Catholicism, and her identity as a Catholic, would have been vital to a girl who was told, "That's the *Jew* in you," whenever she displeased her mother's family.

Perhaps I would have heard such remarks—though not from anyone in my mom's family—had we stayed in the Chicago area, where we lived near my Broderick grandparents until we moved to Lansing, Michigan, when I was eight. I made the transition from childhood to adolescence in a postwar suburb where religion and ethnicity were rapidly losing their once-defining importance. Hardly anyone thought about Jews—or, for that matter, any other minority—in Lansing, the state capital and home of the Oldsmobile division of General Motors. Awareness of ethnic origins was even more muted in Okemos, where we bought a house when I was eleven. The new houses, most of them surrounded by lots denuded of trees, were purchased by white-collar state employees, professors from nearby Michigan State University, and small businessmen like my father. (Our lot on the inappropriately named Greenwood Drive was a departure from the treeless norm: my parents had paid extra for the two beautiful maples in our front yard.) Whatever church anyone in the neighborhood attended, religion was not a central part of life. Although many of the parents had grown up in tight-knit blue-collar communities, they now defined themselves not as Catholics or Protestants, Italian-, Polish-, or Irish-Americans, but as residents of one of Okemos's "subdivisions"—Forest Hills, Indian Hills, Chippewa Hills, Ottawa Hills, Tacoma Hills, and Hiawatha Park.

New parish schools were built as more and more affluent Catholics moved to the suburbs, but most college-educated Catholics, like my parents, pulled their children out of the parochial system when they reached high school age. It was well known that the aim of Catholic secondary schools was to prepare students to enter Catholic colleges or the still-flourishing network of seminaries and convents. Catholic state officials, professors, doctors, lawyers, and accountants did not set such limited goals for the next generation. Like my parents, they wanted to give their children unrestricted opportunities.

Judging from the last names in my high school yearbook—in which only two students (including me) out of a graduating class of 119 bore names that hinted at a Jewish background—the presence of Jews in Okemos must have been minuscule. In this bland suburban environment, no social importance whatsoever was attached to my father's status as a Catholic convert. I have no real way of knowing whether there was any validity to my father's belief that our relations with our neighbors would have been altered, subtly or crudely, had they known he was not only a Catholic convert but also a Jew.

Because I was directly and intimately involved in my father's earthbound transformation into a Catholic, I never imagined his conversion in the mystical terms used in *Lives of the Saints*, a tome familiar to every parochial school student in the fifties. It is hard to think of conversion as a blinding light on the road to Damascus, or as a highly spiritual or intellectual process, when the light comes from a flickering television screen, the voice of the deity is Bishop Sheen, and you have drilled your father on his catechism answers. Doubts take years to ripen, but my own misgivings about Catholicism, of which I was fully cognizant by the time I was eleven or twelve, certainly began while I watched (and helped) as my father prepared for the magical transformation that would take place at the actual moment of baptism. I was troubled from a young age by the idea that pouring water over someone's head could change both his relationship to God (what if my dad had died the day before the ceremony?) and his status as a human being.

ONE TRUTH: I loved my father so much that I was slightly insulted, even as a small child, by the notion that some words from a priest, and a splatter of holy water, were needed to make him a better man.

I have an image of him—it may be my earliest memory—running toward me along the elevated train platform near the south Chicago apartment where we lived until I was three and a half. He works in a tall building downtown, and when he calls to say he's on his way home from the office, my mother and I often walk to the station to meet him. I see him darting through the train door, occasionally tripping over his own feet in his eagerness. I smell the half-smoked Camel he always stubs out just before sweeping me up in his arms, feel the springy texture of his hair, hear him asking, "Are you my little girl?"

Another truth: During the period of these idyllic memories, my father was on the verge of wrecking his life and losing everything and everyone he loved.

MY FATHER certainly did want to leave his Jewish past behind, but he was battling another, more immediate demon—the gambling compulsion of the Jacoby men—when he started paying attention to the message of Bishop Sheen. Dad had more in common with Augustine of Hippo than with Saul of Tarsus: he turned to the structure of the Catholic Church in an effort to overcome a character weakness he had not been able to vanquish on his own, or even with the support of my mother and her family.

Soon after my brother (named Robert James Jacoby, after both my father and Grandfather Broderick) was born in 1948, we left our apartment, with its proximity to Lake Michigan and an endlessly fascinating array of delicatessens, butcher shops, and bakeries, for a tiny "ranch house" in the suburb of Hazel Crest. We were only a ten-minute drive from my grandparents' old-fashioned two-story house in Harvey, where my grandfather owned a real estate business and a combination bar and bowling alley called Bowl Center, a plain name that sounded utterly exotic to me as a child. My father would no longer be working in the city, I was told, because he would be helping out in Gramps's businesses.

A few years later, when I was old enough to understand such concepts, I was told that my father had lost his job (he had been the comptroller of a Chicago advertising agency). Two decades would pass before Dad told me why he had been fired: he simply had not done his work. He was bored by the job—and he had started gambling again. He had given up what he called "the vice of the Jacoby men" when he met my mother, but the old lure proved too strong. There were days when he failed to show up at the office because he was spending his time playing cards or betting at the track. After Dad was fired, my grandfather created a job for his son-in-law, who was reduced to helping out with the bookkeeping and bowling alley. As a bookkeeper, Dad was certainly overqualified: his formidable computational skills were only a notch below the wizardlike talents of his elder brother. At age twenty-one—before he began his sixty-year career as a contract bridge player—Uncle Ozzie had become the youngest person in the United States ever to qualify as a licensed actuary. During World War II, he served in the navy as a code expert, eventually reaching the rank of lieutenant commander. Whenever my father and Ozzie were together as adults, they would compete with each other as human adding machines, totaling six-digit figures in their heads. Ozzie nearly always won, managing to add at least one more row of figures than my father. I have always found it ironic that both men, with mathematical abilities that gave them a far better grasp than the average person has of the odds against winning, were unable to apply a rational calculus to their own chances of success at the gaming tables. But then, my father and my uncle were examples par excellence of the irrationality at the heart of addictive behavior. Not that they would have called themselves addicts. Fifty years ago, gambling was regarded not as a disease but as a character failing (a social and moral judgment my father fully accepted).

When I began to ask my father about his past, he was in his mid-fifties. He was much more willing to talk about his gambling—indeed, he volunteered information I would have had no way of knowing otherwise—than about his Jewish origins. His conversion, he insisted at the time (an opinion he later revised), had nothing to do with wanting to conceal his Jewish parentage. "I thought I'd already accomplished that before I became a Catholic," he emphasized. At the time of his conversion, he had been working for my grandfather for nearly four years and had begun to despair of ever finding another job. With a gap in his résumé and a recent employment history that did not square with his educational credentials and previous experience—keeping books for a tavern and bowling alley was hardly likely to land him a position with a large firm—my father had no choice but to tell prospective employers that he had been fired from his postwar job with the advertising agency. As soon as they heard the truth, they showed Dad the door.

IT IS 1975—I am thirty and he is sixty-one—before he tells me the whole story. "Having lost your job was like having a prison record," my father recalls with a grimace. "I thought of trying to lie at job interviews, but your grandfather reminded me—he was one of the smartest men I ever knew—that lying, or at least avoiding the truth, was what got me into trouble in the first place. I was so discouraged that I was afraid at that place in my life that I would go back to gambling."

Dad tells me that he gambled heavily as a single man, gave it up when he began dating my mother, but started again when I was about a year old. (I wonder whether Mom knows that Dad returned to the gaming tables so soon after their marriage. Maybe not, since he managed to keep his surface life in order, in spite of the gambling, for several more years.) Dad continued to gamble even after losing his job but quit for good after a confrontation with my mother and grandfather. One of my mother's cousins informed Gramps that Dad had been spotted in an after-hours blackjack game. "There's always the temptation to try it one more time," Dad tells me. "It's just like booze. Your mother had told me she would give me one more chance, but that she'd take you and Robbie and leave if I ever gambled again. I knew she meant it. I was terrified of losing you all. But I needed something more than my family, and the something more was the Church. In those days, the Catholic Church spelled out the rules for living. I thought those rules could help me. No meat on Friday, Mass every Sunday, confession once a month, Holy Days of Obligation, giving up something for Lent—all of it reminded me of what I needed to be doing to stay on the straight road. Later on, I didn't need the rules so much. But I did then . . . I did then. And every Sunday, I prayed that someone would give me a second chance. It wasn't that your gramps ever made me feel I owed him for giving me a job, but I *did* owe him. Without that job, you'd have gone hungry. But that's no way for a man to live, knowing he can't make it on his own. I give the Church a lot of the credit for my resisting the temptation to fall back into my old ways. You kids and your mother were the main reason I kept on, but the Church helped. Don't ever think it didn't."

This is my father talking, not giving himself much of the credit for the strength of character and the love that helped him overcome such a powerful compulsion. Love, I think, is what did it. Love for my mother, brother, and for me. But he believes the Church gave him strength, and who am I to argue? Who other than the tempted can speak with authority about the strength of temptation?

IN RETROSPECT, it is a tribute to my mother and father that my early childhood years—so filled with pain, shame, and anxiety for both of them—were unmarred by any sense of insecurity. My mother, with a three-year-old, a new baby, and the knowledge that there wasn't much more than $100 in the bank, may have been even more devastated than my father. "I don't think I slept through the night for years," she says today. If she lay awake, her children never knew. Of course, the possibility of my mother's returning to work never occurred to either of my parents in 1949, although she had loved her personnel job as a single woman and would demonstrate her ability in the same field when she reentered the labor force in the 1970s. Another irony: my father always had an aptitude for domes-ticity—from his baking to his instinctive understanding of small children and the pleasure he took in their company—that my mother lacked. But who knows what it would have done to a man with a frag-ile ego if he and his wife had attempted an outright "role reversal"? And my father so needed protecting—from his own mother, who had criticized him relentlessly as a child and continued to mock his achievements as an adult, and from the memory of a father whose ruined life left a legacy of dissolution for both of his sons. Yet the paternal specter also served as a powerful force for good in Dad's life. Although he did not fully comprehend the extent of his father's self-sabotage—for he was only a baby when the senior Oswald Jacoby's life began to disintegrate—he was nevertheless terrified of reproduc-ing the pattern. Somehow, he summoned up the strength to overcome the character failing, sickness, sin—regardless of the label, the conse-quences were disastrous—that could have shattered yet another gen-eration. Perhaps the Catholic Church, with its emphasis on the possibility of redemption, did help. In any case, it filled an empty space left by his family's outright rejection of Judaism as a religion.

•   •   •

CAN THERE be Jews without Judaism? A Talmudic question, to which most rabbis answer no (and the more Orthodox they are, the more unequivocal the answer). To the Jewish fundamentalists—the fanatics who are mistakenly regarded by many Americans as synonymous with all Orthodox Jews—the question itself is a blasphemy. At any rate, a half-Jew (and one who, by virtue of her mother's Christianity, is not a Jew at all according to traditional Jewish law) is not ideally situated to respond to the question. But I am certain of one thing: whatever it means to be "culturally Jewish"—a complicated mix of behavior and values that can mean anything from a tendency to pepper conversations with "schmuck" and "schmaltz" to a serious knowledge of Jewish tradition and history—the schmuck-schmaltz school of cultural Jewishness provides an inadequate foundation for moral decision making or for confronting a serious personal weakness like gambling. My father, in his thirties, did not qualify as "culturally Jewish" (and would not have wished to do so) even by the schmuck-schmaltz standard. He was a man with no Jewish education of any kind, a vessel emptied of Jewish content, open to the magical metamorphosis promised by conversion.

NOT LONG after his conversion (the two events were always linked in my father's mind) Dad answered a classified ad placed by a small accounting firm in Michigan. He traveled to Lansing for a personal interview with the firm's president, a dour man named Fred Vorn. Vorn, who combined rigidity and rectitude in equal measure, did not, at first glance, seem like a boss who would hire a reformed gambler, or anyone with a gap in his employment history, as his right-hand man.

Nevertheless, he gave my father his second chance and we moved to Michigan in the summer of 1953. For Dad, the move meant the opportunity not only to rebuild his career but to regain his self-respect. Over the years, he would continue to pay dearly for the mistakes of his early thirties. Fred Vorn turned out to be an eccentric autocrat who kept all of his employees in a state of economic uncertainty by giving them a large chunk of their annual salaries as a Christmas cash bonus. Dad worked endless hours—especially in tax season, when he was sometimes gone from five in the morning until ten at night—but he never knew until the annual office Christmas party whether he had had a good, bad, or average year. One of my most vivid childhood memories centers around the Christmas bonus of a thousand dollars that my father received when I was nine. I remember the thousand-dollar bill (something I had never seen before and have never seen since), which my mother made my father deposit in the bank before we left Lansing to drive to Illinois to celebrate the holiday with my grandparents. Dad wanted to show Gramps the actual cash—it would have been a literal demonstration of his trustworthiness as a husband and provider, a man who had learned from his mistakes—but my mother prevailed when she pointed out that Christmas Eve was probably a profitable day for robbers. I remember that Christmas as the happiest of my childhood; from the fuss my grandparents made over my father when they heard about the bonus (as they did the moment we walked through the door), you would have thought that Dad had, at the very least, announced his appointment as the president of a major corporation. Gramps declared repeatedly that he had known all along that Dad would make a great success of his new job in Michigan. What balm all of this praise must have been to a man who had received so little encouragement and approval from his own parents!

The tale of the bonus of course has another side, one belonging more to the nineteenth than to the twentieth century. The "bonuses" weren't really bonuses but a portion of my father's well-deserved salary that his boss chose to keep a secret until the last possible moment. He handed out the annual bonuses at the office Christmas party (just in time to deduct them as business expenses), and the employees had to grovel and thank their boss without knowing whether the amount inside the envelope would make this a merry or a dreary holiday season. When Vorn finally retired many years later and sold the business to my father, one of Dad's first actions as the new owner was to abolish the practice of uncertain, end-of-the-year cash payments.

However long and faithfully he serves his new employer, a man who has been fired from his previous job is never in a good negotiating position. That was the main clause in the unwritten contract between my father and Fred Vorn: Vorn would, out of Christian charity, overlook the blot on Dad's record, and Dad would play Bob Cratchit to his employer's Mr. Scrooge. We were as solidly middle-class as everyone else in our neighborhood (my father made enough not only to meet the mortgage payments on the new three-bedroom house in Okemos but also to pay for figure-skating lessons, camp, and two-inch-thick porterhouse steaks once a week), but I always knew that Dad was afraid to push his boss too hard. In a family with so many secrets, my parents were surprisingly frank about the true nature of my father's position. After September, whenever my brother or I asked for something that would cost more than a small amount, the answer was always, "We have to wait and see how much Dad's bonus is this time." And every year or so, there would be tense discussions about whether Dad should bring up the subject of a raise or wait for Vorn to make an offer. "Why don't you get another job?" I asked when I was twelve or thirteen. That was when Dad told me, for the first time, that he had been fired when I was a baby. "Thank God you were too young then to realize it," he said. "I could never take that chance now with the future of my family." I never repeated the question.

By then, I had absorbed a strong sense of my father's deep insecurities, even though I did not know that his shame about being a Jew was one of them. Having seen the way Dad's own mother belittled him, I developed strong protective instincts toward him at an early age and deeply regretted having asked him a question that could be interpreted as a challenge to his decisions about how best to support his family. I knew, without anyone saying so, that my job as a daughter to my father was twofold—to excel in school (for that was the one thing I knew Jacobys had been expected to do for generations) and to provide some of the emotional protection Dad needed. I succeeded at the first task and failed, too often (as I saw it then and see it now), at the second.

When *I* needed protection—usually at school—I turned to my mother. Whenever there was trouble with the nuns, Mom was the parent who sailed into the fray and defended me. There was trouble with Sister Misericordia in sixth grade after the spider-under-the-dress affair; trouble with Sister Stephen in seventh grade when I expressed doubt about the logic of the Holy Trinity (Sister had offered a paper shamrock into evidence and became enraged when I remarked that the existence of four-leaf clovers didn't prove there were four persons in one God); trouble with Sister Cyril Therese in eighth grade after she dunked a girl's head under the water faucet because she had copied a provocative, tousled hairstyle from *Photoplay* magazine. With its photographs of scantily clad actresses, Sister proclaimed, *Photoplay* constituted an "occasion of sin." I was furious because Sister Cyril—one of those butch nuns who had it in for any girl with a hint of sex appeal beneath her green serge school uniform—had chosen to humiliate Barbara, whose sweetness and lack of self-confidence, combined with early puberty, made her a perfect target for bullies of all ages and vocations. Imagine a thirteen-year-old led back from the lavatory (we were told explicitly at St. Thomas Aquinas School that the word *bathroom* was almost as vulgar as the truly unmentionable *toilet*) with her once-fluffy head soaked, dripping onto the starched white collar of her regulation blouse. As Barbara's tears mingled with the runoff from her hair, Sister Cyril looked to the rest of the class for support. "I had no choice," she screeched. "I had to teach you all a lesson." After Sister Cyril had ranted on about *Photoplay*, I spoke up and said, "It was a mean and wicked thing you did." No one talked that way to a nun; Barbara was so astonished that she stopped crying, and everyone else beat a hasty retreat before Sister had time to begin the usual prayer before dismissal. For a moment, I thought Sister Cyril was going to hit me, but she knew my mother was due to pick me up for an after-school den-

tal appointment. My impeccably dressed, impeccably polite mom—
I can still see her in the blue shirtwaist dress that was *her* uniform—
drew herself up to her full height of five feet, four inches, after the
outraged nun had proferred her version of the story. "Of course, Sue
should never have spoken to you that way," she said mildly, "but I'm
sure she must have thought she had a good reason." Then she asked
for my version of what had happened, her mouth tightening as I
described Barbara's public humiliation. She turned back to Sister
Cyril and said, "If you ever did that to my child, I would remove her
from the school immediately and write a letter to the bishop." *A letter to the bishop.* Sister Cyril, for once, had nothing to say. As we left
the classroom, my mother offered a parting shot. "I believe *Photoplay*
was allowed to photograph Grace Kelly's wedding to Prince Rainier
inside the cathedral in Monte Carlo," she informed Sister. "Surely if
Photoplay were an occasion of sin, the cardinal who performed the
marriage ceremony would never have allowed this." My mother may
have made this up on the spot, but I was awed by her performance.
She had made her point *without raising her voice*—a talent I admired
but would never master.

It was clear to me that Mom liked it when I talked back to the
nuns, even though she was disappointed by my failure to learn how
to express my opinions in ladylike fashion. She had been stuck in convent school (not a regular parish school) during her teenage years,
and she encouraged me to assert myself in ways that her own parents
would not have countenanced. My father, as a convert, was both in
awe of and mystified by the nuns, and he left my mother in charge of
virtually everything to do with Catholic education. He was equally
mystified by the frequency and intensity of my disputes with the sisters and, later, with the priests who took over religious instruction
for the upper grades (providing the superior male intellect presumably required to resolve moral dilemmas above the sixth-grade level).
"Just think what you think and keep it to yourself," Dad would say.
"But how can the pope be infallible?" I would sputter. "The pope's
just a *man.*" "I'm infallible," was my father's reply, "so why shouldn't

the pope be?" Dad was as uninterested in theological debate as he was bemused by my aunt Edith's pursuit of apparitions and miracles on pilgrimages to Lourdes and Fatima. What mattered to him was that he was a Catholic, married to a Catholic, bringing up Catholic children in a setting far removed from his pained and turbulent youth.

Even though my father had converted, my background as the child of a "mixed marriage," as Sister Misericordia's comments suggested, was never entirely forgotten by the arbiters of Catholic education. When a Catholic married a non-Catholic before the reforms of the Second Vatican Council in the early sixties, the non-Catholic spouse had to sign a promise to allow any children to be brought up in the True Faith. Even so, mixed couples received a second-class version of the marriage ceremony, performed not in church but in the rectory. By denying the bride and groom the right to pledge themselves to each other before the altar, the Catholic hierarchy voiced its deep reservations about intermarriage even as it bowed to the realities of people who did not necessarily stick to their own kind when they sought a mate.

Although the nuns explained that truly believing Protestants (no one mentioned truly believing Jews) could go to heaven, the constant drumbeat was that it was much, much better to be a Catholic. We were drilled to declare, "I am a Catholic," when any form of temptation appeared. A Protestant friend offered you a bite of a hot dog on Friday. "I am a Catholic." You were invited to a movie condemned by the Legion of Decency. "I am a Catholic." Later on, "I am a Catholic" would be the appropriate response to a boy who made an "impure suggestion." Unless the boy was a Catholic himself, in which case an indignant "*You* are a Catholic" would suffice. The older nuns longed for the days, as they often said, when Catholic children lived in heavily Catholic immigrant neighborhoods and the questions raised by Protestant friends never came up. The nuns were particularly eloquent on the dangers of dating non-Catholics. "It may not seem like an occasion of sin now," they would say, "but when you are of an age to marry, it can lead to mortal peril for your soul." I often wondered whether the nuns would have advised my mother to declare, "I am a Catholic," when my father first asked her out on a date. The thought made me giggle inwardly, but I restrained myself from putting the question to Sister Cyril. I wasn't sure I could count on my mom to threaten Sister with a letter to the bishop more than once in a school year.

For all of the space that Catholicism occupied in my mental world, we were not a particularly observant family. We went to church on Sundays and Holy Days of Obligation, and that was pretty much it. Both of my parents were openly contemptuous of Catholics who paid attention to what the Church had to say about immoral books and movies. Since my parents had only two children (many of my friends in Catholic elementary school came from huge families with a child in nearly every grade), they must have interpreted the Church's ban on artificial birth control in a less than rigorous way. Because she had been brought up as a Catholic, my mother understood my struggles with religious training far better than my father did. To Dad, religion was not a belief system that was supposed to make sense but a set of helpful moral road signs calling attention to falling rocks, dead-end streets, and dangerous curves. Doubting Thomasina was one of his nicknames for me, but I am certain he did not know that my doubts, by the time I reached the age of thirteen, had hardened into an outright rejection (one I could not voice at the time) of the faith that had given him so much solace. Dad, who had been a star Latin student in high school (one of the few facts I knew about his childhood), had a habit of reciting Mass, sotto voce, along with the priest. *Domine, non sum dignus* (Lord, I am not worthy), he would intone, striking his breastbone along with the celebrant on the altar, eliciting a shush from my mother, and demonstrating that he could not possibly have been born a Catholic (for cradle Catholics of that generation, even if they understood Latin, would not have dreamed of usurping the priest's prerogative by joining in the chant). Thanks to Dad, I knew exactly what the words of the Mass meant by the time I was eight or nine—and that knowledge set me apart from my friends and provided more fuel for my doubts. How could someone be God and man at the same time? How could the Host, delivered from some holy bakery, actually *be* Jesus? "The Host isn't Jesus himself, it's to remind us of Jesus," my theologically incorrect father would say in exasperation. "Daddy, the priest says *corpus Christi* during the Mass. That's what transubstantiation means. Not that the Host is a symbol of Christ but that it really, truly *is* the body of Christ—even though it looks like a wafer." By fourth or fifth grade, Catholic schoolchildren were expected to be fluent in the technical language of church dogma. Terms like *transubstantiation* and *incarnation* were as familiar to us as, and had something in common with, the formulas for diagramming sentences.

At the end of one of these disputations, my father shook his head and said, "You remind me of old Uncle Dano." I'd never heard of an uncle named Dano, and Dad explained that he was an argumentative great-uncle, long deceased, whom he had known and loved as a child. "He was just like you, always cornering people about religion and politics." "Was he a Catholic?" I asked. Dad said Uncle Dano had probably been an Episcopalian. Forty years later, I would discover that "Uncle Dano" was Daniel Jackson, a younger brother of my great-grandmother, Eve Jackson Jacoby. He was a pawnbroker at the turn of the century in Manhattan's financial district. And he was definitely not an Episcopalian. Many years ago, Aunt Edith gave me a tiny gold watch that had belonged to her aunt, suspended from a much older gold pin that she said was a Jackson family heirloom of unknown origin. I didn't realize then that the pin was a precise replica of the traditional three-balled pawnbroker's symbol, derived from the Medici coat of arms.

III

German-Americanization

⟅⟆

"MY FATHER HARDLY EVER talked about being Jewish," Uncle
Ozzie told me just before his death in 1984, "but I knew how he felt.
Being a Jew meant you were better than other people. It also meant
you were worse."

By the end of the nineteenth century, the myths that would shape
the Jacoby family's image of itself for most of the twentieth century
were firmly in place. In the morgue of *The New York Times*, which
includes clippings from other publications as well, I found a glowing
1907 tribute to my grandfather, who had been selected as a worthy
profile subject by *Men of Affairs in New York*. Printed on the creamy,
heavy, enduring paper used for substantive periodicals and books at
the turn of the century, the account of my grandfather's family background and early accomplishments as a lawyer was misfiled in a much
thicker envelope of clippings on his elder son's twentieth-century
tournament bridge career. The long opening paragraph of the article,
which summarizes the circumstances of my great-grandfather's
departure from Germany, provided me with my first glimpse of the
way the family saw itself—and wanted to be seen by others—long
before my father was born.

Oswald N. Jacoby, counselor at law, was born in the city of
New York on December 24, 1870. He is descended from a
German family, his father having come to this country a
short time subsequent to the German revolution of 1848.
This stirring period in the history of Germany had inspired
the elder Jacoby to seek in the New World that freedom of
opinion which the efforts of the revolutionists had failed to
secure in his native land. He was possessed of considerable
means and within a few years, he had established the importing and publishing house of Jacoby & Zeller, at 104 and 106
William Street, which continued to do a prosperous business
at the same locality for nearly 50 years. Mr. Jacoby was married to Eve Jackson, the daughter of an old New Yorker of
prominence.

This excerpt forced me to revise my long-held belief that there
was about as much substance to the legend of the Jacoby family's
lost fortune as there was to Uncle Ozzie's claim that Copernicus was
a distant Jacoby ancestor. I had never placed much credence in my
father's tales (since the money was long gone by the time he was
born) or in my hyperbolic uncle's memories of a Rubens painting
that had once hung in his grandfather's house (though Ozzie was old
enough—barely—to remember a grandfather who died in 1907).
But I would soon conclude, after I learned from other sources that
the firm of Jacoby & Zeller was an art importing and publishing
house with close ties to German, Austrian, and Dutch art dealers,
that the Rubens story is not entirely implausible. Valuable artworks
are, after all, among the first possessions to be sold when a once-
affluent family comes down in the world.

The *Men of Affairs* profile is as interesting for what it attempts to
conceal as for what it reveals about the family's origins. The claim of
German descent was common among second-generation American
Jews of my grandfather's background; German antecedents were
considered far more prestigious than Polish or Russian origins by

Jews and gentiles alike. By 1907, when New York was being transformed as a result of the huge migration of poor, Yiddish-speaking
Jews from the shtetls of Eastern Europe and Russia, it would have
been important for an ambitious man like my grandfather (and his
elder brother, Harold, who had just been appointed director of
Columbia University's astronomical observatory) to distinguish
himself from the rabble of the unassimilated by emphasizing his
German background. (A decade later, when the United States
declared war on Germany, the German connection would not seem so
desirable for Jewish or non-Jewish German-Americans.)

Maximilian Jacoby was just eighteen when, in order "to seek in the
New World that freedom of opinion which the efforts of the revolutionists had failed to secure in his native land," he left Germany from
the port of Bremen as a second-class passenger on one of the transatlantic steamers that were just beginning to replace sailing ships. Born
in 1831, he belonged to a generation of German-speaking Jews who—
particularly if they attended German universities—were more and
more likely to cast off their Hebrew first names. Moseses were transformed into Maximilians; some Miriams even went so far as to take
that most Christian of all feminine given names, Maria. Maximilian
Jacoby's name attested to his own acculturation, while his second-class
ticket (most immigrants traveled in steerage) attested to the relative
affluence of his family. Still more suggestive is the fact (omitted from
the *Men of Affairs* article but included in later writings by his sons)
that the young man had been a student at the University of Breslau
before his departure for New York in 1849. Only the most ambitious
Jewish families, with at least some money to spare, could have afforded
to send a son to a university. Maximilian's political opinions may well
have played a role in his decision to emigrate, since assimilated, well-
off Jews were much less likely than poor Jews to leave Germany in the
1840s and 1850s. The tumultuous events of 1848–49 had drawn many
university students and faculty into the agitation for democratization.
When the movement failed, many of the participants, however marginal their involvement may have been, concluded that they had no

future in Germany. Moreover, politically involved Jews were doubly vulnerable as a wave of post-1848 governmental repression was, inevitably, coupled with a rise in popular anti-Semitism. (In 1852, Bismarck made a threat that, while not specifically anti-Semitic, summed up the threatening nature of the political environment for educated, urbanized Jews—and anyone else—with democratic sympathies. Cities, he declared, did not reflect the values of "the true Prussian people," who were to be found in the countryside. "If the cities were ever to revolt again," Bismarck warned, the true Prussia "would know how to make them obey, even though it had to erase them from the face of the earth.")

When my great-grandfather landed in New York, he was part of the second wave of Jewish immigration, between, roughly, 1820 and 1880, often described by historians as the "German" period of American Jewish history (as distinct from the earlier Sephardic period and the post-1880 era dominated by immigrants from Eastern Europe and Russia). In fact, a considerable proportion of the so-called German immigrants from 1820 to 1880 were extremely poor, Yiddish-speaking Jews who had lived in Posen and Silesia. (The regions became part of a unified Germany in 1871 but remained a source of contention between Poles and Germans. Much of the territory, including the city of Breslau, was ceded to Poland at the end of World War II.) The Jewish immigrants from these eastern areas— especially those who came from small towns—did not have family roots (as the Sondheims of Frankfurt did) that extended back several generations on German soil.

While Maximilian Jacoby was far from poor, his family background in the Old World would not have impressed the Our Crowd merchant princes and bankers who could trace their lineage in Germany for centuries. Although my great-grandfather spoke German, was a student at Breslau's old and distinguished university, and was as well versed in German culture as any of the Our Crowd Jews, his family probably came from somewhere farther east. Breslau was one of the cities that, in the first half of the nineteenth century, served as a magnet for Jews moving westward, seeking better economic prospects and fleeing the anti-Semitic persecutions that were more virulent in the small towns and rural areas of Poland and Russia than in Germany. The growing city was a center of Jewish as well as secular learning, and there a Jew might, if he were so inclined, acquire the dual education espoused by proponents of the Jewish Enlightenment. (But there is no evidence whatsoever that my great-grandfather was exposed to serious Jewish learning or, for that matter, to the rudimentary Jewish education required to become bar mitzvah.) In cities like Breslau, Jews—especially if they had been there more than a generation and achieved a modicum of economic security—identified with the better-educated Germans rather than with the Polish (and German) peasants who were also emigrating from the countryside.

In any event, Maximilian's enrollment at a prominent German university makes it clear that his parents, whatever the degree of their own assimilation, wanted their son to make his way in the German society that had, since the last decades of the eighteenth century, been expanding (albeit grudgingly, slowly, and unevenly) the economic and civil rights of Jews. While generally barred from owning land or entering most professions at the start of the nineteenth century, small numbers of German Jews nevertheless moved into the middle and upper middle classes through trade and finance. And while the overall German middle class was still relatively small in the 1840s, it was huge by comparison with the virtually nonexistent bourgeoisie in a Polish society divided between a tiny upper crust of landowning aristocrats and an impoverished peasantry of near-feudal status. Some Jews managed to accumulate capital in spite of numerous discriminatory taxes, residence restrictions, and legal obstacles to Jewish marriages. With perseverance and money, the same Jews could obtain a secular education at both the secondary and university levels. The late-twentieth-century view of the history of German Jewry, colored as it is by our knowledge of the Holocaust, makes it difficult to appreciate that for a Jew in the middle of the nineteenth century, even before full legal emancipation, Germany was nevertheless a far more desirable—and safer—place to be a Jew than the lands farther east. In my great-grandfather's generation, significant numbers of German Jews began to consider themselves Germans first, Jews second (and to assume that their non-Jewish countrymen shared this view of the Jews in their midst).

Even after the transatlantic migration, Jews like Max Jacoby demonstrated a lifelong, unbreakable attachment to the German language, German literature, and German culture as a whole. Max made sure that each of his three American-born children learned to read and write German; both of his sons spoke German fluently and enjoyed reading German poetry. My grandfather, who loved Shakespeare deeply and passed that love on to his children, wrote a paper during his sophomore year at Columbia analyzing several nineteenth-century translations of Shakespeare from English into German.

IN 1967, a year after my grandmother's funeral, Stephen Birmingham's *Our Crowd*, an account of the rise of the German Jews in New York, became a best-seller. Knowing little more than the bare fact of the family's long-hidden Jewishness, I was struck by Birmingham's observation that "in future generations, in New York, it would become a matter of some importance whether such and such a Jewish family, with a German-sounding name, had been a true *native* German family . . . or a stranger from the east, passing through." The passage revived a long-forgotten image of my stern New York grandmother, waving her hand dismissively as she talked about the Polish origins of the Jacoby family. Max Jacoby, she said repeatedly, had been only one generation removed from a village in Poland when he came to America. "It takes more than one generation to make a gentleman," she would add, grudgingly acknowledging that her father-in-law had been a well-educated man and had spoken accentless, perfect German ("though he still spoke English with an accent after fifty years in New York"). Then she would use a word that sounded in my child's ears as "osjuice," something I presumed to be a variant of orange juice. "My father said he never expected a Sondheim would marry one of the osjuice," she explained—as if I should know what she meant—"but that this was America, and who you were before did not matter so much." When I asked Dad what his mother was talking about, he shook his head and said he had no idea. Thirty years later, reading a passage about Hitler's expulsion of foreign-born Jews from Germany, I realized that she could only have been referring to the *Ostjuden*, the Eastern Jews who still evoked the disdain of a Sondheim of Frankfurt even as her own children proceeded to obliterate the memory of having been *Juden* of any kind. A friend has suggested that my grandmother must have combined the German *Ost* with the English "Jews." I know better. Like my father, Granny Jacoby regarded the word *Jew* as an unspeakable vulgarity.

IN 1871, Max took his wife, Eve, and their three children—nine-year-old Geppy, six-year-old Levi Harold, and the year-old Oswald Nathaniel—on a trip to Europe. In Vienna, they posed for a formal family photograph in evening dress. This is a precious document to me, since it is one of only two pre-1890 pictures of the Jacobys that have survived.

At forty-one, Max is a slender, youthful-looking man, with dark brown eyes, a neatly trimmed beard, and reddish-brown hair just beginning to gray (if the color wash of the photograph is reasonably accurate). Unsmiling (like nearly everyone who posed for photographs in the Victorian era), he nevertheless projects a hint of the sensuality that is so much more obvious in the snapshots of my beardless grandfather at the same age. Eve Jackson Jacoby, at thirty-six, personifies what used to be called "a fine figure of a woman." A massive gold pendant, framed by a low (as low as was proper in 1871) portrait neckline, sets off the creamy, slightly fleshy shoulders that were a hallmark of female beauty in the nineteenth century. With her dark hair swept upward to reveal a high forehead and sharp gray eyes (my father's and my eyes) that look as though they miss nothing, Eve conveys the gravity of a powerful matriarch.

The only member of the family who "looks Jewish" is Levi Harold, a lanky boy much darker and swarthier than his parents or siblings. Geppy is a carbon copy of her mother and Oswald a golden-haired pudding of a baby, his head swathed in the ringlets Victorian mothers refused to cut off until their little boys were well out of the toddler stage. (As Harold reached middle age and began to gray, he would become much less "Jewish-looking" than the younger brother who had been a fair-haired baby.) The portraits leave no doubt that the Maximilian Jacobys have become a wealthy family with a secure place in the world: if Max's parents did indeed start out in a shtetl, their son traveled even farther in twenty-five years than they could have expected when they sent him to the university in Breslau.

IT IS probable that Max already possessed some capital when he arrived in New York, because he managed to acquire an older partner, Jacob Zeller, and to establish himself in business on William Street, by 1857. Max was only twenty-six when the house of Jacoby & Zeller began importing decorative and fine art objects, publishing art books and monographs in German, and producing high-quality lithographs. The firm also mounted art exhibitions; the New York Public Library's precomputer card catalog includes an entry for a portfolio from an 1866 Jacoby & Zeller show. For me, the catalog entry proved to be a cruel tease, because the actual portfolio has disappeared from the library's permanent collection.

The 1850s were wonderful years for anyone attempting to build almost any kind of business in New York. The previous decade had marked the beginning of the transformation of New York from a seafaring town into a mercantile capital. Fueled by the gold pouring into the American economy from California, prices on the New York Stock Exchange rose in a heady spiral as irresistible to contemporary speculators as the bull market of the 1990s would prove to be for their great-grandchildren. Even the panic of 1857, during which only one commercial bank (owned by the German Jewish Seligman family) managed to remain open, failed to slow the growth of New York for long. Within two months after the reopening of the New York banks, gold deposits had more than tripled.

A firm selling expensive art and decorative objects with European cachet could hardly have failed to do well in a city with a burgeoning *nouveau riche* population eager to furnish its newly built homes and advertise its prosperity. Moreover, the publication of books in German reinforced the Jacoby & Zeller firm's marketable connection with European art, taste, and culture. There was a substantial and growing market for German-language publications in the 1850s and 1860s, spurred not only by the desire of recent immigrants from Germany to read books in their native language but also by the high regard for German culture among educated Americans. Private German tutors were in great demand, and many well-educated but impecunious political émigrés found their first jobs in the homes of New Yorkers who wanted their children to acquire a cultural background money alone could not provide. (This aspect of New York life in the decade after the Civil War is exemplified by the character of Professor Bhaer in Louisa May Alcott's *Little Women*. The impoverished professor, a recent émigré from Germany, courts Jo with lines from Goethe while teaching German to the children of their New York landlord.) For a man like my great-grandfather, there were both business and social advantages to be gained by stressing his links with Germany.

At thirty, only three years after the founding of his business, Max had attained enough financial success and stability to win the hand of the daughter of "an old New Yorker of prominence." The marriage was a step up for a man who had been in the United States only twelve years, for, regardless of how prominent Eve's father may or may not have been, the family was well off and had settled in New York in 1814. Eve was born in Flushing, Queens, in 1840. According to a biographical sketch supplied by my grandfather for the Columbia University alumni files, the Jacksons were "of English extraction."

Eve Jackson, like her husband, was Jewish—and her family may also have come originally from Poland. (Before their name was Anglicized, the Jacksons might have been Jacobys themselves.) A century ahead of the great Jewish migration to America from Eastern Europe, Jews from Poland and Russia began settling in England, which became a permanent home for some but served as a way station on the road to America for many others. Like the Jews who had been in Germany for only one generation before moving on to the New World, the Jewish immigrants from England dropped any mention of their eastern origins after a generation in America. To be known as a German Jew was better than to be known as a Polish Jew; to be "English" was better than both. This accretion of social distinctions and small snobberies, stripped of Jewish associations, was to remain important to the Jacobys well into the twentieth century.

Uncle Ozzie gave me a plausible explanation of the Jackson family's decision to come to America, though I don't doubt that he embellished the story he heard from his father. According to Ozzie, the Jacksons were cloth merchants in England, suspected of having evaded the British blockade by shipping wool to the former colonies during the War of 1812. With the war over, the Jacksons decided (perhaps one step ahead of His Majesty's tax collectors) to set sail for the country that had provided them with a handsome profit. Flushing was a logical place for a family of merchant Jews to settle. By the beginning of the nineteenth century, the town already had a 150-year history of religious tolerance. The first settlers, in 1643, were English Puritans who had immigrated to Holland to escape religious persecution and then made their way to America. These Flushing Puritans proved to be much more tolerant than their co-religionists in Massachusetts. At the end of the seventeenth century, Flushing welcomed Quakers who were being persecuted and driven out of New England. In the 1820 census, six years after the Jacksons apparently settled in Flushing, three Jackson families are listed in nearby census tracts. One is a Daniel Jackson, and Eve's younger brother—Dano the pawnbroker, born in 1845—was named after his dead grandfather. The Jacksons of that generation were apparently Jewish enough to follow the custom of not naming children after living relatives.

When an entire family buries its origins, it is reasonable, in the absence of an obvious trauma, to assume that the process occurred over several generations. Though it seems highly unlikely that Max and Eve Jackson Jacoby were observant Jews—none of their children received any sort of Jewish education—the names they gave the children in the 1860s suggest that they were still attached to certain Jewish naming traditions. Their only daughter, born in 1862, was given the peculiar name of Geppy, which sounds like a nickname but is actually the legal name on her marriage certificate. Since the Jacobys preferred Teutonic names, Geppy may have been a Germanization and feminization of a Hebrew name like Gedaliah. Max and Eve's first son, Levi Harold, was the last Jacoby who would bear a definitively Jewish given name.

IN 1995, I tracked down Uncle Harold's file in Columbia University's collection of materials, called Columbiana, on alumni and faculty. It is a voluminous record, for my great-uncle spent his entire academic career at Columbia, from his undergraduate years through graduate school to his appointment as Rutherford Professor of Astronomy and director of the university's observatory. The clippings chronicle a life filled with scholarly honors. They also, in unambiguous black-and-white, reveal a progression away from all that the name Levi signifies. He enters the university as Levi Harold and is still Levi Harold when he graduates with the Class of '85. A few years later, as a graduate student and teaching assistant, he becomes L. Harold Jacoby. Before he marries Annie Maclear, the initial has also been eliminated. In the newspapers, my great-uncle is always Professor Harold Jacoby or "the distinguished Professor Harold Jacoby." With the twentieth century, the name Levi vanishes forever from the Jacoby family tree. What, I wonder, did old Max think of this?

. . .

SOON AFTER finding Harold's curriculum vitae in the Columbia archives, I managed to track down his one surviving grandson, Maclear (Mac) Jacoby Jr., a mathematics teacher and tennis coach at Landon School in Bethesda, Maryland. Mac's father, Maclear Jacoby Sr., was married in 1921, to Margaret Augusta Platt, by an Episcopal bishop who was a cousin of the bride. When I met Mac for the first time—neither of us had been aware of the other's existence before 1995—he told me that no one in his generation had any idea that Harold Jacoby had begun his life as Levi. His grandfather's Jewish origins had been as taboo a subject in Mac's by then impeccably Episcopal family as in mine. "I once asked my mother whether Grandfather's family was Jewish," Mac recalled, "since I was pretty sure Jacoby must be a Jewish name. She said, 'Oh, well, they weren't *really* Jews.' " My father, who had heard of his uncle Harold's existence but knew nothing about the fate of Harold's children and grandchildren, had no idea that Harold's descendants had not only become genuine Episcopalians but had married into a clerical family.

By the time my own grandfather was born in 1870, his parents placed his Jewish name—Nathaniel, after Max's father—in the middle and gave him the non-Jewish first name Oswald. This was (and is) a common strategy among acculturated Jews who wish to honor their origins in some subtle way. Such strategies amount to a private tip of the hat to the past; they neither require the owner to consciously abandon his Jewish name nor leave a printed record of deracination for nosy descendants. When I began looking into my grandfather's and great-uncle's lives, I wondered why, in view of their obvious desire to distance themselves from their origins, neither man changed his last name. The answer now seems quite simple to me: both men achieved success at an early age, and a name change would have been more trouble than it was worth. Harold and Oswald had both published articles in professional journals by their mid-twenties; a change of last name is no asset for someone whose professional identity is already established. Moreover, Max lived until his elder son was in his forties and the younger in his late thirties: a father may look with equanimity upon a son's sloughing off a Jewish first name but be deeply disturbed by a rejection of the family name.

In the next generation, perhaps more surprisingly, neither Uncle Ozzie nor my father ever considered changing his name. Ozzie laughed uproariously when I asked him why he hadn't, since he had lied about his religion (he declared himself a Congregationalist) at the time of his marriage in 1932. "I was already famous as a card-player," he said, "and I'd made a name for myself as Jacoby. Maybe I could have changed my name to something distinguished early on— 'the bridge whiz Oswald James, a distant relative of the distinguished writer Henry James . . .' Seriously, seriously, I never thought about it. Don't you think that would be disrespectful to my ancestors?" My father said much the same thing, even though his refusal to consider a name change ran directly counter to his desire to conceal his Jewishness. "What you call your religion isn't really that important," he said. "God is God is God—I know, you don't believe in God at all, but for me He matters. But who can respect a man who changes his name? My father and his father were Jacobys. I was born a Jacoby and I'm going to die a Jacoby. My grandchildren are going to be Jacobys."

No one can accuse my uncle and my father of suffering from a foolish consistency. They probably would have shared the reaction of Joseph Seligman, the German-born founder of the powerful nineteenth-century banking house that earned the Seligmans the label "the American Rothschilds," when his brother suggested in the 1870s that it was time for the distinguished family to change its name to something less Jewish. "I agree that you should change your name," Seligman was said to have told his brother. "I suggest you change it to *Schlemiel.*"

MY GREAT-GRANDPARENTS could not have raised their family during a more auspicious period for Jews in America than the two decades after the Civil War. Though the American Jewish population quadrupled as a result of immigration between 1850 and 1880—from roughly 50,000 to more than 210,000—the influx of German Jews had not aroused the conspicuous anti-Semitism that would greet the much larger immigration, of less assimilated Russian and Eastern European Jews, in the 1880s and 1890s. Jews like the Jacksons and the Jacobys were virtually indistinguishable from other Americans in appearance and behavior. Even the manner of worship of more observant German Jews did not set them apart from Christian Americans; Reform Judaism, with services mainly in the vernacular rather than in Hebrew, had arisen in Germany out of the modernizing spirit of the Jewish Enlightenment and proved to be an even more perfect fit for a country founded upon the separation of church and state. If that formal separation sometimes broke down in practice, the Bill of Rights nevertheless provided a freedom and protection that Jews had never known in even the most enlightened parts of Europe. In New York, where a third of American Jews were concentrated by 1850, the descendants of Sephardic Jews—who had arrived before the American Revolution—often evinced more discomfort than gentiles at the growing presence and influence of German Jews in the city. Whatever anti-Semitism existed in New York before and immediately after the Civil War, it was not translated into institutionalized discrimination that would impede a man in his attempts to make money, provide his children with a better education, and live more or less where he pleased and how he pleased.

New York, which had prospered during the war, also experienced a sustained economic boom as soon as peace was restored. The number of millionaires in the city increased at least fiftyfold during the decade after the war. My great-grandfather was not a millionaire, but everything about the way he lived, traveled, and educated his children suggests that his business fared extremely well during this period.

In 1861, Max brought his bride to a townhouse in the Murray Hill area. This was not the fashionable location it would later become as society moved uptown, but the East Thirties were a good address for a man who had started a business only four years earlier. Some of the money may have been Eve's; the massive sterling silver tea service she brought to her marriage (Granny Jacoby passed it on to Uncle Ozzie) suggests that the Jacksons of English descent had done very well indeed in the New World.

Max traveled at least every other year to Europe, always stopping in Germany and Austria and always taking his wife, one of his children, or, as in 1871, the entire family. The September 14, 1880, edition of *The New York Times*, in a column chronicling customs violations of affluent New Yorkers (part of the news then considered fit to print), offers a revealing glimpse of Max's way of life. "Among the passengers on the ship Brittania," the *Times* reported, "was Max Jacoby, the William Street lithographer. He was traveling with his wife and daughter and declared that his five trunks contained nothing dutiable. Customs seized $1,000 worth of cloaks, underclothing, silk stockings and other fancy articles. Mr. Jacoby declared that part of the clothes had been worn and the rest were purchased for the use of his daughter, who fell ill and was therefore unable to wear them." One thousand dollars in 1880 translates into more than $25,000 today—a formidable stock of fancy articles by the standards of any era. This episode not only attests to Max's affluence but suggests a certain ethical elasticity (at least where money was concerned) that was replicated, in one form or another, in the next two generations of Jacoby men. Max must have made amends to customs and changed his ways (or been more careful not to get caught), because there is no further evidence of his having had anything other than a spotless business and personal reputation.

Meanwhile, Max was pursuing his version of the American Dream by educating both of his sons in private schools, with the rigorous background in the classics and modern languages required by the Columbia entrance examination. His daughter, as was the custom in most upper-middle-class homes, was tutored privately. Another generation would pass before even the wealthiest, most cultivated Jewish (and non-Jewish) families gave any thought to preparing daughters for a higher education.

AN ATTEMPT to reconstruct the lives of one's ancestors provides a focused lesson, in a way no impersonal history can deliver, on the invisibility of most women's lives before the twentieth century. The only sources of information about ordinary (and even many extraordinary) women are their letters and diaries, and the Jacobys preserved almost no personal papers. As far as the Jacoby men were concerned, it was my good fortune to find public records of their doings in the Columbia alumni files and the morgues of the city's newspapers. But my great-grandmother and great-aunt, like most women, left no public traces of their existence. They owned no property, attended no universities, wrote no books, joined no professional organizations. When they died, their lives as wives and mothers were not considered important enough to merit obituaries. Family photographs, and a silver plate entwining her initials with her husband's on the occasion of their twenty-fifth wedding anniversary in 1886, offer the only concrete evidence (apart from her children) that Eve Jackson Jacoby existed. Her daughter, Geppy, left even fewer traces—but the only surviving photograph of her as a young woman reveals a good deal about the family's willingness to discard whatever attachment it had retained to Judaism as a religion.

On June 29, 1881, at age nineteen, Geppy married Albrecht von Liebenstein, a German baron, in a civil ceremony in New York's City Hall. The marriage ceremony, with the groom in the full regalia of a Prussian officer, was witnessed by the German consul in New York. This was the family's first mixed marriage, for the Baron, as he was called respectfully by the next generation, was definitely not Jewish. The civil ceremony suggests that Geppy did not convert to Christianity in order to marry her baron; that the marriage was witnessed by the German consul indicates that the young couple planned to live in Germany at some point. It seems unlikely that a man who chose to be married in full German military uniform, clutching the distinctive Prussian helmet in his arm while posing for his wedding pictures, would stay in America forever.

Geppy may have met her husband on one of her many trips to Germany with her father. Marriages between Jews and gentiles were unusual but far from unheard of in the newly unified Germany of the 1880s, where Jews had finally been granted full civil rights. (A half century later, the descendants of such couples would find the course of their lives drastically altered by the 1935 Nuremberg Laws, which classified them as Jews or Aryans according to the number of Jewish grandparents. Geppy's and the Baron's children, half-Jews, would have been classified as first-degree *Mischlinge*—literally, "mixed breed"—and their legal status would have been determined by whether they themselves had married Jews or gentiles. Their grandchildren, quarter-Jews—assuming that Geppy was their only Jewish grandparent—would have been deemed second-degree *Mischlinge*, retaining the rights of German citizens. These distinctions did not, however, survive the Final Solution. By 1942, second-degree *Mischlinge* with an "especially unfavorable appearance in racial terms" were to be classified as Jewish *solely* on the basis of their appearance. In some of these cases, sterilization was proposed as an alternative to extermination. In the end, most of the *Mischlinge* trapped in wartime Germany were deported to extermination camps.)

At first, I intended to make every effort to trace the Liebenstein family in Germany in order to find out what happened to my great-aunt, but I soon concluded that Geppy did not live long enough to have children. After her wedding portrait—the petite Geppy is a full head shorter than her dashing groom with the handlebar mustache—my great-aunt disappears from the family records. Whether or not Geppy returned to Germany with her husband, she surely would have appeared in the many post-1890 family photographs if she had been alive. Max and Eve continued to travel widely after their children married, and they would have kept snapshots of their first grandchildren. When Aunt Edith was born in 1907, she was given Geppy as a middle name in memory of her aunt. In typical

Jacoby fashion, the details of Geppy's death—when, why, and how—were never discussed. Ozzie said his father had adored his older sister, who was nine when Oswald Nathaniel was born and who used to call him "my baby." Geppy had been her father's pet, and my grandfather told Ozzie that Max had been ecstatic at his daughter's marriage into "a fine old German family." When Geppy died, Max was so heartbroken that he never talked about her again. At first I doubted the truth of this story, wondering whether Max might have been less than ecstatic at his daughter's marriage to a Prussian officer. However, everything I have learned about my great-grandfather argues against his having been an inflexible patriarch who would have cut his daughter out of his life because she had married a gentile—even if he disapproved of her choice. And there is no reason to suppose that he did disapprove of mixed marriages. The family album shows him on good terms with his son Harold after he married a Christian—and not in a civil ceremony but in a full-fledged Episcopal church service. My guess is that Geppy died in childbirth, still a common occurrence even in well-off nineteenth-century families with access to the best contemporary medical care.

Who was that sweet-faced girl, the young bride who left only her niece's middle name as evidence that she was ever a part of my family? Did she have any ambitions beyond being her father's pet and her husband's darling? Was she as smart as her brothers, who entered one of the best universities in America when they were only fifteen? Did she love Goethe and Schiller, as her father did? I know only that by virtue of her marriage to a German aristocrat, Geppy escaped the peculiarly American dilemmas of her younger brothers, who began their adult lives at a time when America was reinventing anti-Semitism in a form far less virulent than its counterpart in the Old World but no less psychologically painful to its targets.

IN 1877, four years before Levi Harold Jacoby began his freshman year at Columbia, the community of "Forty-Eighters"—as German Jewish immigrants of my great-grandfather's generation were known by then—was shaken by the first widely publicized case of anti-Semitic social discrimination in the United States. This episode, now forgotten by everyone except historians of American Jewry, was especially traumatic to the German Jewish community because it involved Joseph Seligman (the same Seligman who had sneered at his brother's suggestion that they change their last name), the most influential and prominent Jew in America at the time. As a banker who had helped finance the Union Army during the Civil War, Seligman was so devoted to his adopted country that he hired the quintessentially American booster, Horatio Alger, to tutor his sons. (Alger was also Benjamin Cardozo's tutor while he, like my grandfather, was preparing for the Columbia entrance exam.) Seligman had always stayed with his family at Saratoga's elegant Grand Union Hotel during his annual summer vacation in upstate New York, but when he arrived in June 1877, having reserved his usual suite, the eminent banker was greeted by a desk clerk who told him, "Mr. Seligman, I am required to inform you that Judge Hilton [the Grand Union's administrator] has given instructions that no Israelites shall be permitted in the future to stop at this hotel." Unlike many such insults, the whole matter became front-page news—especially in New York—when Seligman issued a public letter describing the incident in detail and accusing Hilton of "shameless bigotry." Hilton replied in his own open letter. "As the law yet permits a man to use his property as he pleases, I propose exercising that blessed privilege, notwithstanding Moses and all his descendants may object."

At the time, my great-grandfather already owned a summer home near Saratoga Springs. As a Jew who was both successful and acculturated, he must have been painfully affected, if only in a psychological sense, by the Seligman-Hilton affair. If a man as powerful as Joseph Seligman could be turned away, how much more vulnerable was a Jew who was merely, as the *Times* put it, a William Street lithographer. And a man whose German origins were of fairly recent vintage.

Although the New York establishment press generally condemned the action of the hotel owner, "Hebrews Need Not Apply" signs began appearing outside resort hotels in vacation areas throughout the country. To avoid the humiliation of being turned away, German Jews established their own hotels and summer vacation communities. Two decades later, the new Jewish immigrants from Eastern Europe would in turn be excluded from the Our Crowd resorts.

The visible success of so many German Jews, the beginning of the influx of poorer Jews from Eastern Europe, and the social pretensions of the Gilded Age all contributed to the development of new, informal American forms of social anti-Semitism (as distinct from the institutionalized discrimination in the Old World) that closed doors open to Jews only a generation earlier. During the Seligman-Hilton controversy, the New York City Bar Association blackballed a Jewish applicant for the first time—a more significant form of discrimination, because it involved a professional organization, than any restrictions at a resort. Soon afterward, Greek-letter fraternities at the City College of New York banded together to exclude Jews. The thought of exclusionary fraternities playing an important role in the social life of City College, known for extending higher education to generations of poor immigrants, is a comical one today. But in the 1880s, when Uncle Harold and my grandfather entered Columbia, college men, at both public and private institutions, took fraternities seriously. My great-grandfather had prepared his two sons to enter an elite institution of higher education and to become whatever they wanted to become in America. At just that point, it was becoming clear that some American possibilities did not extend to Jews. The social restrictions of the 1880s and 1890s prefigured the restrictive covenants and "gentleman's agreements" that began to proliferate before World War I.

The social anti-Semitism of the Gilded Age pushed upper-middle-class German Jews in two not always mutually exclusive directions. Many retreated into their own organizations, which continued to emphasize German, as distinct from Jewish, antecedents until America went to war with Germany. Others, especially those who looked like gentiles and had attenuated ties to the Jewish community, began to disappear into the larger society through intermarriage. In the 1880s, my great-grandfather began attending meetings of the Society for Ethical Culture, an organization that attracted Jews, mainly of German descent, who were ready to abandon traditional Jewish observance but were not about to become Christians. The society had been founded in 1875 by Felix Adler, the son of the rabbi of New York's Temple Emanu-El. Adler graduated from Columbia and was ordained a rabbi in Germany, where he went on to study at the University of Heidelberg. There he was exposed to the newest biblical criticism, based on many recent linguistic and archeological discoveries, that questioned previous interpretations of both the Torah and the Christian Gospels. And there the young rabbi lost his belief in divine revelation. Ethical Culture evolved out of Adler's attempt to construct a spiritual basis for living, absent belief in a personal God. While the organization would eventually attract financial support from some non-Jews (mainly upper-class mavericks like John D. Rockefeller Jr.), its American leaders were almost entirely Jews of German descent. In the last decade of the nineteenth century, Ethical Culture was a way of staying just a little—a very little—bit Jewish, of maintaining some sense of connection to Jewish ethical traditions while abandoning Judaism as a religion. That is why it was rejected not only by the new and more traditionally observant immigrants from Eastern Europe but also by most of the older generation of Reform Jews, who had so effectively adapted the form of their religion to their new country. Ethical Culture was a product of the scientific discoveries and rationalism that posed a challenge to all traditional religions in the latter decades of the Victorian era; the society was devised by men who were filled with doubts but still longed to hear something more than Matthew Arnold's "melancholy, long, withdrawing roar" of what had once been the sea of faith.

I doubt that Max was surprised or horrified either by his elder son's marriage to an Episcopalian or by his younger son's agnosticism. But I suspect he would have been utterly astonished, in view of his adherence to a creed based on humanist ethics and rationality, at the notion that three of his grandchildren would end their lives, nearly a century later, as converts to the Catholic faith.

Neither my father nor my uncle Ozzie had any real understanding of how their father's Jewishness had affected his life, but I believe the family's twentieth-century rejection of its origins was rooted in the experiences of those two brilliant young men, Levi Harold and Oswald Nathaniel, in the New York of the 1880s and 1890s. Their father had built a business that enabled his sons to go to school with members of the true American upper class—but the upper class, at that very moment, was inventing new social barriers designed to keep out not only "the wrong kind" of Jews but also all "Israelites." The Jacobys considered themselves the right kind of Jews, but both Harold and Oswald, as they entered adulthood, must already have become attuned to the double message that neither my father nor Uncle Ozzie ever forgot in the following century: Jews are better than other people. Also worse.

IV

Brothers

FOR MUCH OF MY adult life, I was fascinated by the complicated relationship between my father and his elder brother—a tense and rivalrous, but always loving, connection that deepened by the end of their lives into understanding and acceptance of each other's foibles and strengths. Growing up in a home with aggrieved parents—so disappointed in each other that there was never enough love to go around—Ozzie and Dad might easily have become strangers or enemies. They had no model of brotherly love, for their father and his elder brother had long been estranged by the time they died, within a year of each other, in the early thirties. As brothers and as men, my father and his brother managed to avoid replicating the pattern of the previous generation. It was a near miss, though, for Dad and Ozzie bore the dual burden of memory and memory loss—the personal memory of their father's ruined life, the family's lost memory of the social and psychological history that helped make Oswald Nathaniel Jacoby who and what he was. Today, I cannot think about the two brothers I knew without conjuring up the earlier pair of Jacoby brothers I never knew, the brothers who, by the end of the nineteenth century, seemed poised to fulfill the deepest hopes that impelled their father to leave Breslau fifty years earlier.

IN 1886, a year after his elder brother received his bachelor's degree, fifteen-year-old Oswald Jacoby entered Columbia College School of Arts, as the undergraduate division was called at the time. Of the seventy-four entering freshmen, at least seven, judging from their last names, were Jews. That total—more than 9 percent of the class—offers one indicator of the success attained by many German Jewish immigrants of my great-grandfather's generation, who by then were able to afford the best possible education for their sons. Moreover, the class may have included more Jewish (or half-Jewish) students, with last names that did not reveal their origins. At the time, the small student body was drawn mainly from well-off, old New York families that had sent their sons to Columbia for generations. Benjamin Cardozo, who entered Columbia as a freshman a year before my grandfather, was one of the few students who was a Jew as well as a representative of "old" New York. His mother's family, immigrants from England, had settled in the city around 1750. One of her ancestors, Gershom Seixas, was the first Jew (and the last, until Cardozo himself) to serve as a Columbia trustee.

WHAT WAS it like to be a Jew at Columbia during the 1880s? The answer may have been very different for Cardozo from what it was for Max's sons, who definitely belonged to the "new" New York. Harold, who focused on a future in science from an early age and evinced little interest as an undergraduate in activities unconnected with his academic pursuits, may have seen the matter differently from Oswald, an extrovert of wide interests and a member of numerous student organizations. The yearbook of Oswald's graduating class records that he was a coxswain in the annual Columbia spring regatta, a violinist in the Columbia College orchestra, and a member of both the popular undergraduate Shakespeare Society and the Barnard Literary Association (the college debating society). He and

Cardozo may have become friends through their common involvement in debating, one of the few extracurricular activities that attracted the future Supreme Court justice. Cardozo, not a joiner by temperament, might have pledged a fraternity had he so desired—in spite of his being a Jew and in spite of the tarnishing of the once-spotless Cardozo family name by a political scandal involving his father. However, Columbia classbooks from that era make it clear that by the 1880s, most Jews were already excluded from social fraternities.

My grandfather was a young man who would have wanted to belong to a fraternity. Unlike Cardozo, Oswald was gregarious, athletic, and physically precocious. Standing nearly six feet tall when he entered Columbia at fifteen, he projected the brand of male charisma that earns a young man the admiration of his contemporaries. After winning a scholarship in English literature in his junior year, he was elected president of the Shakespeare Society as a senior (an honor that had as much to do with popularity among other students as with academic distinction). Yet neither his academic honors nor his friendships could get him into a fraternity. Uncle Ozzie remembered his father's bitter words on the subject. "When I was a freshman at Columbia in nineteen nineteen, Father told me not even to think about pledging a fraternity because they didn't want anyone who was too smart. It still rankled with him that he hadn't been asked to join. Didn't bother me a bit. I told Father I had no desire to be around dummies. Being left out of a fraternity isn't the blow of a lifetime, you know. But for Father—yes-yes-yes-yes—it was a great insult." (Ozzie, like my dad, spoke in such rapid-fire fashion that it was often hard to understand him. In moments of excitement, he would sometimes break into a stream of yesses that resembled the barking of a dog.)

"Yes-yes-yes," Ozzie growled, "there was a lot of Groucho Marx in Father—you know the line, 'I wouldn't want to belong to any club that would have me as a member.' But he did want to belong to clubs that *wouldn't* have him." Ozzie himself took considerable pleasure in the knowledge that his status as a bridge champion had earned him an invitation to join the Dallas Country Club, an institution not noted for its hospitality to Jews or anyone else perceived as less than a full-blooded, white, Christian (but not Hispanic Christian) American. In 1964, when Barry Goldwater was running against Lyndon Johnson for the presidency, Ozzie looked around the table at his card-playing cronies and declared, "You know the difference between us? You'll vote for Barry Goldwater for president but you wouldn't want him in this country club. I'd let him into the club but I sure don't want him in the White House."

From a late-twentieth-century perspective, it may seem petty to emphasize the importance of an anti-Semitic social slight to my grandfather, a young man who, after all, had everything else going for him. But the young do take such matters seriously: it has often been noted by biographers that the financier Bernard Baruch never got over his anger at having been blackballed from a fraternity at the City College of New York. Moreover, my grandfather was an extremely ambitious young man, and his social experiences at Columbia must have taught him the bitter lesson that however much he achieved, and however well liked he was as an individual, some doors would still be closed to him as a Jew.

His elder brother, who had an even more brilliant academic career as an undergraduate, clearly drew the same conclusions about the social and professional liability attached to being unmistakably identified as a Jew. One wonders whether Annie Maclear's parents would have welcomed a son-in-law named Levi as enthusiastically as they welcomed Harold. Annie and Harold met while he was spending several months in the vicinity of Capetown in order to conduct astronomical observations for his doctoral thesis; the area around the Cape of Good Hope had long been a favorite site for astronomers studying the skies of the Southern Hemisphere. It was not surprising, in view of the prominence of Annie's grandfather, the Astronomer Royal, that a visiting scientist would be introduced to the Maclears. Harold's and Annie's granddaughter, Eve Van de Water

Thew (another of my newly discovered cousins, she was named for our great-grandmother, Eve Jackson Jacoby), says the Maclears, whose professional and social standing in Capetown was far higher than their financial standing, regarded the obviously affluent young American as a good catch for their daughter. Mrs. Thew is the child of Harold's only daughter, Eve Marion, who married Edward Ter-hune Van de Water in 1923 in yet another Episcopal ceremony, presided over by a priest who was a relative of the groom. The younger Eve grew up (like her first cousin, Mac Jacoby Jr.) knowing that there had been a terrible falling-out between her grandfather and my grandfather but not knowing why. "No one ever explained," she says. "I'm sure that Granny Annie—that's what we called her— knew, but it wasn't something that was talked about. I just under-stood as a child that *we*—the descendants of Harold—didn't have anything to do with *them*—'the other Jacobys.' We were very well aware that we were related to the famous bridge columnist, but no one reached out and tried to get in touch with him. That's how sen-sitive the subject of 'the other Jacobys' was in the family."

Of course, the children of the estranged Jacoby brothers were first cousins. Uncle Ozzie, who was already a teenager by the time of Harold's and Oswald's falling-out, certainly did know his cousins, even though he never talked about them in later life. The long-lost family photo album includes several pre-1915 pictures of the two Jacoby families together. In a later snapshot, the teenage Ozzie is clowning around a swimming pool with his cousin Eve (Mrs. Thew's mother). But a few years later, there would be no trace of "the other Jacobys" at Eve's wedding.

Now in her seventies, Mrs. Thew spent her girlhood in Westport, Connecticut (on the same street as her cousin Mac), where Harold and Annie lived after his retirement from Columbia. At that time, restrictive covenants were the rule in most upper-class, old-line WASP Connecticut towns within commuting distance of New York. Westport had only a handful of Jewish residents in the thirties and forties (though it was never as tightly closed to Jews as nearby

Darien, cited in the postwar novel and movie *Gentleman's Agreement* as a prime example of a community determined to maintain its anti-Semitic restrictive covenants). Mrs. Thew says she doubts that either her mother or Mac's father knew that Harold's real first name was Levi. "I don't even know whether my grandmother knew that," she says, "though she obviously must have known that the Jacoby family was originally Jewish. I certainly didn't know as a child that Jacoby was generally a Jewish name, but I feel that she must have known. It didn't come up for me, since my name was Van de Water. But I can remember later, much later in life, when my cousin Mac came to visit, people would sometimes ask, 'What kind of a name is Jacoby?' With a little edge to the question. As I got older, I began to wonder more and more what really happened in the previous generation."

The marriage between Annie and Harold—unlike my grandparents' marriage—seems to have been an unqualified success. Annie, a learned young woman with a deep interest of her own in science and history, was an asset to her husband in his role as a rising young star at Columbia, not because her grandfather had been the Astronomer Royal at Capetown (although that didn't hurt) but because she was a socially adept woman of great charm and vivacity, capable of carrying out to perfection the duties of a faculty wife. Invitations to her afternoon teas, a Columbia faculty bulletin noted, were prized because of the liveliness of the discussions and the excellence of the cake and sandwiches. Harold, who became an expert in the application of rapidly evolving late-nineteenth-century photographic technology to astronomical observation, rose swiftly at Columbia. At twenty-nine, even before receiving his doctorate, he had been appointed an adjutant professor. From 1904 until his retirement in 1929, he was a full professor and, for most of those years, director of Columbia's observatory.

Ozzie said his father always described his brother as "a brilliant bore." My dad, who was only a baby when the elder Jacoby brothers broke off contact with each other, seems never to have met his scholarly uncle. By then, my grandfather had ample reason to envy his brother, who lived in a beautiful house near the university on Morningside Heights (while the Oswald Jacobys lived in Brooklyn's inelegant Flatbush section), had achieved an unbroken string of professional successes, and was widely quoted in the New York press on every conceivable scientific issue.

Professor Jacoby was always in the news; the architects of the new Grand Central Terminal thought so highly of him that they commissioned him to prepare a map of the constellations for the main lobby's glorious azure ceiling. That ceiling, glowing with all of its original brightness since the renovation of Grand Central in the mid-1990s, has been beloved by generations of New Yorkers but was a source of some embarrassment to the original builders—and Harold—when the station opened in 1913. An observant commuter pointed out that the constellations, while certainly beautiful and impressive, were reversed on the ceiling. The contractors passed the buck to Uncle Harold, who had supplied the map, but he maintained with considerable indignation that either the contractor or the workmen had turned his chart the wrong way when they began transferring the paper design to the ceiling. I believe my great-uncle's version of the story, since it seems unlikely that the head of the Columbia Observatory would have failed to place the stars in their proper order.

Until I looked up Harold's file in the *Times* morgue, I had no idea that he had anything to do with the creation of the Grand Central ceiling. If my father, Edith, or Ozzie ever knew about the connection between their uncle and a famous New York landmark, they had forgotten it by the time I began asking questions about the family. That in itself suggests the depth of the breach between Harold and my grandfather: silence and distance bred more silence and distance. Had Harold not been prominent enough to receive considerable press coverage, and lengthy obituaries, I would never have known anything about him other than the fact that he had once been a professor at Columbia.

In addition to a distinguished career, Harold also enjoyed delightful-sounding hobbies. An article in a 1954 issue of *Boats*, a magazine chronicling the history of recreational boating in America, paints a charming picture (mainly from Harold's diaries and his son's reminiscences) of the life my great-uncle built with his close-knit family—the harmonious and satisfying domestic life my grandfather never had. Professor Harold Jacoby, the article explained, was typical of "skippers" who owned small craft and sailed for pleasure in the first two decades of the twentieth century. Accompanied by his wife and son, Harold cruised around Long Island Sound and Cape Cod in a twenty-seven-foot catboat in the days when, as the magazine pointed out, " 'yachting' was generally considered the preserve of bankers, railroad presidents, and oil men." In 1906, Harold traded in his sails for a twenty-eight-foot power boat, one of the earliest raised-deck cruisers on Long Island Sound. In winter, he moored his cruiser in Greenwich, Connecticut, "and on clear weekends the Professor and young Mac [his son] proceeded to Greenwich of a Friday evening, walked out on the ice to the boat, and clambered aboard. Before he even changed his clothes, the Professor would fire up the galley stove and have a pot of tea brewing. Saturdays they fished through the ice, went iceboating, and visited their oystermen friends. Saturday night's dinner was a full-pot oyster stew. . . . the good Professor had found, as have many professional men since, that a boat is a perfect place in which to leave shore routine far behind." In 1912, Harold traded in the cruiser for a houseboat, so that his entire family could spend the summer on the water. Mac Jacoby Jr. recalls his father, the young "Mac" in the article, telling loving stories about the time the family spent together, and he and his father spent by themselves, on their succession of boats. My grandfather had also owned a sailboat, but it was sold in 1915—presumably to pay off debts. More to the point, by the time Oswald was in his forties, he rarely spent an entire weekend—on land or sea—with his family.

If my grandfather really thought his brother was a bore, he was wrong. Delving into a murky family past is a process that produces

many surprises, and the discovery of my great-uncle's large published body of work has been a source of pure enjoyment. The more
I read him, the more I realized how much I would have liked him. He
was a popularizer of science, gifted with the capacity to explain
abstruse matters in down-to-earth, vivid images and language intelli-
gible to a population that was simultaneously fascinated by the rapid
turn-of-the-century advances in science and consumed by superstition. Reading Uncle Harold's books and essays, directed toward readers who were the equivalent of today's audience for the writings of
Stephen Jay Gould, I have been struck by the parallel between the
ambivalent attitude to science at the turn of the last century and the
combination of reverence and ignorance that shapes public attitudes
toward science and technology today. Harold Jacoby, like most educated men of his generation, was convinced that fundamentalist religious creeds, as well as belief in older superstitions like astrology and
fortune-telling, would fade away during the twentieth century. And
why not? The proliferating inventions and scientific discoveries in
the last three decades of the nineteenth century were, in many
respects, far more transforming, and more conducive to belief in the
triumph of rationality, than the computer revolution in the closing
decades of the twentieth century. From the X ray that, for the first
time, laid bare the body without cutting it open, to the electric light
that finally gave men power over night, late Victorian science and
inventiveness stripped away the mystery of what had previously
been unseen and therefore unknown and unknowable. In this environment, my great-uncle attempted to explain the difference
between real science and pseudoscientific, crackpot exploitation of
the new discoveries.

His first collection of essays, *Practical Talks by an Astronomer*,
was published by Scribner's in 1902. Throughout the book, which
covers subjects ranging from advances in navigation to the scientific
uses of photography, Professor Jacoby took up the cudgels on behalf
of rationality. "The public attitude toward matters scientific is one
of the mysteries of our time," he observed.

It can be described best by the single word, Credulity; simple, absolute credulity. Perfect confidence is the most remarkable characteristic of this unbelieving age. No charlatan, necromancer, or astrologer of three centuries ago commanded more respectful attention than does his successor of to-day. . . . We have had the Keeley motor and the liquid-air power schemes for making something out of nothing. Extracting gold from sea-water has been duly heralded on scientific authority as an easy source of fabulous wealth for the millions. Hard-headed business men not only believe in such things, but actually invest in them their most valued possession, capital.

My great-uncle's talent for bringing abstractions down to earth—a quality that must have served him well as a teacher—is evident in a lengthy 1927 interview on the subject of Albert Einstein's genius. "Years ago if I were to direct you to a certain man's address," Professor Jacoby told a reporter for the *New York Evening World*, "it would have been sufficient to say that he lived at 118th Street and Broadway. Then, as time went on, I would have to make that more explicit by saying that he lived at 118th Street and Broadway on the eighteenth floor. In other words, I had to give you three dimensions, instead of only two.

"Then Einstein came along and said the time element was important: that you would have to add to the other directions the time, say 1927, and that your complete directions would now include, '118th Street and Broadway, the eighteenth floor, and 1927.' That was original, for previous scientists regarded time and space as different entities, to be considered separately. Yet Einstein insisted that both should be considered together, for otherwise, if you left out the time, it would mean you had reached the given address at the wrong time and found the building crumbled away in old age."

There is no evidence that Harold's career at Columbia was hampered by his being a Jew—in part because he entered academia before administrators and trustees of elite universities became concerned about the rising number of student applications from Jews and began instituting measures, formal and informal, to deal with what they perceived as a "Jewish problem" on their campuses. In *A History of the Jews in America*, Howard M. Sachar cites a remarkable and revealing statistic: throughout the 1920s, in the entire country, fewer than one hundred Jewish professors were employed as full-time faculty in the arts and sciences. Considered from that perspective, it is easy to understand why Harold's Jewish origins remained a sensitive subject, to be downplayed and concealed from the next generation, long after he had become the much-lionized Professor Jacoby, a fixture on the Morningside Heights campus. My great-uncle established himself at Columbia, as a student and a teacher, before university officials (at Columbia and throughout the Ivy League) became deeply concerned about the rise in Jewish student enrollment as a result of the post-1880 immigration. Upper-class anti-Semitism intensified as the Jewish student presence at first-rank universities became more visible at both undergraduate and graduate levels. In 1905, a year after Harold Jacoby was promoted to full professor, the newly wed Eleanor Roosevelt, who only later discarded the prejudices inculcated by her upbringing, mentioned casually in a letter to her mother-in-law that it must be terrible for Franklin to be surrounded by so many Jews in his classes at Columbia Law School. Such ingrained prejudices, typical of that era and social class, were shared by many of the trustees and administrators of Ivy League universities. If Harold had earned his doctorate after 1900, he probably would not have had the chance to rise through the academic ranks and become one of those fortunate one hundred exceptions.

As a LAWYER starting out in the 1890s, in a profession where social contacts counted for a great deal, my grandfather would have been affected more directly than his elder brother by anti-Semitism. The old-line, non-Jewish New York law firms were of course closed to him: he could choose between going into practice for himself or joining a Jewish firm. But before Oswald was permitted to begin law school, his father insisted that he give the family business a try.

I felt my first flash of empathy for my grandfather—for I had considered his life only in terms of its impact on my father—when I spotted a three-year lacuna in his generally triumphal youthful vita. He had dreamed of becoming a lawyer since childhood—years later, Cardozo alluded to those youthful ambitions in an inscription to my grandfather on the flyleaf of a book—but Max insisted that his younger son go to work for him upon his graduation from Columbia in 1890. Harold, as a budding scientist, was exempted from the common Victorian paternal mandate that a son follow in his father's footsteps. Oswald, who had graduated first in his class, was tethered to the business for two years. At the end of 1892, Max relented and allowed his son to enroll in New York Law School. (Since Columbia was the preeminent law school in the city, it is somewhat surprising that my grandfather studied elsewhere. One wonders whether he had had enough of being the younger brother at an institution in which the elder brother was already making a name for himself on the junior faculty.) In his law school graduating class of two hundred, Oswald took first prize for a graduation essay titled "The Doctrine of Latent Equities as Affecting the Rights of Assignees." The essay was reprinted in a publication of the New York State Bar Association, a signal honor for a young man who had not yet been admitted to the bar. This nugget of information, describing a youthful achievement in such great detail, appeared in 1914 in a puff piece in which all of the material had obviously been supplied by the subject. That my grandfather chose to focus on a twenty-year-old honor is, in itself, a poignant comment on his state of mind and professional status in midlife.

At age twenty-four, as soon as he was admitted to the bar, Oswald chose to open his own law office in the financial district instead of joining the Jewish law firm where he had worked as a clerk while studying for the bar examination. He began to build a broad general practice that included civil and criminal cases, with a specialty in the lucrative field of fire insurance law. Oswald did extremely well financially during those early years; in 1900, when he married Edith Sondheim, his annual income was more than $20,000 a year (more than $150,000 today). Oswald frequently wound up with large settlements for his clients because he was noted for his ability to win over juries; even in an era of primitive safety laws, damage awards were rising. Especially after Theodore Roosevelt replaced the assassinated William McKinley as president and ushered in an era of more progressive social legislation, many insurance companies preferred negotiating a settlement to facing an aggressive lawyer—which Oswald definitely was—in a jury trial.

In addition to his insurance specialty, my grandfather took on a variety of quixotic cases in which he usually wound up on the side of the underdog (though not necessarily an innocent underdog). In fraud, libel, and divorce cases, he represented both defendants and plaintiffs. Oswald Jacoby's choice of clients sheds considerable light on his character: he repeatedly and successfully represented con men who, instead of bilking widows and orphans, had applied their deceptive talents to large companies. These clients, while not Robin Hoods, tended to be sympathetic figures to juries.

My grandfather's career was also influenced by the fact that he, like many German-descended Jews before World War I, was a progressive Republican who believed in activist government in both domestic and foreign affairs. German Jewish Democrats were the exception rather than the rule at that time. Even the exceptions, like Henry Morgenthau Sr. (whose son, Henry Jr., would become Franklin Roosevelt's secretary of the treasury), carefully described themselves as "Cleveland Democrats." While they had strongly supported former president Grover Cleveland, they wished to distance themselves from William Jennings Bryan, the Democratic presidential nominee in 1896, 1900, and 1908. (Bryan's Christian fundamentalism was naturally viewed with great suspicion by Jews, and his most famous metaphor, "You shall not crucify mankind upon a cross of gold," did nothing to ameliorate those suspicions.) Teddy

Roosevelt, who, as police commissioner of New York, had maintained excellent relations with wealthy German Jews as well as with representatives of the newer, poorer Eastern European immigrants, was a Republican who enjoyed particularly broad support within the city's Jewish community. As president, his advocacy of laws to ease the plight of the poor—coupled with such gestures as his 1906 White House invitation to a delegation from the American Conference of Rabbis—reinforced the esteem in which he was held by Jews. My grandfather, who did not care about rabbis but did care about social legislation, supported Roosevelt as the Republican candidate in 1904 and as the Progressive third-party candidate in 1912.

IN 1908, many of Oswald Jacoby's affinities—his delight in the spectacle of respectable executives with egg on their faces; affinity for rogues; talent for swaying juries; and Republican political sympathies—came together in a grand larceny trial that made front-page news. He served as the defense attorney for a colorful political hanger-on and shady behind-the-scenes manipulator named Broughton Brandenburg, who seems to have been an Edwardian combination of Lucianne Goldberg and Dick Morris.

The extensive newspaper accounts of my grandfather's behavior during the trial, and his subsequent attitude toward the case, offer real insight—as well as the only confirmation from sources outside the family—into the character of a man who enjoyed living on the edge and whose own ethics were flexible. The glamorous and sometimes unscrupulous patriarch, as described by both my father and uncle, was very much on display in Oswald's conduct of the Brandenburg case. Yet the Brandenburg affair would fascinate me even without the family connection, for it also offers a cameo portrait of what has, and has not, changed in journalistic and legal ethics since the beginning of the twentieth century.

Brandenburg was charged with forging Cleveland's signature on a political essay and then selling it to *The New York Times*. The "literary agent," as the *Times* described the defendant, had ties to both

Democrats and Republicans. He turned up in the offices of the *Times* in August 1908, bearing a typewritten manuscript, with a handwritten signature allegedly written by Cleveland. In the essay, the former Democratic president made it clear that he favored the Republican presidential candidate, William Howard Taft, over Bryan, the nominee of his own party.

Hot news, but there was one small problem: Cleveland had been dead since June 24. Backed up by the executor of Cleveland's estate, Brandenburg convinced the *Times* that the former president, assuming that Bryan and Taft would be nominated by their respective parties, had written the article and authorized its sale before his death. The *Times* went ahead and published the piece, on the front page of its Sunday magazine section, on August 30, and a delighted Republican Campaign Committee obtained the reprint rights, again through Brandenburg, for $300. Soon afterward, much to the chagrin of the *Times*, Cleveland's widow protested the publication of the article and claimed that the signature had been forged (though she and everyone involved agreed that the piece accurately reflected the late president's well-known anti-Bryan and pro-Taft convictions).

The willingness of the *Times* to deal with Brandenburg in the first place is something of a mystery, for the thirty-one-year-old hustler already possessed an unsavory reputation. He had been publicly implicated in an attempt, inspired by the National Association of Manufacturers, to blackmail Samuel Gompers into resigning the presidency of the American Federation of Labor. In an era when labor had few rights but workers were beginning to organize, big business correctly regarded Gompers as a formidable adversary, and Brandenburg, acting on behalf of the manufacturers' lobbying organization, had offered the AFL president permanent financial support in return for a signed "confession" that he had been living an "immoral" and "evil" life. The *Times* itself had reported the failed blackmail scheme after Gompers and the AFL leaked the story to one of the paper's Washington correspondents.

A particularly embarrassing detail, brought out by my grandfather during Brandenburg's trial and seized upon gleefully by the *New York World* and *New York Herald*, was that the *Herald* had rejected the manuscript before Brandenburg successfully peddled it to the *Times*'s Sunday editor. Moreover, the *Times* had compounded its embarrassment with an accompanying editorial, under the headline "Grover Cleveland's Article," painting a portrait of the hardworking statesman composing the thought-provoking essay in his study, "just before his last illness."

Two months after the article's publication and Mrs. Cleveland's disclaimer, Brandenburg was arrested on the charge of grand larceny. With extraordinary chutzpah, he compared himself to the unjustly accused victim of French anti-Semitism, Captain Alfred Dreyfus. Brandenburg did not claim to be the target of anti-Semites but instead declared himself a victim of conspiratorial Democrats wishing to discredit Cleveland's endorsement of Taft. The newspaper stories do not reveal whether Brandenburg himself was Jewish, but his last name (even though there may also be non-Jewish Brandenburgs of German descent) and the Dreyfus comparison are certainly suggestive. That Brandenburg picked a Jewish lawyer to defend him is also suggestive but hardly conclusive in New York City, where Jewish lawyers were certainly no novelty by 1908. No doubt the determining factor in the choice of Oswald Jacoby was his reputation as a litigator who possessed—as he would demonstrate in Brandenburg's defense—a keen sense of how best to appeal to sophisticated New York jurors.

During the trial, Oswald confounded the district attorney, who had lined up a parade of handwriting experts to testify for the prosecution, by having his client freely admit that he was the one who signed the article. Oswald then led the jury to focus on the judgment of the *Times* editors who bought the manuscript rather than on the behavior of his client. The jury had already learned from defense witnesses that Brandenburg had met with Cleveland several months before his death, discussed a prospective series of articles, and received authorization to act as the president's agent. Moreover, the executor of the estate had reaffirmed Brandenburg's commission (to him and to the *Times* editor who asked whether Brandenburg was authorized to sell the rights) after Cleveland's death. One of Oswald's shrewdest maneuvers was to keep Mrs. Cleveland's testimony—she had no firsthand personal knowledge whether her husband had or had not written the article—out of the record. My grandfather understood that he was much more likely to win his case by grilling evasive Timesmen than by cross-examining the grieving widow. As the *Times* noted mournfully, "Mr. Jacoby . . . put so much opposition in the way of Mrs. Cleveland's testimony that her journey from Tamworth to New York specially to take the stand was of practically no avail."

Oswald's defense of his client boiled down to the contention that Cleveland wrote the article and Brandenburg simply added the signature. And if Brandenburg had tinkered with the original manuscript to make it more readable, Oswald suggested, well, that was exactly what editors were paid to do. Reading between the lines, it seems clear that neither the *Times* nor Cleveland's executor had been eager to inquire too closely into whether the president had actually finished the article before he died or whether Brandenburg finished it for him. Brandenburg, his hyperbolic comparison to Dreyfus aside, was probably right in his contention that there was a "conspiracy among the Democrats" to discredit Cleveland's endorsement of Taft and that Mrs. Cleveland may well have been pressured into disavowing the article after its usefulness to the Republican campaign became evident. The clear intent of my grandfather's defense was to imply that everyone had been in on the scam, if scam it was, but his client was the only one charged with a crime.

As the *Times* fairly reported, "Mr. Jacoby argued that a verdict for the defendant would mean the vindication of the article. He declared that it was unimportant to consider if the signature was genuine or not. The real question [was whether] the article itself was Mr. Cleveland's. That was proved by the style which had convinced an editor of the *Times*." Oswald concluded with a tongue-in-cheek comment about the vagueness of the editors' recollections of their handling of the manuscript, suggesting (even though he had already conceded the forging of Cleveland's signature) that the original might just as easily have been spirited away from the newspaper offices by autograph hunters or Bryan supporters. In a closing argument reminiscent of a well-known scene from the movie *Miracle on 34th Street*—in which a young attorney convinces a judge to keep an open mind about the existence of Santa Claus—Oswald informed the jury that "we cannot tell what happened in the *Times* office. . . . We do not say the *Times* did it. We do not say the *Times* did not do it. . . ." The *World* succinctly summed up my grandfather's argument as the "*caveat emptor* defense."

Acquittal was far from a foregone conclusion, for Brandenburg— in addition to his less than illustrious record as an agent and blackmailer—also managed to get himself charged with kidnapping his stepson during the course of the trial. The prosecutor, over my grandfather's strenuous objections, persuaded the judge to allow testimony on the pending kidnapping charge. In a defense attorney's courtroom nightmare, Brandenburg then confessed on the stand to the kidnapping (motivated by a tangled custody-divorce suit straight out of today's headlines).

"Mr. Jacoby was aghast," the *Times* recounted—not least because the judge refused to allow him to cross-examine the witness at that point. But Brandenburg wasn't through opening his mouth. "Was the lady you were living with . . . your wife?" asked the prosecutor. "I think so," Brandenburg replied. The jury, however, proved capable of evaluating the forgery charge without being swayed by Brandenburg's behavior as a husband and stepfather. Concluding that Brandenburg had technically violated the law but had not violated contemporary journalistic norms, the jurors returned a not guilty verdict the same day.

Years later, my grandfather told a legal writer that the *caveat emptor* defense had been entirely ethical and appropriate for a case involving an institution with the resources of the *Times*. "If Brandenburg had sold the article to some schoolgirl, it would have been an entirely different matter," Oswald said, "but the *Times*, as we know, is not a schoolgirl. The DA's case was, in essence, that this two-bit con man was brilliant enough to deceive the attorney for the late President, the President's widow, and the editors of the country's most respected newspaper. Brandenburg just wasn't that smart."

BY THE time I read the accounts of this trial, which portray my grandfather in the ebullient prime of his career, I already knew that Oswald Jacoby was an extremely complex man. His resistance to authority and disdain for conventional respectability—two traits shared by both of his sons—were displayed during the trial and in his later comments on the case. Yet there was another equally important side to my grandfather's character—a craving for social status. His desire to move up in the world played a major role in his marriage to Edith Sondheim in 1900.

When I began to form a picture of my grandfather as a young man, I assumed that his marriage must have been a purely calculated move, designed to attain some sort of social advantage. On one level, this was surely the case. Like Max Jacoby, the Sondheims were Forty-eighters. Unlike Max, they could trace their lineage in Germany for several generations. This was something my grandmother Jacoby never forgot and presumably never let her husband forget. Perhaps Oswald was as impressed with the name Sondheim as my grandmother was. (After her mother's death, Aunt Edith became convinced that we were related to the composer Stephen Sondheim. I would like to claim him as a relative, but it seems unlikely in spite of our common last name.)

Granny Jacoby's father, Simon Sondheim, was a classics scholar who had studied at the University of Heidelberg before he left Germany. His family of china merchants had lived near Frankfurt since the middle of the eighteenth century. His wife, Sarah, whom he married in 1872, also came from Frankfurt. The Sondheims had settled in Brooklyn, where Simon and Sarah ran a school for young ladies. Simon believed that girls, like boys, should be rigorously schooled in the classics, and he put this conviction into practice in the education of his children. My grandmother, the only one of the Sondheim daughters to marry, did not attend college, but she had been taught by her father to read both Greek and Latin. Her sisters, Mabel, Carrie, and Adele, who had to earn a living, all went to Hunter College and became teachers (two of them principals) in the New York City public school system. Her brother, Simon (like my uncle Ozzie, he had been named after his living father in defiance of Jewish naming traditions), spent several years in China as a trader in the Oriental bric-a-brac so popular before World War I. A peculiar sideline was his dealing in human hair (because of its thickness, Asian hair was often used to augment the coiffures of European and American women with thinning hair) and hair ornaments. Like his sisters, Si eventually became a public school teacher.

I knew Granny Jacoby's other siblings, because they all lived into their eighties. "The aunts," as they were known collectively, kept house for Si and a younger brother, Walter, who was said to be "simple" (a Victorian euphemism for mentally retarded). They were a jolly bunch, given to old-fashioned amusements, from singing around the piano to amateur theatricals, and visiting them was one of the few experiences I genuinely enjoyed during our family trips to New York. They were so very different from my severe grandmother that I found it hard to believe she was their sister. But, then, they hadn't been married to my grandfather.

It is easy to see what she saw in him in 1900, regardless of how much she eventually came to regret her choice. He was a handsome, charming, sexually charismatic, successful young man on the way up. And he had money—something the Sondheims lacked. It is harder to figure out what he saw in her. As a young woman, my grandmother was plain and awkward; the family snapshots reveal a sharp contrast between her stiff demeanor and the born-to-have-his-picture-taken ease of her new husband. If Oswald was looking for someone pretty and socially adept enough to help him get where he wanted to go, he picked the wrong woman. I am also somewhat surprised that, of Max's three children, my grandfather was the only one who married a Jew (especially one who would twit him about the "Polish" origins of his family). I have two theories about my grandfather's motivation—one cynical, the other more charitable. I suspect that by 1900, though everything looked good on the surface and though his law practice was flourishing, Oswald's private life wasn't going quite as well as he wanted everyone to believe. Gentile families of substance would not have regarded a cocky young Jewish lawyer, with no apparent connections to the better-known Our Crowd families, as a desirable suitor for a daughter. And the successful Our Crowd families would have scrutinized Oswald's qualifications as a suitor just as skeptically and just as thoroughly. I am not at all certain that my grandfather would have emerged unblemished from a discreet and exhaustive inquiry into his finances and personal habits at age thirty. The Sondheim family, scholarly and proud but relatively poor, was in no position to be choosy about a son-in-law. My grandmother's social origins, in the world of German-descended New York Jews, were a cut above my grandfather's, but she would not have been considered a desirable match for a Guggenheim or a Straus even if she did share a piano teacher with them.

But I may be doing my grandfather an injustice, since I know him mainly as the bad father he became to my own father. For there was more to Oswald Jacoby than narrow professional ambition. He was a genuinely cultured man, fluent in German and Spanish, with a passion for the arts and a wide-ranging love of literature. In this, my grandmother was a match for him. "They both loved opera—all forms of classical music—and painting," Aunt Edith recalled during one of our conversations after my father's death. "The times I think of them as happy were when they were talking, usually arguing, about painting. Mother, who was quite a good amateur painter herself, was very interested in the new art we were beginning to see from Europe—Picasso, the work of Monet in his later years. Father was strictly a seventeenth-century Dutch and Italian Renaissance man. He was convinced that the Impressionists would be completely forgotten in his children's lifetime. Of course, he had been exposed to fine works of art his whole life, and his taste was formed by his father. He and Mother could argue about art for hours; they'd get very animated and interrupt each other, and you could see they were happy. Really liking each other. For a few moments, maybe they could see in each other what they saw when they were courting."

Before Aunt Edith entered the last stages of Alzheimer's disease, I prodded her for more happy memories of her parents' life together. At first she said there were none, but then, as she cast her mind deeper into her childhood, she came up with some poignant images. "Mother was a very accomplished pianist—so good that Father used to say she could have played professionally. I can see them together in the parlor, I was seven or eight maybe, I know it was before the war [World War I] because after that he was hardly ever home. Father would take out his violin—I think it was a very expensive, very fine old instrument that Max had bought for him when he was selected for the Columbia orchestra—and she would sit down at the piano. I can hear them playing Beethoven sonatas for violin and piano—the Kreutzer Sonata was their favorite, and you know how difficult that piece is. Mother's face glowed—you probably don't remember her ever smiling. I can see her, perspiring, her hair falling out of its topknot because playing was hard work. She was not a pretty woman, but she came close to being beautiful at those moments. At the end, when the last note died away, Father would bow to Mother. He took her hand as she got up from the piano bench and they would both bow to the rest of us, as if we were in a concert hall. Once he had roses delivered from the florist at the end of their 'performance'—this was when we were still living in Manhattan. Mother cried and kissed him. Your dad didn't have any memories like this. . . . Mother and Father had grown to hate each other by the time he was born."

My grandfather's attitude toward Judaism, and his own Jewishness, seems to have been one source of friction between him and my grandmother. When I asked Uncle Ozzie whether his father had ever taught him anything about what it meant to be a Jew, his answer was immediate. "Oh, *God, no.* Father was an atheist. He said everything that had to do with religion, all religions, was pure superstition. This was a problem for Mother, because while she didn't believe in the religion, her family—especially her brother—still considered themselves Jews. Your uncle Simon went to temple on the Sabbath for many, many years. You didn't know that? Of course you didn't. No one would have mentioned this around your aunt Edith. I'm sure her brother's attitude influenced Mother in her reluctance to convert when Edith started pressuring her. Once in a while, around what I suppose were Jewish holidays, Mother would bring out special dishes that we never used the rest of the year. It was around Easter. Father would make fun of her, asking her which holiday she was celebrating. It was Passover. But you know, I don't think I ever heard the word *Passover* until I was thirty. I was in a bridge tournament, and my partner had to back out because he said his mother would drop dead if she knew he was playing cards on the first night of Passover."

THOSE DISHES are now among my most cherished possessions. My Sondheim great-grandparents brought them to America from Frankfurt in 1848. My grandmother, having already bestowed Eve Jackson Jacoby's silver tea service on Ozzie and his wife, gave the Sondheim china to my mother at some point during the 1950s. My mom handed down part of the set to me a few years ago, and she has left the rest of the dishes to me in her will. I intend to pass on the Sondheim china to my nieces when I die. They are the finest English stone chinaware, in a pattern manufactured between 1825 and 1835, with flowers and butterflies delicately traced over a pale blue background. These may indeed have been Passover dishes, carefully stored away for the rest of the year, because they are still in flawless condition. I use them on holidays too, washing them by hand. Their vibrant reds, blues, and golds have scarcely faded over nearly two centuries, leaving a visible heritage of care from generations of women. I wonder if my grandfather was really a man who would make fun of his wife for using special dishes on a holiday that had lost its religious significance for the family? I feel, for the first time, a smidgeon of sympathy for my grandmother. I wish I had known the young woman who loved to play Beethoven and Brahms. I wish she had known I would take good care of her family's china. In recent years, I have begun bringing out the dishes whenever I have friends over for dinner—as I usually do—during Passover and Hanukkah. According to Ozzie (who heard it from his mother's brother, Simon), my Sondheim great-great-grandfather was a rabbi in Germany. Maybe, maybe not. Every Jewish family, even one as far removed from Judaism as mine, hopes to find a learned rabbi in the family tree. Before the Sondheims went into the china business, they sold chess sets and playing cards at village fairs. That I do believe. Uncle Si had fantastic collections of carved chessmen and old playing cards in his chockablock house. When he died, Aunt Edith got rid of nearly all of his possessions. Including what I now realize was a menorah.

NEAR THE end of 1907, Max Jacoby died at the age of seventy-six. His wife had died several years before, and he left an estate valued at approximately $200,000 (between $800,000 and $1.2 million today, depending on the value of the works), to be divided equally between his two sons. Included in the estate was a cottage near Saratoga, various paintings and "works of fine art" (though no Rubens), and more than $100,000 worth of government and railroad securities. Both Oswald and Harold should have been set for life—or at least until the stock market crash of 1929.

Harold was set. He lived in Manhattan throughout his years at Columbia, his children were educated in private schools, and the newspaper clippings chronicling his career showed that my greatuncle, like his father, was able to afford European travel throughout his lifetime. Even if he did lose money in the crash—professors being no more immune than other Americans to the lure of the everexpanding stock market bubble—there was enough left for him to retire to affluent Westport upon his retirement.

Oswald was not set. Indeed, the legacy from his father—"found money"—may have fueled the destructive tendencies that ruined a once-promising life. "You know how it is," explained Uncle Ozzie. "If you get some money you didn't expect, it's not gambling if you bet it. You didn't have the money the day before, so what does it matter if you don't have it the day after? Of course, you may bet money you *did* have the day before once you've lost the found money."

In a 1936 magazine essay describing his introduction to contract bridge, Ozzie evoked the psychology of compulsive gambling, handed down from Jacoby fathers to sons, in revealing language. The words *addict* and *addiction* appear over and over, in an era when such terms were not customarily applied to behavior like drinking and gambling. "My father before me was a bridge addict," Ozzie explained. "His suffering was often indescribable—particularly when he had to play with my aunts, my mother being immune to the game. So, although I do not believe that bridge is actually a hereditary ailment, I am sure that I must have come into the world with a constitutional weakness, or predilection, for it. Although a great deal is known to science about the nature and progress of bridge, its devastating effect and the misery it inflicts upon the human race, no reliable cure or adequate preventive measures have ever been devised, and the germ itself has never been isolated."

Ozzie began to master bridge at age six, when he contracted measles, mumps, whooping cough, and chicken pox, one after another, during a six-month period. He played with his father and his Sondheim aunts, since his mother adamantly refused to learn any card game. Under his father's tutelage, young Ozzie soon moved on from bridge to blackjack and poker, thereby expanding the scope of his "addiction" to cards. Bridge was largely a game of skill (even though, of course, one could be dealt a bad hand), but Ozzie was quick to "reinvest" (his term) earnings in pure gambling, from the roulette wheel to sports gambling. High-stakes poker fell somewhere in between games of skill and games of chance. From my uncle's description of his father's habits, it could not be clearer that the gambling "virus," "addiction," or "germ" was passed on from father to son in the Jacoby family.

My grandfather must have gambled away a small fortune between Max's death and my father's birth in 1914. He closed down his private practice in 1910, serving a two-year stint as assistant district attorney for New York County. Around the time of my father's birth, the family moved from Manhattan to Brooklyn, where my grandfather reestablished a private legal practice. (All three children had been born in Brooklyn; my grandmother, when her due date neared, would move back into her mother's home to give birth.) Edith and Ozzie had attended private schools, but my father entered kindergarten in an ordinary Brooklyn public school in 1918. From that point on, there are no more pictures of the family in evening dress, no snapshots of the Jacobys playing croquet on the lawn of a summer home, no evidence of ocean crossings on passenger liners or stops at fashionable hotels in Europe. After 1920, there were no more pictures of Uncle Harold and his family.

My dad, Aunt Edith, and Uncle Ozzie all said they had no idea what had come between their father and his elder brother. While there is no hard evidence, I feel certain, in view of my grandfather's predilections, that money must have been involved in some way. It would hardly be surprising if Oswald had borrowed money from his brother and failed to pay it back. Perhaps Harold turned Oswald down when he needed still more money to pay off his gambling debts.

Oswald Jacoby's "weaknesses," as Miss Frankfurter termed them, were not limited to gambling. He was also a longtime cocaine addict and a frequenter of brothels. Cocaine use, it must be noted, did not have the criminal connotations that it has acquired today. Nineteenth-century physicians frequently prescribed cocaine (and morphine and opium) for a variety of medical conditions. Aunt Edith said her father became addicted to the drug as a teenager, when the family doctor prescribed it for the treatment of infected sinuses. (The physician must have been thinking about the numbing, rather than the inflaming, effect of cocaine on the nasal membranes.)

He continued to use cocaine in some form—it was easily obtainable in New York during the twenties—for the rest of his life. But even though there were fewer legal risks attached to the use of cocaine than there are today, the drug can only have encouraged my grandfather's erratic behavior and exacerbated his character weaknesses. The gambling, the cocaine, the use of prostitutes: all add up to a portrait of a man in deep trouble. Perhaps Harold had simply had enough, or perhaps he feared that his own family would be tainted by association. One would not have to be a prig and a bore, as my grandfather described Harold to Ozzie, to be fed up with a brother who was a gambler and a compulsive liar.

Mac Jacoby Jr. says his father and Uncle Ozzie saw each other occasionally during the 1930s—Mac remembers meeting Ozzie at least once when he was a boy—but that they were not close. "Whatever happened in the previous generation must have been very bad," Mac says, "because it kept my father and Ozzie apart even though I know my dad loved Ozzie. He would talk about him once in a while in a way you would talk about a brother who had died."

In a real sense, my grandfather and his elder brother did die to each other, and that death in the family separated their children forever. The way I found my cousin Mac—by a pure stroke of luck— illustrates the completeness of the breach between the two branches of the family. In 1995, not long after I had discovered the records of Harold's academic career at Columbia, I made a trip to Dallas to look through old family photographs, jammed in boxes in the house that once belonged to Uncle Ozzie. The house is now owned by Judy Jacoby, the widow of Ozzie's elder son, Jim. While I was staying with Judy in Dallas, she mentioned in the course of a phone conversation with her sister in Washington, D.C., that I was visiting and was thinking of writing a book about the Jacoby family. Her sister said she knew a Maclear Jacoby who was a teacher and tennis coach and asked whether we might be related. Judy had never heard anyone mention a relative named Maclear, but I knew instantly that this unknown teacher must be a descendant of Great-Uncle Harold and his wife, Annie Maclear. How many Maclear Jacobys can there be in the world? When I phoned Mac, who hadn't even known that Uncle Ozzie had a younger brother, he was delighted to hear from a previously unknown Jacoby relative. Having taught high school math for more than forty years, he had inherited the family aptitude for numbers (but not the "gambling gene," which seems to have been limited to my grandfather's descendants). Nearly twenty years my senior, Mac was five—just old enough to remember his grandfather—when Harold died in 1932. He grew up in a family in which Harold Jacoby's memory was as deep a source of pride for his descendants as Oswald Jacoby's was a source of humiliation for his children. "My grandmother and father were very proud of his [Harold's] career as a scientist," Mac remembers, "but he was also a success as a father. A real family man. I never heard anything but praise for him from anyone who knew him."

Perhaps the saddest element in this tale of two brothers is the silence, so emblematic of the Jacoby family style, that enveloped the rupture. As a child, I knew of Harold's existence—Aunt Edith and Uncle Ozzie referred to him as "the stargazer"—but I was under the misapprehension that he had died not in 1932 but around 1915. Edith and Ozzie both gave me that impression, probably because they did not want to discuss the break between Oswald and Harold.

For both brothers, the severing of family ties must have been a significant emotional event. As I formed a picture of the two men from the many articles written about them and from their own writings, I came to realize how much they must have shared in spite of their sharply contrasting characters. Both were men of broad intelligence and fierce rationalism; both loved sailing, classical music, and German and English literature. Moreover, both were accomplished and witty writers and public speakers. I never realized, until I discovered Uncle Harold's books and published accounts of my grandfather's courtroom speeches, how far back a facility with words could be traced in my family. "A way with words and gambling—our dominant genes," Ozzie said.

But when it mattered most, at least two generations of Jacobys had no words. Whatever pained and shamed them remained unexamined and unspoken. In their heritage of warm paternal memories, the "other Jacobys" could not have been more different from my father and his siblings. Yet the two branches of the family—one descended from the good son, the other from the bad son—were united in their denial of the Jacobys' Jewish origins.

ONE POSITIVE legacy my grandfather did pass on to his children was his love of the written and spoken word. Learning poems and plays at his father's knee was one of my dad's few sweet childhood memories, and he loved to quote from Oswald's favorites, which ranged from Shakespeare's sonnets to Edward Lear's "The Owl and the Pussycat." Another of his father's favorites was John Webster's seventeenth-century play, *The White Devil.* "I do not look, / Who went before nor who shall follow me. / No, at myself I will begin and end." Dad said he could still hear his father reciting those lines. When I was growing up, it did not occur to me that this was a strange philosophy—"at myself I will begin and end"—for a parent to pass on to a child. Now it seems to me that the quote embodies the error and the tragedy of my grandfather's life, along with the burden of secrets bequeathed by both Jacoby brothers to the grandchildren and great-grandchildren they never knew.

V

Brothers: Second Generation

DURING THE SUMMER OF 1916, fourteen-year-old Ozzie Jacoby wrote several letters from his family's rented beach cottage on Long Island's north shore to his best friend from school. They are filled with teenage ennui at being stuck with his family for the entire summer, love of sailing and the sea, and pride in his ability to beat everyone in the house, including his father, at bridge. In each of the letters, there are touching references to the baby of the family. "Robert can float in the ocean—which is some going for a two-year-old!!" "Robert begged me to take him sailing with my friends. I could not say no to those eyes. I let him think he was the one who caught the fish." "If only Robert could play bridge—he would give me a good game. Next year." "Taught Robert the 'Jabberwocky' last week. He recites it almost all the way through. A true Jacoby!"

In 1995, when I found these letters at the bottom of one of the boxes in Ozzie's home, he had been dead for eleven years and my dad for nine. I had a deep affection for my uncle—although I knew that Dad's love for his elder brother was tinged with his envy of a life played out on a larger and more flamboyant stage than that available to an accountant in Lansing, Michigan. Ozzie had always been larger than life—whether he was running away from home at fifteen, in 1917, to join the U.S. Army before the fighting in Europe was over (he made it into the army but the war ended before he made it into combat); confounding his superiors at Metropolitan Life at age twenty-one when, as the youngest licensed actuary in the United States, he solved a mathematical problem in two hours that would ordinarily have taken an adding machine and several actuaries a week to resolve; winning every national and international bridge championship in the thirties, forties, and fifties; serving as a navy code expert during World War II; writing a classic book on canasta that became the second best-selling nonfiction book in 1949 (nosing out Thomas Merton's *Seven Storey Mountain*, which the *Times* described as "a religious book of another kind"); fighting a $250,000 back tax bill from the Internal Revenue Service in the sixties with the argument that he had gambled away more money in Las Vegas and with his country-club poker-playing cronies than he had earned from his professional bridge tournaments and books; or, just before his death from colon cancer at eighty-one, becoming the oldest competitor ever to win bridge's prestigious Reisinger Trophy.

My father, who shared many (though not all) of Ozzie's talents and personal weaknesses, was a more life-size character. While Ozzie traversed the globe in search of master points in international bridge standings (and side action in casinos and clubs when the tournaments were over), leaving his wife, Mary Zita, with most of the responsibility for bringing up their two sons, my father stayed close to home and got to know his children. That was an achievement Ozzie recognized. "Bobbie was a better father than I've been," my uncle told me. "I was too selfish, you know, to pay much attention to my children when they were little. Yes. I've always been interested mainly in myself."

That wasn't entirely true. Ozzie's old letters, written at a time in life when everyone is interested mainly in himself, evince a precocious tenderness for the little brother who was the unwanted last child of a disintegrating marriage. And Uncle Ozzie never told me one of the most important facts of his life as a young man: at age twenty-one, he assumed the chief financial responsibility for his mother, sister, and brother. It was Aunt Edith who, a few years before her death, told me that Ozzie had paid for her last two years at Smith College, my father's expenses at private prep school, and the first two years of Dad's tuition at Dartmouth College. Only when Ozzie became a father himself in 1933—two years after his own father's death—did he step back from his role as the primary contributor to his original family's finances. The change in Ozzie's circumstances would have a major impact on my father's life, since he then dropped out of college to go to work. But that is hardly a criticism of my uncle; he had already shouldered far more financial responsibility for his younger siblings than most men in their twenties would have undertaken—a responsibility that should, of course, have been borne by his father.

The years between the end of World War I and the beginning of the Depression were crucial ones for all three Jacoby siblings. Their parents' marriage and the family finances went from bad to worse, as my grandfather's life spun more and more out of control. Dad, who was only five years old in 1919, was affected most profoundly, because he was the youngest, by the fall in the family's fortunes. In the streets and the playground of his public school, Dad was exposed to the ungenteel anti-Semitism—from schoolyard beatings to epithets—that had not been a part of his sister's and brother's experiences in private schools. Small for his age and unathletic (except in sports, like swimming, that had no self-defense value), my father was easy prey for tough kids who made fun of his proper, non-Brooklynese diction.

SIXTY-FIVE years later, when I pressed my father for a description of his schooldays, he responded with long-suppressed rage. This was not his usual outburst of temper, dissipating almost as soon as he raised his voice, but an uncharacteristic, simmering resentment at my persistent questions about his childhood. But the year was 1975, I had just turned thirty, and I no longer had the sense, as one does in one's twenties, that time and possibilities stretched out limitlessly before me (much less before my parents). Filled with an unfamiliar sense of urgency—even though my father was then a healthy and extremely active sixty-one-year-old—I pushed him when we were talking on the telephone one evening. "All right," he said furiously. "All right, you want to dig all this up. You're in second grade, and this is what they sing in the schoolyard. 'All the girls do dance / with tomatoes in their pants / and the dance they do / is enough to kill a Jew.' You take a swing at them, though you don't have any idea what a Jew is. They beat you up, rip your shirt, tear some pages out of your books. You run home, the cries of 'baby Jew-boy' ringing in your ears. You're afraid they'll get you again on the way. Your mother sends you to your room without dinner as punishment for fighting. You're too ashamed to tell her why you got into a fight. It wouldn't make any difference anyway. 'A gentleman settles arguments with his brains, not with his fists,' she would say. Ozzie would understand, but he's living in the city now. Is that what you want to know about? Is that what you want to write about?" Then the anger died out of Dad's voice. "Of course, I had a friend. There was Freddie."

The friend was Fred Groff, who grew up just a few blocks from the Jacobys in Flatbush and went to the same elementary school as my dad. He eventually became a doctor and established a practice in Schenectady, New York, and we always used to stop there overnight on our way to visit Aunt Edith and Granny Jacoby. "Dr. Fred" was the only figure from Dad's childhood—apart from his family—whom I ever met. A gentle giant of a man, Fred was as big for his age when he was a boy as my father was small. Descended from a family of German (not German Jewish) immigrants, Freddie became my father's protector on the playground. Not long after Dad's old anguish erupted during our phone conversation, I happened to be home for a visit when Fred turned up in Lansing to see my parents and to play in a golf tournament for the benefit of the American

Cancer Society. My dad told his old friend that I was interested in what it was like to have grown up Jewish in the 1920s, and Fred said, "I thought you didn't want the kids to know." "She figured it out," Dad replied, in a tone of exasperation mixed with pride.

Then the two men began to talk about the way Fred had defended Dad throughout elementary school. "The smallest kid always gets picked on," Fred recalled, "and I always hated that. When I heard those kids using words like *sheeney* and *kike* and *yid*, I didn't even know what they meant. I came home and asked my mother, and she said those were words that ignorant people used for the Israelites in the Bible. Like *kraut* for the Germans. I said I was going to hit those boys the next time they called Bobbie a kike. She said fighting wasn't the way, but I should speak up and if someone hit me, I could hit back. I didn't wait for them to hit first, I pounded away. I figured they'd already hit Bobbie, and that was hitting first. They didn't have to get the first punch in at me too." Tears came to my father's eyes as he listened to that recapitulation. "I never thanked you," he told his old friend. Dr. Fred replied, "Sure you did, Bobbie. Don't you remember all the help you gave me with my arithmetic? If it weren't for you, I'd probably have flunked fourth grade and I never would have gotten into medical school." Then he turned to me and said, "You know, you *should* write about this someday. People don't realize what this kind of thing does to a sensitive kid, that you carry it your whole life. It was the same as being called a nigger. And there are people today who don't understand what that must mean to a child with brown skin. Some become angry at the whole world. Some become ashamed of themselves. Isn't that right, Bob?" Dad put his hand over mine and said, "That's right. And some of us became angry *and* ashamed."

MY FATHER must have been a very lonely little boy. Ozzie never lived at home full-time after he enlisted in the army in 1917—with his father's tacit approval and over his mother's bitter objections. Ozzie's account of his military service, which appeared in a 1950

New York Times profile by Gilbert Millstein, provides yet another example of the Jacobys' habit of fictionalizing their family history. His father raised no objections, Ozzie told Millstein, because the family had a long military tradition going back to the War of 1812. (Needless to say, Ozzie's Jacoby forebears were nowhere in the vicinity of the young United States of America in 1812.) The only break in the family tradition of military service, he added, occurred during the Civil War, when one of Eve Jackson Jacoby's great-uncles, supposedly a major in a Connecticut regiment, missed the entire conflict as a result of injuries sustained in a fall from his horse. That may or may not have been true. One thing is certain: Ozzie, Aunt Edith (who was a lieutenant in the Waves), and my father were the only Jacobys ever to serve in the U.S. military in any era. My great-grandfather, Max, did not enlist in the Union Army during the Civil War; Great-Uncle Harold and my grandfather belonged to one of those fortunate generations too young or too old to be conscripted for any large-scale war. The only ancestors in Ozzie's pantheon who had anything to do with the military were Sondheims; my grandmother kept several pictures of older male relatives (including her father) in full uniform, taken in Brooklyn before they went to join their Union Army regiments. Why did Ozzie, in telling the colorful (and true) story of his own enlistment in the army at fifteen, find it necessary to invent a family history of distinguished military service? This can be seen either as pure self-aggrandizement, for Ozzie loved anything that added to his own legend, or as yet another attempt to hide the family's origins: *If we fought in the War of 1812, we can't be Jews.* In any event, Uncle Ozzie's abbreviated war was spent in upper Manhattan, billeted in an abandoned home for the blind and playing poker with the other members of his outfit waiting to be shipped out. The armistice came first, and the Great War was over. When Ozzie entered Columbia in the autumn of 1919, he had a stake of $500 from his poker winnings to finance his social life as an undergraduate. Ozzie told Millstein that he received just one piece of advice from his father before entering Columbia with his poker stash. "You're going to be cursed by being a good cardplayer," he told his son, "but if you have to be one, I want you to remember two things. Always take the worst of it in a situation and never hide the deck." Cheating at cards seems to have been one of the few social offenses my grandfather never committed, and Uncle Ozzie would have been justifiably offended had anyone ever suggested (and no one ever did) that he needed to cheat in order to win.

Unlike his father and uncle, Ozzie dropped out of Columbia after two years. This may have been entirely a matter of personal inclination: it is hard for me to imagine my uncle willingly consigning himself to classrooms for four years. Unless there was money to be made (or lost) at a card table, Ozzie almost never sat still or stopped talking for more than two minutes. Formal education would have been—must have been—a torture for him. But Ozzie may well have had to leave school in any case because his father's law practice had fallen off and the family was in desperate need of money. The eldest child came to the rescue, working as an actuary at the Metropolitan Life Insurance Company from 1921 to 1928, when he quit to devote himself full-time to tournament bridge and backgammon. In the 1950s, Ozzie was still remembered vividly by his old colleagues at Met Life. One of them described an occasion on which his boss handed the twenty-two-year-old Ozzie a multicolumn set of insurance figures that had already been checked separately by two teams of company actuaries. Glancing briefly at the two sets of calculations, Ozzie looked up and said, "They're both about a hundred thousand dollars off." Ozzie was right; he had produced a nearly accurate total straight out of his head, while the other actuaries had spent hours working on mechanical calculators and come up with numbers that were way off.

Edith, who entered Smith College in 1924 and was old enough to join in some of her elder brother's social activities, naturally saw much more of Ozzie than my father did throughout the twenties. "If we had known what it was like for Bobbie in public school," she told me a few years before she died, "I'm sure Ozzie would have come up with the tuition for private school. But since money was scarce, we thought he could finish out the eighth grade in public school and transfer to a prep school the following year. By then I would be through at Smith and I could get a job and help out. The truth is that no one really paid attention to Bobbie during those years. Father was—well, God knows where he was half the time. You know about Mother. Ozzie was her favorite, and there was just no room in her heart for anyone else. I don't think Bobbie existed for her at all. I feel guilty now that I didn't spend more time with Bobbie, take the trouble to find out what was going on in his little head. But I wanted to be out of that house. On vacations, I'd beg Ozzie to let me stay with him in his apartment in the city. Bobbie just fell through the cracks. One night, he showed up at Ozzie's apartment in Greenwich Village around ten o'clock at night, having run away from home because Mother and Father were fighting again. I took him back to Brooklyn the next morning; Ozzie had been out in an all-night poker game. Bobbie cried and begged me not to leave him there. I'd forgotten that little face until now: I blame myself for that. But your father turned out very well, better than either Ozzie or me in some ways. Still, I should have made more of an effort. I was Bobbie's big sister."

I don't blame my aunt for what she considered her unsisterly behavior: like my father, she had developed serious emotional problems (though of a quite different nature) as a result of being her parents' daughter. Edith, her father's favorite, had adored him as a child, and even though she was aware that his gambling had destroyed the standard of living the family had once enjoyed, her love for her unreliable parent survived into early adulthood. But one day in 1926, she arrived home for her summer vacation from Smith—her mother was visiting a friend on Long Island—and found her father in bed with another woman. When she told Ozzie, he said their father was in the habit of bringing prostitutes home when he thought the house would be empty. "I hardened my heart against Father after that," Edith said. "I could hardly stand to look at him. That he would do this in his and Mother's bedroom . . . it was too much for a girl to accept. Later, he tried to justify himself by telling me that he and

Mother had not had marital relations since Bobbie was born—and that may very well have been true. As an adult woman, I can have some sympathy for him today. At the time, though, I was furious at him for trying to get back into my good graces by telling me about his intimate life. I thought, 'I should not be hearing this. You should not be telling me this.' I wish now that I had been more forgiving of him. Then, my reaction was just to get out of there and stay away, stay away as much as possible. It meant that I didn't see much of Bobbie, but I didn't think about that then."

If it is true, as psychologists like to say, that each child of the same parents grows up in a different family, the generalization applied to my father more than it does to most children. His older brother and sister had spent their preadolescent years in an environment of material comfort and financial security, with parents who, whatever the strains in their marriage, had not yet given up on each other. Their father still spent considerable time at home, telling his children tales from Greek mythology, reading them Shakespeare, playing the violin, and teaching them how to play bridge, poker, and pinochle. By the time my father came along, the financial security was gone and his parents were estranged at their best, openly warring at their worst. Dad was seven years younger than his sister and twelve years younger than the brother he worshiped.

Moreover, the split between my grandfather and his brother Harold meant that my father would never know his first cousins, who had been very much a part of Ozzie's and Edith's childhood. Granny Jacoby discouraged my father's friendships with public school classmates, whom she regarded as uncouth and inferior in every way (with the fortunate exception of Fred Groff). Young Bobbie tried to spend as much time as possible at Fred's house, but Granny Jacoby usually refused permission when he asked to stay overnight or eat with the Groffs. Her younger son's table manners, she frequently said, weren't fit for company. After Edith went off to Smith, the lone child left behind usually had only his mother for company at the dinner table.

For an isolated little boy, the one bright spot was the companionship of his Sondheim uncle, Simon, and the Sondheim aunts—Carrie, Mabel, and Adele. At some point during the twenties, Dad's maternal grandmother, Sarah Sondheim, moved in with her daughter in Brooklyn. Nana Sarah, as all of the children called her—though my father didn't remember much about her—seems to have been as gentle and encouraging a woman as her daughter was harsh and negative. "Never were a mother and daughter more different from each other," said Aunt Edith. "Nana Sarah was a lovely woman, the kind of woman children are naturally drawn to. To her, every child was the handsomest, the prettiest, the smartest, the nicest. Everyone in the family loved her. I'm surprised your dad doesn't remember more about her, because he was her special pet. But maybe the influence of Mother was so overwhelming, her constant criticism so harsh, that it pushed out his other memories."

As I would learn when I met them thirty years later, Uncle Simon and the Sondheim maiden aunts were also extremely fond of my dad. Si was the clown of the family. Well into his seventies by the time I met him, he had the playfulness and energy of a much younger man. During my dad's childhood, Uncle Si provided some of the physical horseplay for which my grandfather, who turned fifty in 1920, was already too old. The Sondheim aunts engaged their nephew in quieter pastimes: like my grandfather, they attempted (successfully) to instill a love of English verse in the little boy. When we visited the aunts in New York, they would talk about my dad's having had the best memory in the family for poetry, and I was thrilled when they would ask my father to recite some of the verses that had been his favorites as a child. "Jabberwocky"—which must have stuck firmly in his mind since he first heard it as a two-year-old from Ozzie—was one of Dad's specialties, and he acted out the verses with sound effects and broad gestures. "One, two! One, two! And through and through / The vorpal blade went snicker-snack! / He left it dead, and with its head / He went galumphing back." In their seventies, the aunts seemed as delighted by my dad's recitation as they undoubtedly were when he was a little boy, and I saw that their love had been a bright spot in a childhood filled with too little praise and encouragement. None of this, however, made up for my dad's isolation from friends his own age or his father's absence and his mother's disapproving presence.

IT IS PAINFUL for me, even today, to think about the lifelong impact of this upbringing on my father. In many respects, I believe the burden of my grandfather's absence was more permanent in its effects than the obvious negativism of my grandmother's presence. A parent who clearly favors one child over another, and does it over a lifetime, can eventually be seen for what she is. In recent years, I have often thought that my father compensated for his deficit of motherly love by becoming more maternal in relation to his own children, and more available to other children, than most men of his generation.

My brother's and my friends, with fathers cast in a more rigid paternal mode, were always hanging around the house because they adored my dad. "I remember two things about your dad," says Rose Glennon, my best friend from grade school. "He always listened to what you had to say as if it were the most important thing in the world. And if he lost his temper, he'd always apologize right away. 'I'm sorry' was not in the vocabulary of most of the fathers we knew."

I don't believe my father ever got over his own father's defection, in part because my grandfather, for all his character flaws, was a man who did know how to show love when he was around to do it. When my brother and I were playing outdoors, my dad would summon us with what sounded like a war cry in a foreign language but had actually been my grandfather's favorite way of summoning the family dogs: "Berrups, Berree, Berrowowee, Har!, Fee, Rah! Battle." Or he would recite Tennyson's "The Eagle," prompting an exasperated, "Oh, *Daddy*," when I reached the age at which children become deeply embarrassed by any sign of eccentricity in their parents. My friends, however, were enthralled by his recitation, complete with a diving gesture at the end—"The wrinkled sea beneath him crawls; / He watches from his mountain walls, / And like a thunderbolt he falls." Everyone was especially impressed by Dad's version of "The Owl and the Pussy-Cat." He would twirl and prance, as he said his father had done, when he reached the final stanzas:

> *They dined on mince and slices of quince,*
> *Which they ate with a runcible spoon;*
> *And hand in hand, on the edge of the sand*
> *They danced by the light of the moon,*
> *The moon,*
> *The moon,*
> *They danced by the light of the moon.*

My dad's face would light up when he recited these poems—perhaps the only unclouded legacy from his father. And the memory of the pleasure and yearning in his face hurts more than the memory of the times he evaded my questions with the assertion that he hardly knew his father. As an adult, my dad longed, unassuagably, for what he never received as a child. For what his mother could not give and what his father might have been able to give but was rarely around to provide.

THE JACOBYS' pervasive ambivalence, verging on shame, about being Jewish was only one strand in the fabric of this unhappy family, but the thread was woven tightly through the psyches of all three children.

It was Ozzie who told me that Uncle Si had once been an observant Jew—observant enough, at least, to go to synagogue on most Saturdays and the High Holidays. But my grandfather, who was quite fond of his Sondheim in-laws, explicitly told Si that he did not want his children to learn anything about Judaism. When I asked Ozzie whether his father had any connection to Judaism at all—

whether he had been bar mitzvahed, for instance—my uncle replied, "No, no, no. Father had about as much respect for traditional Jewish customs as he did for human sacrifice. We knew we were Jews—it wasn't like with you kids, who grew up not knowing. But we didn't really know what being Jewish meant. Though Si was a modern Jew, we basically thought of religious Jews as those men in long black coats with side curls. Father was adamant that we were to have nothing to do with any of this superstition, and he ruled the household on that point. At the same time, he and Mother would both talk about how Jews were envied and hated because they were smarter and better educated than other people. It was all very confusing. Not that my parents talked about this very often. But it was there, a sort of undigested lump. A lump of brisket, maybe. On holidays when other people would make ham, Mother would make brisket and sponge cake. We had brisket for Easter."

It is important to understand that my father grew up in an America that, in certain respects, had become "worse for the Jews" than the society in which my grandfather was raised. Even without the family's economic comedown, my father would undoubtedly have encountered more manifestations of anti-Semitism than his parents—and even his elder brother—did in their early lives. Recent Jewish immigrants from Eastern Europe—many still poor, many still sharply distinguishable, in dress, language, and religious customs, from other Americans—were a more visible presence in New York City than anywhere else in America. Before the wave of immigration that began in the 1880s, the city was already home to the largest Jewish population in the country. Established New York Jewish families like the Jacobys were fearful of being lumped with the as-yet-undigested immigrants, most of them the dreaded *Ostjuden*. My father's generation would grow up with the knowledge that the fear had become a reality in many aspects of American life. Restrictive housing covenants and attempts to discourage the enrollment of more Jews in private universities became increasingly common after 1910; during the twenties, measures to discourage Jewish applicants would harden into explicit Jewish quotas in elite undergraduate institutions as well as professional schools.

When my father entered Brooklyn's Polytechnical Preparatory Country Day School in 1927—the beginning of what he always said were the happiest four years of his youth—the all-male student body was drawn mainly from affluent Protestant families. Although the school was officially nondenominational, students were required to attend daily chapel where Protestant hymns were sung and Christian sermons preached. This requirement was taken for granted, and accepted, by assimilated Jewish families that sent their sons to such institutions. Judging from the last names in his school yearbook— inappropriately named *The Polyglot*—there were eight or nine Jews in my father's graduating class of seventy-eight. In view of the city's large Jewish population, including a significant number of affluent second- and third-generation German-descended Jews with the means and the desire to send their children to private schools, a Jewish enrollment of just 10 percent indicates that Poly, like private universities in the area, was already taking steps to ensure that its student body would not look "too Jewish."

Founded in 1854, Poly Prep is situated on 25 pastoral acres of ponds, trees, and gardens, with a spectacular view of the Verrazano Narrows. Even today, the grounds convey the dignified aura of a New England landscape rather than the claustrophobia of an enclave wedged between the water and a down-at-the-heels neighborhood pockmarked by aging discos. In the more civil, optimistic New York where my father grew up, Poly's air of dignified immunity from urban pressures, coupled with its academic excellence, already offered significant inducements for parents unwilling to entrust the education of their children to the city's public schools. In today's infinitely harsher city, civility remains a palpable characteristic of, and attraction for, a student body that is now a genuine polyglot mixture, including every imaginable race and ethnic group.

My father's schoolmates, by contrast, were all white males, most with Anglo-Saxon or Scandinavian names and pedigrees. (The Bay

Ridge area surrounding Poly Prep had long attracted Norwegian immigrants, and by the 1920s, some of their descendants were affluent enough to send their sons to a private prep school that would have been out of reach a generation earlier.) Catholics were a distinct minority, perhaps a smaller minority than Jews, at Poly. Wealthy Irish Catholics of that generation were still inclined to send their children to exclusive Catholic institutions rather than Protestant prep schools; Joseph P. Kennedy, who sent his sons to Choate precisely because he wanted them to associate with well-connected, old-line WASPs, was an exception. Poly was not as old, or as socially exclusive, as Exeter, Choate, and Lawrenceville: a Brooklyn location—even in what was then a near-bucolic setting—was not compatible with top-drawer social status. Nevertheless, Poly was in the same academic league as the better-known boarding schools. For the most part, the school's graduates went on to Harvard, Yale, Princeton, Columbia, Williams, and Dartmouth. In 1931, Poly sent thirteen members of my father's graduating class to Dartmouth, the fourth-largest number from prep schools considered feeders for the Ivy League.

Dad was able to enroll at Poly (he had started his freshman year at Erasmus Hall, an outstanding public boys' high school in Brooklyn) only because Uncle Ozzie, who by 1927 was on his way to making (and losing) his first fortune, paid the tuition. Between 1925 and 1929, Ozzie made more than a quarter of a million dollars in the stock market. Having quit his job at Met Life in 1928, he became a full-time professional at cards only after he lost virtually everything in the 1929 crash.

For my father, Poly provided a welcome change from his unhappy experiences with anti-Semites in public school (though a selective public academic high school like Erasmus would probably have served the same purpose). His good memories of Poly were underscored by annual donations to the school alumni fund (he gave almost nothing to Dartmouth) until the end of his life.

Dad had a moon face as a teenager, and that earned him the nickname "Fat"—which he did not resent at all—under his senior class picture. It was clear that Fat was one of the smartest young men in the Class of '31. The class scribe reported that "Fat makes a practice of winning one or two General Information and Intelligence Tests every year. Therefore we don't see why he should wear that sheepish expression all the time. . . . He blushes frequently, which *is* something to see in this day and age." A cartoon mockingly naming my dad as "Class Social Lion" shows an embarrassed, slightly chubby boy sitting at the far end of a couch from a girl who is unsuccessfully trying to get him to move closer. Dad was a member of the lacrosse and swim teams and assistant manager of the school football team (a customary job for a boy who can't make it as a jock) in his junior year. He was also a member of *Cum Laude*, a junior Phi Beta Kappa for prep school students, with chapters at other high-ranking private academies like Phillips, Lawrenceville, Choate, the Germantown Friends School, and the William Penn Charter School. (Although only about 10 percent of the students in my father's graduating class were Jews, they made up 40 percent of the *Cum Laude* membership.) What emerges from the yearbook is a portrait of a bright, studious, socially unpolished young man. But he was also a young man who knew how to have a good time and who made friends easily (as he did not in grade school).

"Bob was very, very funny," said Charles Wardell, a surviving classmate and friend, when I tracked him down in 1995. "But he was very popular because he didn't have any meanness in him. You know how some kids with a comic talent will do impressions of other kids that are downright cruel. Bob never made fun of people in a hurtful way. The fun was more at his own expense, or the expense of the universe." My dad and Charlie Wardell would take the subway into Manhattan to study together in the reading room of the New York Public Library at Fifth Avenue and Forty-second Street. They went to Dodger games together at Ebbets Field, and they sneaked off to the movies as the new "talkies" began to banish silent films. What they did not do, however, was double-date or visit each other's homes. And that, Charlie Wardell told me, was because he was a Christian and Dad was a Jew—and there was an unacknowledged but real barrier that permitted a private, one-on-one friendship but did not extend to social and family activities.

"Of course," said Wardell, "I didn't think this through at the time. I never really thought about it until you asked me. But I know it was so. There were fraternities, and I was a member of one, but the Jewish boys were never asked to join. Looking back, I can see this was a terrible thing, but no one ever thought about it then. There was a social line. For instance, I went to ballroom dancing—Miss Hepburn's, it was—where I first met my wife, and the Jewish boys didn't. I suppose I assumed they had their own. Although we spent a lot of time together, I never met either of Bob's parents—and he never met mine. Now that I look back, I see what was unusual is that I did have one Jewish friend. I think we first got to like each other because we both loved Latin, but we couldn't admit it because all of the other fellows would have made fun of us. But I didn't know any of the other Jewish boys in the class. I remember that years later, I was on a fund-raising committee for the school with one of our most successful classmates, a fellow named Dan Fradd who was a college football all-American and later on a very prominent businessman— and I hadn't known him at all in school. It had to be because he was Jewish. There weren't that many boys in the class, I knew almost everyone else. You see, it was all so unconscious back then. Christians and Jewish people, different worlds. People like me didn't think much about anti-Semitism until after the war. That is, until we'd seen where it could lead."

WHILE MY father was enjoying his high school years at Poly Prep, his older brother was beginning the professional bridge, canasta, backgammon, and writing career that would make him famous and rich (or, to be more precise, the career that would have made him rich had he not gambled away such a large proportion of his professional earnings at games where pure chance played a much larger role). From 1930 to 1960, the heyday of bridge and canasta (on which Ozzie was also an expert) as middle-class pastimes, the top tournament players were national and international celebrities. In America, Puritan objections to cards had lost their force, and families across the nation turned to cards, especially bridge, for diversion. Until television subsumed all other forms of entertainment, bridge was a staple in college dormitories, at luncheons like the ones my mother and her friends gave or attended every week, and at Saturday-night after-dinner gatherings of couples. Newspaper bridge columns were as well read as the sports pages, and grandmasters like my uncle and Charles Goren were frequently written about (and wrote about each other) in mass-circulation magazines. Some of the liveliest articles about my uncle appeared in women's magazines, for bridge and canasta, unlike poker, did not conjure up images of cigar-chomping, hard-drinking, tough-talking men in the sleazy back room of a bar. Whenever he was interviewed by a women's magazine, Ozzie always made a point of talking about the bridge and backgammon tournaments in which he and his wife were partners. (He always had a male partner, of course, in the most serious high-stakes tournaments.) Few of my contemporaries recognize Ozzie Jacoby's name when I mention that he was my uncle, but nearly everyone over sixty-five (except for those who had no interest in bridge) remembers him as a celebrity.

Uncle Ozzie won his first bridge match, the Eastern Pairs, after being "discovered" in 1929 by one of the leading members of the Knickerbocker Whist Club. In 1931, he was selected by Sidney Lenz, then the *éminence grise* of the bridge world, as his partner in a rubber match against Ely Culbertson (a young man who would also go on to cardplaying fame). The match, held in Philadelphia, was chronicled in front-page newspaper stories and followed by ardent fans across the country. Lenz and Ozzie had a falling-out over Ozzie's unorthodox bids, and my uncle withdrew from the match. While Lenz went on to lose the match (with another partner) by a huge margin, the upstart Ozzie earned an instant national reputation for brilliant, unconventional play. He became a key member of the Four Aces team, which dominated bridge throughout the thirties. Ozzie had certainly picked a curious profession for a man who wished to distance himself from his Jewish origins, for Jews had long played as conspicuous a role in world-class competitive bridge as they did in chess. Short of becoming a psychoanalyst, my uncle could hardly have made his living in a way more calculated to bring him into social and professional contact with Jews.

Given the nature of his talents, it is not surprising that Ozzie proved to be among the minority of Americans who did extremely well during the Depression. Sports, games, and gambling of all kinds (including betting on sports and games) flourish in tough economic times; bridge and backgammon, in which skill is generally more important than chance, were perfect for my uncle. A great professional cardplayer must possess the talent and coolheadedness to cope with bad luck in the form of a bad hand, and Ozzie definitely knew when to hold and when to fold. But he was incapable of taking his own advice about the need to respect the line between games in which the ability to think several bids ahead, or make a crucial bluff, can overcome a bad hand and those in which no degree of skill can affect the outcome (unless your skill happens to be loading dice or fixing a roulette wheel).

While Ozzie was launching his career, and putting his sister through college and his brother through prep school, my grandfather was representing fewer and fewer clients. One curious episode suggests how desperate for money Oswald Sr. must have been during the twenties. He filed a $90,000 libel suit against another lawyer on behalf of a female client he was representing in a divorce case. My grandfather contended that his client had been defamed because the lawyer had dictated letters regarding the divorce suit—in which the woman's behavior and character were attacked—to his stenographer. By dictating his letters to a third party, my grandfather argued, the opposing lawyer had "published" defamatory material— though letters between opposing counsel had long been covered by attorney-client privilege. Even in 1924, when attorneys and businessmen relied somewhat less on clerical staff than they would only a decade later, it amounted to a frivolous lawsuit to suggest that dictating a sharp letter to a secretary was the equivalent of defamation in an open forum. My grandfather would naturally have known this but must have been hoping for a percentage of an out-of-court settlement. The other attorney, however, was not intimidated, and the suit was eventually thrown out. This lawsuit was the machination of a sleazy lawyer on the skids, not the work of one of the brightest young members of the city bar, a man who had once been spoken of in the same breath as Benjamin Cardozo. It must have been extraordinarily painful for my grandfather to measure his own tarnished reputation against the distinguished legal career of his old friend, by that time the enormously respected chief judge of the New York State Court of Appeals. Cardozo's achievements merited a biography even before he was elevated to the Supreme Court; my grandfather, contemplating the warm inscription from the friend of his youth, can hardly have been unmoved by the obvious contrast in their status.

Oswald Jacoby's last noteworthy appearance as a defense lawyer took place in 1928, when he represented a swindler who was convicted in large measure because he had been dumb enough to advertise for investors in *The New York Times*. Hell hath no fury like a good gray lady used for black ends. In 1909, my grandfather had won an acquittal of the man who sold the newspaper an article with the fraudulent signature of Grover Cleveland. Nineteen years later, he fared less well in his defense of Edward Arden Noblett, a sixty-three-year-old con man who was convicted of swindling one Amos J. C. Baldwin out of $2,000. Noblett, who had been arrested at least twenty times in thirty years but served only two terms in jail, had billed himself as the representative of a British perfume company. Judging from the account in the *Times*, the arrest resulted from a sting operation organized by the Nassau County District Attorney's Office, the *Times* itself, and the pigeon. My grandfather pleaded for leniency for his client on grounds of his advanced age, but the judge sentenced him to ten years at hard labor in Sing Sing. "Old age is one thing," declared County Court Judge Lewis J. Smith, "but this man never did anything in his life useful or worthy. He has been a swindler ever since he was a young man. He seems to be obsessed with a great case of ego." (Noblett, to be sure, had not helped his own cause by trying to bribe the arresting officers.)

A great case of ego. That phrase would certainly have made an appropriate inscription on my grandfather's tombstone—if anyone had paid for a proper burial. But Oswald Nathaniel Jacoby was cremated after his sudden, unexplained death, at the age of sixty-one, in 1931. Nothing attests more powerfully to the low regard in which my grandfather was held by his surviving family members than their failure to give him a proper funeral. All three children claimed they did not know what happened to their father's ashes and did not remember anything about a funeral. Cremation itself was much less common in the United States seventy years ago than it has become in recent decades, but it may have been my grandfather's preference. He was not only irreligious but known to be antireligious, and even though he sent his children to schools with Protestant church connections, he was not himself a member of any church. But there is something unspeakably (in the most literal sense) sad about a family so angry at its husband and father that he was deemed unworthy of a formal burial ceremony.

There were no obituaries for Oswald Jacoby, save one small notice of his death, cause unstated, in a Columbia alumni publication. The absence of an obituary in the *Times*, which had such an extensive file on my grandfather's early career, is significant. If there is one truism about newspapers, it is that they generally note the deaths of people they have chronicled in life. The *Times* would surely not have failed to publish an obituary for Oswald Jacoby merely because he had occasionally crossed swords with the newspaper in court; it is far more likely that no one in the family called to report the death. The Jacoby family, apparently unable to follow the policy of *de mortuis nil nisi bonum*, settled on *de mortuis nil*.

What was the cause of my grandfather's death? My dad thought his father had died of a stroke, while Ozzie told me the cause was syphilis and a heart attack. Aunt Edith, however (at least in the last years of her life), was convinced that her father had committed suicide. Suicide would certainly explain the mysteries—the silence, the absence of a funeral, the nonexistence of obituaries—surrounding my grandfather's death. His cocaine addiction could, of course, have hastened his death from any cause.

WHEN I look at the last fifteen years of my grandfather's life, I see a man who had ample reason for despair. He was a lawyer of diminished stature, unable to meet his basic financial obligations to his family. He was a man who had squandered immense gifts of intellect, charm, education, and culture—a husband with a cold, unloving wife and a father whose children were so angry at him by the time he died that they would avoid looking at pictures of him for the rest of their lives.

Above all, I see the empty space the following June in the chapel at Poly Prep—the space where my grandfather should have been sitting when his seventeen-year-old son marched up to receive his *cum laude* high school diploma. For my father, that space would never be filled.

OZZIE WAS twenty-nine when his father died, and he and Edith, who had just graduated from Smith and gone to work as a salesclerk, took over the responsibility of supporting their mother. My grandfather, not surprisingly, left no estate. Both my aunt and my grandmother seem to have held the traditional view (bolstered, one may assume, by Ozzie's widely publicized and lucrative triumphs in bridge tournaments) of an eldest son's eternal financial responsibility to the rest of the family. My uncle accepted that responsibility as long as he was single, but that would change when he met Mary Zita McHale on a tennis court in Dallas.

Ozzie was in Dallas for a bridge tournament when he spotted the beautiful Texas women's tennis champion across the court. It was love at first sight: Ozzie and Mary were married just a week later in the rectory (the church itself being off-limits because Ozzie wasn't a Catholic) of the Sacred Heart Cathedral in Dallas. In the wedding announcement in the Dallas newspapers, Ozzie was described as a Congregationalist. He had agreed, as the Church demanded, that his and Mary's children be raised as Roman Catholics. "I was so crazy about her, I would have agreed to have the children raised as Druids," Ozzie told me when I asked him how he felt about signing the papers. The McHale family must have had enormous clout to get the local bishop to marry their daughter so quickly to a non-Catholic; normally, a mixed couple would have been required to undergo weeks of pastoral counseling before a priest would consent to marry them. The counseling was designed not only to acquaint the non-Catholic partner with the requirements of marriage to a Catholic (including the all-important prohibition of artificial birth control) but, if possible, to dissuade the Catholic from entering the union at all. Although Mary McHale was (and would remain) a devout Catholic, she was not about to be dissuaded from marrying Ozzie. At the time she met my uncle, she was teaching in a parochial school. When she told the Mother Superior she was leaving to marry a bridge expert, the nun smiled and said, "Ah, how nice, an engineer!"

Mary's father did not inquire further into his future son-in-law's background when Ozzie announced that he was a Congregationalist. In the late 1970s, when I first enlisted Ozzie's help in reconstructing the Jacoby family's Jewish past, he told me he had presented himself as a Congregationalist "because it sounded quite vague." Ozzie said he was sure his future father-in-law knew the Jacobys were Jews but didn't particularly care as long as there was an acceptable cover story for the local papers. "I really think Mary's father didn't give a damn who I was as long as he thought I could support her and I agreed to be married by a priest," Ozzie speculated. "My mother, on the other hand, was absolutely furious that Mary was a Catholic. In 1928, when Al Smith was running for the presidency, she believed all that rubbish about how a Catholic president would be taking his secret orders from the Pope. I think having all three of her children marry

Catholics was probably her worst nightmare. Of course, she probably wouldn't have liked any woman I married."

Mary Zita McHale Jacoby proved to be a formidable rival. Ozzie brought his bride home to an apartment on East Sixty-third Street in Manhattan—as fashionable a location then as it is today. Aunt Edith and my grandmother, who lived together, expected that the married son would soon bring his mother to live with him. But Mary quickly assessed Granny Jacoby's overbearing, possessive nature, and told her new husband, "It's her or me." After his first son, Jim, was born in early 1933, Ozzie sharply reduced the amount of money he had been sending his mother every month. The depth of the conflict involving Ozzie, Mary, Granny Jacoby, and Aunt Edith is revealed in a rancorous 1934 exchange of letters. Ozzie had, uncharacteristically, hung on to the letters, and I found them in an envelope in Dallas after his death. I could hear my grandmother's demanding voice as I read the yellowing pages:

My dear Oswald,
This is to acknowledge for $80.00 which, as you know, is $20 short of the amount promised by you to be paid monthly for my maintenance and reaffirmed by our telephone conversation late last month. As to the jewelry of mine I had entrusted to you for safe-keeping, I now wish to present to *you* the rosette of diamonds set in silver and gold, which in happier times I had instead hoped to give to a wife of yours. This is a gift; it is not in payment of any real or fancied obligation. It is given solely in memory of the love I once believed you had for me. I have neither the time nor the inclination to answer the numerous charges against me you have trumped up to justify your behavior. You are happier believing me dishonest, false, wicked. I find nothing for which to reproach myself unless it is the fault of loving "not wisely but too well." For the last of all time I wish you every success and happiness. I want you to have all that your heart desires and to forget that you ever had a Mother.

The style of this communication is as recognizable to me as that of a Shakespeare sonnet. Having decided that she didn't like Mary, my grandmother must have asked Ozzie to return the "rosette of diamonds" she had conferred on him long ago. When Ozzie balked, Granny Jacoby made a point of saying she'd changed her mind—not about Mary but about Ozzie's keeping the jewelry. ("I now wish to present to *you*.") Forget that he ever had a Mother? Not likely. Aunt Edith got into the act by informing Ozzie, also in March of 1934, that "Mother talks of trying to get housework to do but hopes she will die before she does." Edith advised her brother that it was his legal duty either to bring his mother to live with him or to support her. "I believe that your sense of decency should make you realize your duty to make every effort to reconcile yourself with Mother and to try to give her a little ease of mind for the rest of her poor life," Edith admonished. She also intimated that Mother might commit suicide if Ozzie did not make amends.

My formidable grandmother, who loved being the center of family feuding, would never have killed herself (though she undoubtedly would have preferred death to life as a cleaning woman). She and Ozzie eventually patched things up and continued to aggravate each other for the rest of Granny Jacoby's "poor life," which lasted another thirty-two years. In 1936, Ozzie and Mary moved from New York to Dallas, ostensibly for Mary to be closer to her family but mainly to escape the face-to-face wrangling with Mother. While Ozzie never broke off relations with his mother, he saw her even less frequently than my father did. My own mother proved to be as leery of Granny Jacoby as Aunt Mary was. After the war, there was some talk of my father's moving his family back to New York, but my mother flatly refused. Granny Jacoby wanted to control both of her sons' lives, but in very different ways. Her possessive admiration for Ozzie was matched by her possessive denigration of my father. Mary and my mom were right: they kept their families out of harm's way by keeping them away from the formidable Jacoby matriarch.

·   ·   ·

DURING THE early thirties, no one in the family was paying much attention to my father. He was away at Dartmouth until the summer of 1933, when he came home at the end of his sophomore year, knowing he would not be able to return to college in the fall. I think my father may have been quite happy to leave the snows of Hanover, New Hampshire. The outstanding student at Poly Prep had turned, for whatever reasons, into a mediocre student at Dartmouth. Dad entered Dartmouth at a time when the alumni and the administration were becoming increasingly concerned about "the Jewish problem"— the presence of too many Jewish students, especially from New York—on the Hanover campus. During his two years there, my father was exposed to a microcosm of the upper-class anti-Semitism that would, only a few years later, deny visas to Jews frantic to leave Nazi Germany. After learning what Dartmouth officials thought, said, and did about the Jews in their midst during the early thirties, it is easier for me to understand why my father found it so difficult, forty years later, to believe that American anti-Semitism had lost the power to circumscribe his children's educational and employment prospects. In his mind, there was still a threat. It was not the threat of an American-bred Holocaust, or even of his children or grandchildren being beaten up by bullies in a schoolyard. In my father's experience, the threat was more subtle and therefore more pernicious. Unnamed powers-that-be might decide, without ever coming right out and saying so, that Jews weren't quite good enough for their university or their club or their offices. Or they would decide, as they had in the twenties and thirties, that only a fixed number of Jews would be able to pass the invisible test that enabled them to pass invisible barriers. The rest would remain outsiders by virtue of the insiders' gentleman's agreements. That is exactly what was happening at Dartmouth, and every other university esteemed by German-descended Jews like the Jacobys, when my father arrived on campus as a freshman in 1931.

VI

The Chosen and the Heathen

⟨⟩

THE INCOMING DARTMOUTH freshman class in the autumn of
1931—the Class of '35—included the largest number of Jewish students in the history of the college. Of the class's 696 members, 75—
more than 10 percent—were Jews. Moreover, that figure included
only those students who stated a Jewish religious preference.
Another 97 incoming freshmen—14 percent of the total—declared
"no preference." My father was one of the no-preference students,
suggesting that the true proportion of Jews in his class (whether
they admitted it or not) was much higher than 1 in 10. Whatever the
real number, it represented more than a fivefold increase over a ten-
year period, prompting the director of admissions, E. Gordon Bill,
to observe sardonically in the alumni magazine that "the triumph of
the chosen and the heathen peoples seems to be a continuing
process. . . ."

Because Bill's impolitic comment proved deeply offensive (much
to his astonishment) to some Jewish alumni, Dartmouth's president,
Ernest Martin Hopkins, advised his acerbic dean of freshmen (the
admissions director's official title) to absent himself from the next

regularly scheduled Alumni Council meeting in the fall of 1931. A full-scale discussion of Jewish undergraduate enrollment by the council—which Bill's presence could only have served to promote and exacerbate—would have made it more difficult for Hopkins to douse the controversy the dean had aroused by publicly voicing attitudes that were usually reserved for the private world of gentleman's agreements.

Although some Jewish graduates of Dartmouth were upset by Bill's comments, others—along with some Jewish undergraduates— were themselves disturbed by the presence of so many Jews in the Class of '35. Like the Jacobys, most of these anxious Jews identified with the "German" sector of American Jewry, and they feared, characteristically, that admission of "the wrong kind" of Jews—those of Eastern European immigrant origins—would stimulate anti-Semitism at Dartmouth. This surging anti-Semitism might, of course, spill over onto the "right kind"—their kind. Jewish alumni had long been enlisted to screen applications from other "Hebrews," in order to ensure that they would not be too religious, too unassimilated—too Jewish—for Dartmouth.

What did it mean to be "too Jewish" at an old-line WASP college in the thirties? In a letter to Hopkins on January 3, 1933, the irrepressibly candid Bill confided, "I am increasingly of the opinion that the actual physical appearance of a Jewish applicant is an extraordinarily important factor in determining selection or rejection. . . ."

Bill went on to clarify his meaning. "In other words," he explained, "I believe that the Jewish boys whom we do not like and who do not seem to fit into the Dartmouth picture and hence should not have been selected, are of a physical type that is unattractive to the average Dartmouth student. This situation pertains to no other race because I believe the more homely and physically unattractive an Irishman is, the better he is generally liked."

Bill reminded Hopkins that all of the applicants for the next year's entering freshman class had been required to submit pictures—which would presumably enable the admissions office to identify those of "a physical type that is unattractive to the average Dartmouth student." After the brouhaha over the large Jewish presence in my father's class, Hopkins and Bill were determined to reverse a trend that they saw as a threat to the social, if not the academic, reputation of the college. In one of his many epistolary exchanges with Bill on the "Jewish problem," Hopkins relayed a comment from a visiting Harvard colleague, "who says that he always had heard that Dartmouth was the one Anglo-Saxon college left, [but] insists that he stood on the Inn corner and that every fourth man who passed him in a period of fifteen or twenty minutes was a Jew. Allowing for his undoubted overemphasis, and his desire to claim that we were picking up the group which Harvard, Yale, Princeton and Columbia are refusing, it still remains a fact that we have too many for our own good or for the good of the Jewish boys themselves."

I CAN EASILY envisage this snooty visitor from Harvard, standing in front of the Hanover Inn (established in 1780), overlooking the eighteenth- and nineteenth-century buildings that form the graceful core of the Dartmouth campus. He was not admiring the architecture or gazing at the surrounding mountains that lend this New Hampshire community so much of its charm. Instead, he was looking for people who did not, as far as he was concerned, belong in such an idyllic New England setting, at a college chartered by King George III in 1769 and charged with the mission of "spreading Christian knowledge among the savages" while at the same time offering "the best means of education" for all of its students. The first objective was soon subsumed by the mission of preparing the sons of the upper classes to take their place in the newly independent United States of America.

How did the emissary from Harvard identify non-Christian outsiders strolling near the Dartmouth Common in 1932? Were they talking with their hands? Talking too loudly? Was my father one of the young men wandering by the Inn, constituting a presence too conspicuous "for the good of the Jewish boys themselves"?

•   •   •

THERE WAS nothing unusual about such attitudes on the part of the men who ran the country's elite institutions of higher education—and nearly everything else—in the decades between the twentieth century's two world wars. Dartmouth was not the first but one of the last elite eastern colleges to take stringent measures to restrict Jewish enrollment. My father came of age at a time when it was much more difficult for a Jew to get into a top-ranking private college than it had been for his father and older brother. In 1919, when Uncle Ozzie entered Columbia, Jewish quotas had not yet been established at most Ivy League schools. In that year, Jews made up more than 40 percent of undergraduates at Columbia, 20 percent at Harvard, and 20 percent at Brown. But 1919 was also the year in which Nicholas Murray Butler, Columbia's formidable president, ordered the registrar to devise a new admissions form featuring a psychological test that would measure "environmental" factors as well as intellectual achievement. For the first time, applicants were required to list their religious affiliation and their father's name and birthplace, to supply a photograph of themselves (a tactic Dartmouth did not adopt until the thirties), and to submit to a personal interview. Such procedures, which soon became a model for all private universities, provided a handy way of filtering out applicants of undesirable races, religions, and social backgrounds. When my grandfather and Great-Uncle Harold entered Columbia in the 1880s, all that counted was their academic performance on a rigorous, classics-oriented entrance examination. One can only wonder whether the distinguished Professor Harold Jacoby, who looked so very Jewish as a young man, would have made it through the post-1920 admissions net. Or whether he ever discussed the new undergraduate admissions procedures (and the decline in Jewish admissions to Columbia's law and medical schools) with Butler, who was a personal friend. Although they were not members of the same class, the two men had known each other since their undergraduate days.

Throughout the 1920s, explicit and implicit Jewish quotas steadily reduced Jewish enrollment at all universities of the first

rank. With its new admissions procedures, Columbia cut the proportion of Jews in its freshman class from 40 percent in 1920 to 22 percent in 1922. By 1928, the percentage of Jews in Harvard's freshman
class had also been halved.

Dartmouth did not have a "Jewish problem" during this period
because so few Jews had applied for admission in the early twenties.
The college's isolated location, near the Vermont–New Hampshire
border, far from any centers of Jewish population, was unappealing
to Jewish families living in the northeast corridor between Boston
and Philadelphia. Moreover, the Dartmouth of the twenties was not
on an academic par with Harvard, Yale, or Columbia. In 1920, when
Columbia and Harvard were struggling to cut their Jewish enroll-
ments, Jews made up fewer than 2 percent of undergraduates at
Dartmouth. Only when the more distinguished eastern universities
began to restrict Jewish admissions did the number of Jewish applicants to Dartmouth begin to rise. Indeed, there was undoubtedly a
direct connection between the developing quota system at Columbia—and its success in cutting Jewish enrollment in half during the
early twenties—and the rise in applications to Dartmouth from the
New York City area.

Nevertheless, Dartmouth had already taken tentative steps
toward limiting Jewish enrollment—without instituting a rigid
quota system—through an admissions procedure called the Selective
Process. Devised by Hopkins in the early twenties, the Process
(always capitalized) was designed to ensure geographical and "occu-
pational" (meaning the occupation of the student's father) diversity
as well as to raise academic standards. Felix Frankfurter, the future
Supreme Court justice and a personal friend of President Hopkins,
expressed concern as early as 1922 that the new admissions system
(modeled to a considerable degree on the procedures already instituted at Columbia) might serve to discriminate against Jews. The
Process seems to have been the subject of an ongoing dialogue
between Frankfurter and Hopkins. In March 1923, Frankfurter
wrote Hopkins that he had taken every opportunity "to give vigor-

ous expression of my conviction that the Dartmouth of which you are the head, cannot conceivably go in for the folly of racial or social lines in the selection of its student body." Nevertheless, Frankfurter added, "Some day I should like to have a long 'jaw' with you on this subject as part of the larger subject of what our colleges, and particularly our universities, are for." The Process did not harden into an outright quota system until my father's class produced such a large representation of "the chosen and the heathen." (Until I read excerpts from this correspondence, I had mistakenly credited Kenneth Starr with the first reverential use of the neutral-sounding "process" to describe a procedure that was anything but unbiased.)

By 1930, Hopkins and Bill had become especially worried about the large number of applications from New York City. In September of that year, Bill wrote Hopkins that he had become "increasingly positive this summer . . . that the Jewish problem in connection with our New York and vicinity application lists should be man-handled. To be specific, I think it would be a good thing if during the next four or five years we take very few Jews from that district. At the present time I feel that they are completely dominating the Dartmouth application lists in . . . New York and if we don't look out, we will get into a rut from which we will extricate ourselves with great difficulty."

Dartmouth's initial failure to "man-handle" the New York Jewish problem was demonstrated by the presence of twenty-seven Jews from the area in my father's class—down by four from the previous year, but still not low enough in the view of the administration. In April 1932, Bill traveled to New York to discuss the problem with Judge Arthur J. Cohen (Class of 1903), a Jewish alumnus who had *not* been outraged by the dean's comments about "the chosen and the heathen." A delighted Bill reported to Hopkins that Judge Cohen was "absolutely in agreement with you and me." The judge, according to Bill, regarded the presence of such a large Jewish contingent from New York as "almost a tragedy." He suggested that Jewish enrollment be limited through private measures rather than publicly announced policies, and Bill assured him that the Selective Process was designed to achieve just that end. Judge Cohen apparently voiced just one reservation. "The only possible difference of opinion we had," Bill reported, "was that he felt that all *brilliant* Jewish students from the New York high schools should be admitted. I told him that he probably had no idea how many such students were applying." This posed a conundrum for President Hopkins, whose main goal at the time was to raise the academic standing of Dartmouth—to place the school on a par with the more prestigious Ivy League schools—by improving the quality of both the student body and the faculty. On the one hand, the pool of Jewish applicants was filled with outstanding scholars. On the other, the presence of too many Jews at Dartmouth might impel the more academically talented WASPs to choose other Ivy League schools that already had strict Jewish quotas in place. A few weeks after Bill's meeting with Judge Cohen, Hopkins acknowledged the dilemma, noting that "any college which is going to base its admission wholly on scholastic standing will find itself with an infinitesimal proportion of anything else than Jews eventually."

Just as there was a conflict between raising the academic level of the student body and keeping out Jews, there was a tension between the increasing secularization of Dartmouth under Hopkins and its pious Protestant history. Dartmouth was not of course unique in its religious origins; all colleges dating from the colonial era were founded by ministers, for the purpose of educating future religious leaders. For much of the nineteenth century, however, theological conservatism was the hallmark of ministers selected as presidents of Dartmouth. The ministers who presided over better-known New England colleges tended to be staunch abolitionists, but Dartmouth's president during the Civil War, the Reverend Nathan Lord, publicly espoused slavery and cited Scripture to support his position. Only in 1893 did the Dartmouth trustees select a president who was both a minister and a progressive—the Reverend William Jewett Tucker, who had already aroused the ire of conservative theologians by arguing that belief in God was compatible with Darwinism. Hopkins, who assumed the presidency in 1916, came from a business instead of a ministerial or academic background; his administration completed Dartmouth's transition from a Protestant-identified college into a basically secular twentieth-century institution of higher education. Before 1925, when Hopkins abolished compulsory chapel attendance, Jewish students at Dartmouth were required to participate in regular Protestant services, including Sunday vespers.

The abandonment of compulsory chapel must have provided yet another spur to Jewish enrollment during the second half of the twenties, yet Hopkins was clearly conflicted over the secularization he himself had promoted. In an article published in 1945 in the *New York Post*, Hopkins declared that Dartmouth was still "a Christian College founded for the Christianizing of its students." A half-century later, that provocative statement would be cited approvingly by neoconservative students—ironically, some of them Jews—associated with the controversial *Dartmouth Review*, dedicated to the proposition that multiculturalism and liberalism were running amok in Hanover. It would be interesting to know if Hopkins ever did sit down for a "jaw" about the Christianizing mission of Dartmouth with his friend Felix Frankfurter. If Hopkins had a fault as a booster of his institution—one of the main roles of any university president in any era—it can only have been that he was more candid than his contemporaries at other colleges. If they felt, as many did, that part of their job was to remain faithful to the Christian and WASP origins of their institutions, they didn't broadcast their views—especially in forums such as a New York newspaper with a large Jewish readership.

My father and his contemporaries did not need explicit instruction in the prevailing attitudes, at Dartmouth and other old-line educational institutions, toward too-Jewish Jews. It is hardly surprising that Jewish students of my father's generation suffered from a serious case of *tsitterdik* syndrome, a condition shared by many Jews, in many social contexts, throughout the nation. The *tsitterdik* sufferer—the word is derived from the onomatopoetic Yiddish *tsitter*, to shake or tremble—was condemned to unending worry about the behavior of his fellow Jews. One Jew's loud voice, pushiness, conspicuous display of wealth—anything, really, that fit anti-Semitic stereotypes—could reflect badly on all Jews. *Tsitterdik* behavior had long characterized the assimilated community of Jews in Germany (though they would soon learn that looking and behaving exactly like their countrymen provided no guarantee against anti-Semitism on the rampage). In America, *tsitterdik* responses by German Jews were intensified by the beginning of the Jewish influx from Eastern Europe in the 1880s; the outpouring of German Jewish money into the settlement houses and educational programs of New York's Lower East Side attested to the nervousness as well as to the charitable traditions of the community. As far as German Jews were concerned, the only cure for these palpitations was the rapid Americanization and assimilation of the new arrivals. Only when the immigrants had abandoned their obviously Jewish and foreign ways would the nervousness of the older American Jewish community subside.

In 1991, Alexandra Shepard—a student at a very different Dartmouth from the institution my father attended—was working in the college archives when she became interested in correspondence during the twenties and thirties among Dartmouth administrators, and from alumni to the administration, concerning "the Jewish problem" on the Hanover campus. Drawing extensively on archival material as well as interviews with surviving alumni, Shepard wrote her honors thesis in history on Jewish students at Dartmouth between 1920 and 1940. Her interviews with alumni are of particular interest, because they illuminate the social insecurity that pervaded the psyches of even those Jewish students who were most successful and most thoroughly assimilated.

In the spring of 1931, Michael Stern (a pseudonym), an editor of the student newspaper, *The Dartmouth*, and a Big Man On Campus, manifested his *tsitter* jitters by requesting a meeting with President Hopkins to voice his concern over a "deterioration" in the kind of

Jewish students who were being admitted. Hopkins agreed, noting repeatedly in correspondence that it was for the good of the Jews themselves that Dartmouth limit the influx of undesirable "Hebrew" applicants from public high schools and places like Brooklyn. The Flatbush section of Brooklyn, where my father's family lived after moving from Manhattan, seems to have been regarded by many college administrators (not only those at Dartmouth) as the wellspring of a new, presumably pushier breed of Jewish immigrant. Jewish students like Stern and my father were acutely aware of the need to present themselves as worthy representatives of their people and of the adverse consequences of being perceived as part of a "racial problem" (as it was often called in the days when "Hebrews" were perceived by many gentiles as a race apart). "I didn't know how Jewish to be," Stern told Shepard in an interview. His requirement that Shepard use a pseudonym certainly suggests that this former BMOC was still conflicted about his Dartmouth experience and about his attitude toward other Jewish students of his generation. My dad, who was not cut out to be a BMOC, must have been as tormented in college as he was in later years by the fear that he could not measure up to a set of amorphous social standards.

ALTHOUGH Bob Jacoby was a graduate of a well-regarded prep school and came from the type of cultivated, acculturated Jewish family favored by Dartmouth's admissions office, his family's economic comedown had also saddled him with an undesirable Flatbush address. But Dartmouth never knew that. On my father's college transcript, and in the freshman "Green Book," his address is listed as 32 Washington Square West in Manhattan. With its Jamesian associations, this was a much better address than any street in Flatbush. Although plenty of Jews lived on, or at least in the vicinity of, Washington Square by 1930 (most of them in decidedly un-Jamesian accommodations), the address still conveyed a sense of Old New York and old money. It was Uncle Ozzie who lived at Number 32 before he married Aunt Mary, and it was he who provided the front for the Dartmouth admissions office. True, Dad had applied to Dartmouth from Poly Prep (which Dean Bill described as "a splendid school" in the alumni magazine). But he also had an identifiably Jewish name and features—a nose, at any rate—that certainly hinted at his origins. A Washington Square address might offset some of those liabilities. While no longer quite "the ideal of quiet and of genteel retirement" portrayed by Henry James in his 1881 novel, the square (in spite of the encroaching bohemia of Greenwich Village) retained an upper-class aura. In the late 1920s, in spite of the presence of several new apartment buildings, one could still recognize the Washington Square of James's nineteenth-century description: "It has a kind of established repose which is not of frequent occurrence in other quarters of the long, shrill city; it has a riper, richer, more honorable look than any of the upper ramifications of the great longitudinal thoroughfare—the look of having something of a social history."

As it happens, the history of 32 Washington Square West offers a neatly ironic microcosm of the constantly shifting social and residential barriers that affected Jews of my father's and uncle's generation. When Uncle Ozzie lived at that address, in a building erected on the site in 1925, he rented his apartment. After World War II, the rental building was transformed into an elegant and exclusive cooperative—a form of apartment ownership largely unheard of outside New York—where, it was well known, Jews need not apply. No Jews were permitted to buy apartments at Number 32 until 1962, when the building's board of directors caved in under pressure from the city's recently established Human Rights Commission. Until that time, co-ops had successfully argued that they were exempt from city policies prohibiting racial and religious discrimination in rental apartments. Uncle Ozzie (even though he had a way of gaining acceptance in venues, like the Dallas Country Club, that were generally closed to Jews) would not, in the late 1940s, have been permitted to buy the apartment he had once rented in New York. It is sobering to reflect upon the fact that for much of the twentieth century, no Jew—however well-off, however well-connected—could take for granted the right to live anywhere he chose in the city with the largest Jewish population in the United States. And if that was true in New York, why should my father not have suspected that it might also be true in Okemos, Michigan?

THE PHONY address on my father's transcript provides one more piece of evidence of the family's thoroughgoing desire to conceal its true social, economic, and ethnic background. What an immense amount of thought and energy must have gone into this accumulation of fictions, great and small, in the service of another identity! In view of the attitudes expressed by men who had the power to keep a Jewish boy out of a good college, it is easy to understand why the Jacobys went to such lengths. What is so striking about the Dartmouth administrators' correspondence on the "Jewish problem" is the matter-of-fact, unashamed tone in which the sentiments were voiced. No one was embarrassed to be talking about how to exclude Jewish students of the wrong kind, and it obviously never occurred to these refined WASP educators that posterity might take a different view of their views.

In 1997, Dartmouth president James O. Freedman (now retired) quoted a telling piece of correspondence at the dedication of a campus center for Jewish students. The letters were exchanged in 1934 between Robert C. Strong, Bill's successor as director of admissions, and Ford H. Whelden, an alumnus from Detroit. Whelden observed that "the campus seems more Jewish each time I arrive in Hanover. And unfortunately, many of them (on quick judgement) seem to be the 'kike' type." The admissions director told Whelden he was "glad to have your comments on the Jewish problem, and I shall appreciate your help along this line in the future. If we go beyond the 5% or 6% in the Class of 1938, I shall be grieved beyond words. . . . It may be that all of the Jewish boys [accepted for admission] will come, in which case we may get up to 6%, but I do not see how it can climb as

high as 8% or 9%." Both Whelden and Strong would surely have
been grieved beyond words, and utterly disbelieving, had they
known that Dartmouth would one day have a Jewish president, and
that the president would cite their correspondence as a prime example of the anti-Semitism shared by many of the college's alumni,
administrators, and students during the first four decades of the
twentieth century.

READING THESE old words in the Dartmouth archives, more than
thirty years after my dad first admitted to me that he was Jewish, I
can finally comprehend, on an emotional rather than a purely intellectual level, the depth of his fear that his children might be
deprived of something they wanted in life simply because their
father had been born a Jew. My father wasn't delusional (as I had
ignorantly half-concluded in 1966) to think that a Jew could never
quite predict when a door might be slammed in his face. Instead of
directing his anger at people who talked about a "Jewish problem" in
the thirties, my father internalized the judgments embedded in President Hopkins's and Dean Bill's letters.

In his formative years, Dad could not have seen these attitudes
for what they were—one piece in an overarching edifice of unexamined prejudices and stereotypes applying not only to Jews but to
everyone outside the WASP elite. Bill, after all, was as certain that
the whole world loved a homely Irishman as he was that the whole
world despised a hook-nosed Jew. His views of black Americans were
cut from the same cloth. In March 1932, Bill took time out from his
incessant worrying about Jews to focus on the much less significant
(in terms of the number of applicants) but still anxiety-producing
question of whether to admit a Negro or two. He was trying to
decide on the application of "a Negro boy from New York City who
is evidently an outstandingly fine member of that race." The young
man, a high school track star, had been recommended by Dartmouth's track coach, who assured Bill that the prospective freshman
"should at least add color to the campus. Inasmuch as this boy can

run a 440 in 52 sec. flat . . . even tho he be a Chinaman we can use him. . . ."

Much to my regret, the question of admitting women to Dartmouth never came up during the thirties. It would no doubt be edifying to read Dean Bill's analysis of the intellectual abilities of female applicants, and his image of what a girl ought to look like in order to gain full acceptance by the Dartmouth community.

I AM SURPRISED at the depth of my anger as I sift through these letters. Most of them were written nearly seventy years ago, yet they retain a certain power over me because the authors, and men like them, wielded a great deal of power over my father. Cultivated men, men dedicated not only to their college but to education itself, the administrators of Dartmouth used part of their power to restrict the opportunities of those whom they regarded as social inferiors. *Tout comprendre, c'est tout pardonner?* Not a chance. Although anti-Semitism was an error bred in the bones of upper-class gentiles at that time, some of Hopkins's and Bill's contemporaries, like Eleanor Roosevelt, made a serious attempt to wean themselves from the prejudices with which they had been raised. It is no excuse, though it is an explanation, to acknowledge that the administrators at Dartmouth, and throughout the Ivy League, were typical products of their social class and generation. Their policies—the logical extension of their ingrained biases—lived on for decades. A Dartmouth alumnus (not Jewish), now in his mid-sixties, tells me that some of his classmates were furious when President Freedman's speech, quoting excerpts from the anti-Semitic letters, was reported in *The New York Times.* "The campus certainly has more than its fair share of Jews now," one of my friend's ex-roommates had said to him, "so what's the point of airing out that dirty linen?"

MY FATHER'S conflicts about his Jewishness formed only one strand in his unhappiness at Dartmouth. The outstanding student at Poly Prep had turned into a C student in college. My father participated in no extracurricular activities (another contrast to his years at Poly), although "well-roundedness" was considered more important than academic distinction in the Dartmouth of that era. Moreover, Dartmouth, unlike a number of other private colleges, does not seem to have placed any barriers in the way of Jewish students interested in extracurricular activities. Jews occupied prominent positions on Dartmouth student publications, in drama groups, and in intellectual discussion clubs—all activities that had attracted my dad at Poly. At Dartmouth, he seems to have formed few lasting friendships. I was unable to track down anyone who remembered my father from college, as Charles Wardell remembered him from Poly, even though many members of his class were still alive when I began working on this book.

The fraternity system at Dartmouth divided Jews and gentiles in much the same manner as it did on all other campuses (though Dartmouth's non-Jewish fraternities did occasionally pledge Jewish BMOCs, which was not true at every school). There was one Jewish fraternity on campus at the time, composed mainly of men from German Jewish families like the Sondheims and the Jacobys. However, I doubt that my dad would ever have joined a Jewish fraternity even if he had been selected as a pledge, and even if his family had been able to afford frills like fraternity initiation fees. Becoming a member of any identifiably Jewish group would have gone entirely against the grain of his upbringing. Jews, he had been taught, should not set themselves apart. And if most Jews could not expect to be invited to join a gentile fraternity, better to be unaffiliated than to appear "clannish." Better to be seen as one of the heathen than one of the chosen.

My father's tight budget was also a social liability—more so at Dartmouth than it would have been at Columbia, which enrolled many day students who lived at home in order to save money. (Columbia did pressure freshmen to live on campus—one way of discouraging applicants from immigrant families, who would find it hard to pay dormitory room and board.) Dartmouth's geographical isolation meant that every student's family had to come up with money for room and board, and this requirement virtually guaranteed a more affluent student population than the one at Columbia or Harvard. My dad told me he began to gamble seriously during his college years (even if he didn't have many close friends, there was never any shortage of gambling buddies) in order to come up with the money he needed to invite a girlfriend to social events like Dartmouth's Winter Carnival and to accept invitations to mixers at women's colleges. The man was, of course, expected to pay for everything, whether his girlfriend visited him in Hanover or whether he visited her at her college. Dad often came up short. "Sometimes I had to throw myself on the mercy of the girl," he recalled, "because of course I usually lost more money than I won in an effort to pay for my share. I would let it be known that my family had lost its money in the stock market crash and there was just enough left for my tuition. Which was partly true. It wouldn't have impressed my dates to learn that I'd lost the money meant for a Hanover Inn dinner in a poker game."

When my father filled out a questionnaire for his twenty-fifth class reunion in 1960—which he did not attend—he noted only, "Did not return to Dartmouth after sophomore year (remember the Depression)."

By the time my father left the college, the Dartmouth administration was well on its way to attaining its goal of a sharply reduced Jewish undergraduate presence. In the fall of 1932, only 5.8 percent of entering freshmen were Jewish, compared with 10.8 percent in my dad's class just a year earlier. The Jewish delegation, Bill reported in an alumni magazine issue published a year after his ill-advised quip about "the chosen and the heathen," was now "back to normal." Furthermore, Bill observed with satisfaction, the number of those stating no religious preference had declined from ninety-seven to *nine*. Given the small furor over his comments about the previous freshman class, Bill would have been well advised to refrain from making any further public statements that could be regarded as anti-

Semitic. Nevertheless, he could not refrain from returning to the
sensitive subject of physical appearance as an admissions criterion.
"One boy was admitted," Bill explained, "because he had such lovely
light hair and blue eyes and was about six feet two in height. Our Phi
Beta Kappa societies are getting so swarthy that it is well to lighten
things up a bit."

FOR MY FATHER, Dartmouth was always a memory tinged with
sadness. I am certain that the emotional turmoil connected with my
grandfather's death must have contributed to his poor academic performance and his overall unhappiness during his two college years.
The death of a parent is a heavy burden for any adolescent; a mysterious death, with no chance to say good-bye, imposes a dual burden
of loss and secrecy. To me, nothing speaks more eloquently of the
crushing nature of this burden than my father's lifelong insistence
that the early death of his father was "not really all that important."

I don't think my dad blamed Ozzie for not paying his tuition
after his sophomore year, although he deeply regretted his failure to
complete his college education. I do blame my grandmother and my
aunt, who were on the scene and could have insisted that my dad finish school in New York City. Of all the dismaying facts I have learned
about my father's family, the worst is its failure to see that its
younger son receive an education commensurate with his brains. If
Granny Jacoby were still alive, I'd ask her why she didn't sell the
damned diamond rosette to keep my dad in school. What was wrong
with a woman who hung on to a hundred-year-old set of china, a
huge collection of sterling silver pieces, and a large array of other
heirlooms while her son dropped out of college? I think it is perfectly
understandable that my father's education wasn't the number one
concern of the newly married Ozzie. But I do not understand
Granny Jacoby—except insofar as "wicked" (if that is the word
Ozzie really applied to her) describes her behavior.

My father might have lived at home and gone to Columbia, which
would have been much cheaper than Dartmouth because he would

not have had to pay room and board. Even with the strict Jewish quota instituted under Butler, my dad would surely have been admitted as a legacy, given that his father, uncle, and elder brother had all been Columbia men. Or Dad could have gone to that great public institution of higher education, the City College of New York. During the thirties, thousands of New York students, most of them from families much poorer than the Jacobys, received a first-rate, free education there. From 1920 through 1950, the City College of New York was arguably the most distinguished public college in the nation (possibly the world).

My grandmother, with her snobbery about being a Sondheim of Frankfurt, may have considered City College so far beneath her that it never even occurred to her as a possibility for her son. But that seems unlikely, since her own sisters were graduates of Hunter College, the city's equally distinguished public institution of higher education for women. Still, Granny Jacoby may well have felt that what was good enough for her siblings wasn't good enough for her children. However socially undesirable City College might seem to the descendants of German Jews, the academic status of that institution was not in question in 1932. My grandfather, during the last years of his life, could hardly have been unaware of the brilliant legal and scholarly career of Felix Frankfurter—a career unimpeded by Frankfurter's undergraduate degree from City College. Born in 1882, the future Supreme Court justice, a Viennese Jew who arrived in New York in 1893 with scarcely a word of English, was already, by the 1920s, regarded as one of the most outstanding legal minds of his generation. My grandfather, who had begun life with so many more advantages, was reduced to defending small-time swindlers. Estelle Frankfurter alluded to the comparison when she told me about having met my grandfather. "*Your* grandfather started out with everything," she said pointedly.

By the beginning of the thirties, the student body at City College was composed almost entirely of Jews—but not Jews like the Jacobys (or the Frankfurters, who, though they were poor, came from a long line of rabbinical scholars). The City College students of my father's generation were, for the most part, the children of uneducated immigrants from Eastern Europe. They were hungry for every form of knowledge, fiercely competitive, and openly ambitious in ways that fit the anti-Semitic stereotypes held at the time not only by the non-Jewish American majority but also by German-descended Jews like my father and his siblings. Had my father gone to City College, he might have rubbed shoulders with Alfred Kazin or Jonas Salk, but my grandmother would have been appalled at the thought of her son associating with Jews who came from Yiddish-speaking homes, were raised in neighborhoods like Brownsville and the Lower East Side, and who spoke English with the coarse accents of the New York streets rather than prep school diction.

THE COURSE of my father's life would surely have been very different had he gone on to finish his education at City College. Fresh out of Poly Prep and two years at Dartmouth, with all that implied about the aping of WASP gentility and restraint, he might have been almost as out of step in his first weeks at City as he had been in a Brooklyn public school. But that wouldn't have lasted long. His natural gregariousness (in spite of his adolescent shyness with girls), love of wordplay, literary and historical erudition, and enjoyment of numbers would have served him well with his classmates at a commuter school for people who could not afford any other sort of higher education. Young Bob Jacoby—who was, after all, in precisely the same boat—might have benefited greatly from being around contemporaries who were determined to educate themselves with or without ivy-covered walls. When I moved to New York in the early seventies and first encountered New York Jewish intellectuals of my father's generation, I immediately felt a sense of familiarity because their manner—quick, funny, impatient, argumentative, openly emotional—reminded me so much of Dad. My father would have fitted in here, in a way he never quite did with men whose idea of a good time was an afternoon spent stalking deer in the Michigan woods.

I am also quite certain that my father would have chosen a very different way of making a living had he completed his education in New York. I doubt that he would have become an accountant—a profession for which he was ill suited, in spite of his mathematical skills, not only because he was chronically disorganized but also because he was more interested in talking to people than in poring over detailed columns of figures. I can see him as a high school history or English teacher, like his Sondheim uncle and aunts, doing work that would have tapped both his love of language and his empathy for kids. And he might have come to terms with his Jewishness had he stayed in the city and gotten to know Jews who hadn't been shaped by several generations of identification with, and the desire to be identified as, Germans or American WASPs. He might even have married a Jewish girl—if Granny Jacoby didn't get in the way. And his child would have grown up knowing she was a Jew— even if she received no Jewish education and her parents were completely nonobservant. But the child wouldn't have been me.

VII

Family Contrasts

⌇

MY FATHER WAS ONLY nineteen when he left Dartmouth in the spring of 1933 and returned to the unhappy home that now consisted of his mother and sister. He knew that he would soon be expected to get a job in order to help support his mother and that he would also be expected to go on living under her roof; he had every intention of fulfilling the first expectation and no intention whatsoever of fulfilling the second. Ozzie used his connections to help his younger brother land a position as a junior accountant with the Fiduciary Trust Company in Manhattan. The young accountant's responsibilities at work did not interfere with his gambling and pursuit of girls, often in the company of old Poly Prep friends who had also been obliged, as a result of the Depression, to go to work instead of finishing college. My dad and his friends were never out of work during the thirties; their families may have lost a good deal of money in the stock market crash, but the Old Boy Network (or, in my father's case, the Young Boy Network represented by his brother) gave them entree into the straitened job market.

When he turned twenty-one, like Ozzie before him, the young-man-about-town moved out of his mother's house and was free to devote himself to having an extremely good time. For my father, the thirties amounted to a lengthy, basically carefree parenthesis, a bridge between his college years and the war. In his early twenties, the shy "Fat" turned into a handsome young man, with a ready laugh and a charm that was rooted in his genuine interest in other people. On the whole, he preferred the company of women to that of men (a trait he would exhibit throughout his life). Women were drawn to him, but they tended to see him as a friend rather than as a lover; he lacked the streak of callousness that piques erotic interest in women in their twenties. (In my early twenties, I introduced my father to a male friend who obviously wanted to be something more. "Of course you're not interested in him *that way*," Dad said with an ironic laugh. "He's too nice. I know the signs.")

Like many of his contemporaries, he felt no urgency about settling down during a decade that began with the Depression and ended with the imminent prospect of war. In the spring of 1940, when Hitler's troops were storming through France and the Low Countries, my father was only twenty-six. While the gathering war clouds propelled some young men into hasty marriages, many others saw the coming conflict as a good reason, as well as a perfect excuse, to put off any serious decisions. It was sensible, as well as more fun, to keep life provisional and uncomplicated. "By the time of Dunkirk, you had to be an idiot not to know we were going to be in the war sooner or later—and probably sooner," Dad recalled. "If you were going to be sent to god-knows-where, maybe to be killed, why would you get married? Well, some guys thought otherwise. They got married because they wanted something to hang on to, someone to come back to. I was pretty immature then, and I was happy to have another reason not to settle down. Actually, it sounds awful, but I looked forward to the war. I thought we should be in it, that fighting the Nazis was something important to do."

Ozzie, twelve years older than my father and as settled down as he was capable of being, also viewed the potential disruption of war with an equanimity that bordered on enthusiasm. The navy, eager to draw on my uncle's special mathematical skills, commissioned Ozzie and assigned him to an elite unit charged with the responsibility of breaking Japanese and German codes. He was stationed in Washington and Honolulu, with occasional top-secret trips to London. The suspension of international bridge tournaments for the duration of the war did not hurt Ozzie's finances: high-stakes poker games with admirals and generals replenished his coffers (though only a fraction of his winnings made their way to Aunt Mary in Dallas). "I never had as much fun in my life as I did during the war," Ozzie said. "Don't let anyone who had a desk job tell you how much he hated the war, what a terrible sacrifice it was to be away from home. Code analysis was fascinating work, but officers with dull jobs loved the war too. How else could they get to be away from their wives and be praised for serving mankind? Sometimes at the poker table, raking in the money from admirals and two-star generals, I'd wonder how the hell guys who had so little talent for bluffing could expect to win a war. I asked Eisenhower that question the one time I met him during a game, and he said, "That's why we have men like you to break the enemy codes—so we don't have to bluff." Ozzie's story about meeting Eisenhower in London may be true, since Ike's enthusiasm for bridge was legendary. The Supreme Commander of the Allied Forces in Europe would certainly have wanted to meet the bridge celebrity and would certainly have had no trouble inveigling him into a game.

My father's war, like everything else about his life, was less colorful than Ozzie's. Legally blind in one eye as the result of his teenage accident, he was deemed unfit for combat. In 1942, however, he was selected for Officer Candidate School (like Ozzie, on the basis of his mathematical aptitude) for noncombat service. In early 1943, he was posted to Chicago, where he worked as an administrator in the Quartermaster Corps until the end of the war. By virtue of its position as a railroad and meatpacking center, as well as its strategic location between the two coasts, Chicago played an important role in the mammoth effort to supply the troops in both Europe and the Pacific. While allocating meat tonnage was hardly as glamorous as breaking

Nazi and Japanese codes, my dad's years in the army gave him far more satisfaction than his accounting jobs had in New York. "I fought the Battle of Michigan Avenue," he observed, in typical self-deprecating fashion, on his Dartmouth twenty-fifth reunion questionnaire. Still, my dad also remembered the war years, even before he met my mother, as a happy time in his life. "You had the sense that what you were doing mattered—to your country and the world," he told me at some point in the late sixties, when America and American families were being torn apart by the Vietnam War. "People my age look back to our war with nostalgia because it was a time—the last time, I think—when everyone was pulling together on behalf of a cause greater than themselves. The war made us who we are; it was the turning point for our generation. It can't be that way now; I personally don't see Vietnam as a just war in the way I saw World War Two."

THE WAR years would also prove to be a turning point in the flight of the Jacoby family from its Jewish past. In 1944, both my father and my aunt Edith followed their brother in marrying Irish Catholics—and Edith became the first Jacoby actually to convert to Catholicism. My aunt, whose earlier marriage seemed to pose an insuperable obstacle to a second union sanctioned by the Church, had nevertheless been romantically involved with the devout Ted Faller for several years. When Edith's ex-husband, "that wretch, Feeney," conveniently dropped dead and made her a widow in the eyes of the Church, she joyfully converted and promptly married Ted. Granny Jacoby disapproved of the conversion—and said so—but did not object to Ted as she had objected to Ozzie's choice of Aunt Mary. With her characteristic maternal solicitude, she told Edith, then in her late thirties, that she was lucky to have found anyone willing to marry her.

In fact, Ted was passionately in love with my aunt. The most successful member of a huge Irish-American family, charged with the responsibility of caring for dependent relatives, Ted was nearly forty when he met Edith. He was so devout a Catholic, and so wrapped up in his duties to the rest of his family, that he seemed destined for a lifetime of fussy bachelorhood. But when he spotted my aunt in Macy's executive offices, he fell in love for the first and last time in his life. In her mid-thirties, the dark-haired, long-limbed, full-bosomed Edith was not a conventional beauty, but she projected a liveliness and sensuality that had always attracted men. And Uncle Ted, used to women who expected men to take care of them, was impressed by a woman with the brains and energy to work her way up to an executive job in a man's world. Any man who would take on a lifelong relationship with Granny Jacoby, Uncle Ozzie once pointed out, *had* to have been head over heels in love with her daughter. Already accustomed to supporting his own relatives, Ted cheerfully added my prickly grandmother to his list of dependents and relieved my father and Uncle Ozzie of any further responsibility for her financial support.

Edith was every bit as much in love with Ted as he was with her. He was the only person in the world who could soften her sharp tone and bring a warm light to her eyes, and he was the only man who received her unqualified approval. Their mutual devotion never wavered, even though both were deeply disappointed when Edith, already in her late thirties at the time of the marriage, proved unable to bear children. Temperamentally, they were opposites. Edith generally regarded pleasure as an indulgence (if not a sin): she dressed plainly, resisting Ted's desire to buy her fashionable clothes, furs, and jewels; set a frugal and unappetizing table (though Ted loved fine food and wine); and allowed herself to spend money freely only on travel to religious shrines and the art capitals of Europe (she was happiest when she could combine the two pilgrimages). One form of pleasure she did not disdain, however, was sex: the physical attraction between these unlikely characters, who touched each other tenderly at every possible opportunity, was obvious. Their relationship was a source of bemusement and amusement to the other members of the family, who had long considered Edith a prissy spinster (in spite of her youthful divorce). Moreover, Ted's obvious physical passion

Great-grandparents, Maximilian and Eve Jackson Jacoby, 1871.

Great-grandmother
Sarah Sondheim, age eighteen, 1868.

Great-grandfather Simon Sondheim at left, off to fight for the Union in the Civil War. (Man at right unknown.)

Great-aunt Geppy Jacoby and her groom, Baron Albrecht von Liebenstein, on their wedding day in New York, 1881.

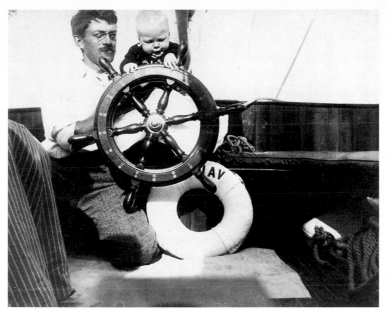

Great-uncle Harold Jacoby, and his son, Maclear,
boating on Long Island Sound, 1897.

Grandfather Oswald Jacoby, age thirty-six, and his first son,
my uncle Ozzie, age four, Manhasset, New York, 1906.

Great-grandfather Maximilian Jacoby, at seventy-six, with Uncle Ozzie, age four, 1906.

Grandmother Edith Sondheim Jacoby, age twenty-eight, 1906.

Great-grandmother Sarah Sondheim, Brooklyn, c.1903.

My father, Robert Jacoby, at age three, with my grandfather, sailing off Long Island, 1917.

Uncle Ozzie, Aunt Edith, and Dad, 1916.

Uncle Ozzie and his first cousin,
Eve Marion Jacoby, c.1920.

Uncle Ozzie with Dad
on his shoulders, 1927.

At four months with Dad,
October 1945.

Dad, Mom, and ten-month-old Susan,
Easter, 1946.

Dad, 1948.

At age five with my two-year-old brother, Bob (Robbie).

Mom, Dad, Susan, and Robbie, Museum of Science and Industry, Chicago, 1953.

for his wife represented a real departure from the repressive sexual upbringing inculcated in Irish Catholics of his generation. I always thought, though I never dared ask my aunt to confirm my suspicions, that Edith and Ted must have broken the laws of the Church by having premarital sex—a mortal sin—during the period before Feeney's death. The romance that began in New York flourished more freely during the war in Washington, when both Edith and Ted took leave from Macy's to serve their country in the military. Ted, as was natural in view of his executive status, became a high-level procurement officer, and Edith's assignments as a Wave lieutenant also drew on her retailing and personnel administration experience at Macy's. Hundreds of miles from his family and hers (for the first and last time in their lives), these two extremely serious and conscientious people were free, like nearly everyone else after working hours in wartime Washington, to have fun.

When Ted was in his seventies, sex with Edith was still so important to him that he put off lifesaving prostate cancer surgery because it would have rendered him impotent. (At the time, impotence was inevitable after prostate removal.) Ted could not, as Aunt Edith once told me with a mixture of pride and guilt, "bear the thought of never having marital relations again." I have never seen a better illustration of the opacity, the ultimate mystery, of enduring love than the bond between my aunt and uncle—two souls who, had they not found each other, would have been condemned to the special hell reserved for those who live on the margins of other people's lives: *Old Maid Edith. Ted-Who-Should-Have-Been-A-Priest—and wasn't it a shame that he had to take care of his brothers and sisters instead of following his true vocation, but the Lord must have His reasons. . . .*

A HALF-CONTINENT away from his mother and sister, the youngest of the Jacoby siblings was also embarking upon a relationship with a Catholic (albeit a far more lax Catholic than the spouses Edith and Ozzie had chosen). For Bob Jacoby, the provisional life of the Depression and the war years would end soon after he met Irma

Broderick. They had known each other for about three months when they were married on July 1, 1944, with the world still at war but an end in sight. The importance of what they didn't know about each other ("just about everything," according to Dad) paled by comparison with their desire to start a family in a world where, in the wake of the successful Normandy invasion, the conclusion of the war in an Allied victory had become a near-certainty in the minds of most Americans. At thirty, my father was finally embarking upon his adult life. At twenty-three, my mother was starting over.

My mother, like my father, had a secret that carries no stigma today. She was divorced—a fact of her life, like so much about my father's life, that I would not discover for many years. She had married, over my grandparents' strenuous objections, only to leave her feckless young husband when she realized her parents had been right about his character. Fortunately, this brief, unwise union produced no children. Unfortunately, my mother and her first husband had been married in a Catholic ceremony, which meant she might forever be precluded from remarrying within the Church. My parents were therefore married in a Lutheran ceremony. My grandparents preferred to see my mother married in any church rather than before a justice of the peace, so the couple went around Chicago from one house of worship to another until they found a minister who wasn't fussy about religious provenance. Their first choice had been a particularly beautiful Episcopal church frequented by Chicago society, but they were frostily turned away after a brief inquiry into their backgrounds. My mother's description of this pragmatic shopping tour for a church, and my Broderick grandparents' equally pragmatic acquiescence, is entirely consistent with the ambivalent messages that would later characterize my religious upbringing.

At the wedding, the groom was in uniform and the bride wore a rose *peau de soie* street-length dress and an orchid corsage. I didn't know that my mother had been married twice until 1966, which turned out to be a big year for the revelation of secrets on both sides of my family. My seventeen-year-old brother was the one who made the discovery; one of his favorite pastimes, when he was home sick from school and Mom had left the house to do various errands, was sifting through my parents' private papers to see what interesting information he could dig up. (As the reporter in the family, I was quite chagrined that I had not thought of employing such sneaky tactics myself.) On one of Rob's fishing expeditions, in the type of discovery scene frequently written into the plots of soap operas, he hit pay dirt—my mother's ancient divorce papers. Like most people, Mom had failed to destroy all of the evidence of her youthful indiscretions. As far as my father was concerned, the secret of my mother's divorce was hers to tell or not tell as she saw fit—just as my mother regarded the secret of Dad's Jewish origins as his private property. And by the late sixties, divorce was a secret with limited shock value. Had she been a member of my generation, my mother later said, she would probably have lived with her first husband for a few months and broken up with him, leaving no stain on her record.

Like so many men and women who married during the war—and far more hastily than they would have in a more settled world—my parents would probably never have met each other in peacetime. They exemplified one of the unanticipated side effects of the war—a substantial increase in the number of mixed marriages cutting across geographic, ethnic, religious, and cultural boundaries. Most of these unlikely couples, like my parents, managed to stay married in spite of differences in their backgrounds that might well have posed insuperable obstacles to their happiness in a less mobile, more tradition-bound era of American history.

My mother's status as a divorced woman who could not be married within the Church certainly made it easier for her to marry a Jew and easier for her parents to accept the marriage. Dad did not have to go through the rigmarole of Catholic marriage counseling or promise to raise his children as Catholics (as Ozzie did when he married Mary McHale). And my Broderick grandparents, partly because my mom's marriage to a Catholic had turned out badly and partly because they genuinely liked my dad, regarded his Jewishness as a relatively minor detail. If Mom's first marriage were ever to be annulled by the Church, she and my father could be remarried by a priest. And if she remained an outcast from Catholicism, well, my grandparents were more concerned about their daughter's happiness in this world than in the next. They were not entirely sanguine about the situation, however, for they urged my mother to seek a Church annulment of her first marriage when my brother and I came along. The annulment was granted, some years before my father's conversion, on grounds that my mother and her first husband had never intended to have children (one of the few grounds for Catholic annulments in those days). It was rumored that my grandfather had paid a bribe to someone in the Chicago Archdiocese in order to grease the wheels, but my grandmother Broderick denied this. "Your gramps could have done it without my knowing," she acknowledged, "but I don't believe it. It's true that we—especially he—wanted your mother to be able to receive the sacraments again, but I don't think he would have paid good money for it. It wasn't that hard to get an annulment if you never had children and you and your former husband agreed to say that you never intended to have them." My grandmother may or may not have been right about what actually happened, but I don't think Gramps would have hesitated for a moment to pay someone off in order to make things right between God and his little girl. And if he didn't do it, he probably enjoyed creating the impression that he was rich enough to bribe God's representatives on earth. In any event, my parents were remarried by a priest after her annulment but before his conversion.

The "blemish" of my mother's mildly wild youth may have been a psychological plus from my father's perspective, because it balanced out what he saw as the far greater liability of his being a Jew. In Bob Jacoby's eyes, my mother was a catch. His knowledge that she had a certain amount of "experience," had suffered a certain amount of hurt and betrayal, may well have been a plus. At thirty, my dad was not looking for a virgin (in the emotional or physical sense). He was looking for a woman strong enough to bring out the best in him, to help him overcome his weaknesses. This my mother was eventually able to do, even though she had no idea of the full extent of those weaknesses when she married him.

My Broderick grandparents were part of the package. Any reservations they had about acquiring a New York Jew for a son-in-law were overcome by his obvious adoration of their daughter. "When she was young, your mother became involved with men who took advantage of her, who didn't give her the love and respect she deserved," my grandmother told me. "Your dad was different. The way he looked at her, you knew he thought of her as a prize. And the proof came later, when he had to choose between gambling and his family and he chose his wife and children."

Part of the emotional fit between my parents was the space my Broderick grandparents filled in my father's heart. It is not hard to imagine what their unfailing love meant to my dad, coming as he did from a family whose fractious members were in the habit of cutting one another off for months, years, or eternity. My grandfather Broderick had his faults: he was an old-fashioned Irish patriarch, steeped (like his contemporary, Joseph Kennedy) in the traditional Irish Catholic dichotomy between good girls and bad girls. When my mother displayed a broad streak of rebellion for a well-raised Irish Catholic girl of her generation, Gramps had no idea how to deal with her. He was a man who was used to getting his own way, and he wanted nothing more than to push my mother back into the mold of a good Catholic girl, but there is no possibility that he would ever, for whatever reason, have cut his child out of his life.

My grandmother treated Dad like another of her children. "I think of him as my son, not as a son-in-law," she would say. It was as natural for my grandmother Broderick to praise as it was for my grandmother Jacoby to criticize, and I noticed the difference at a very young age. In particular, my mother's mother was always telling Dad what a wonderful father he was to my brother and me, something that must have been especially meaningful to him in view of the parental neglect that characterized his own upbringing. Two months after their wedding, my mother became pregnant with me. Couples who married near the end of the war, when nearly all of the news was good (with the exception of the relatively brief Battle of the Bulge), saw no reason to wait to start their families. The baby boom did not begin officially until 1946, when most of the veterans returned to civilian life, but my parents got a jump start. I was born on June 4, 1945, 363 days after D-Day. Before I was three months old, the war would be over.

My parents were both happy at my arrival, but *happiness* was too mild a word to describe Bob Jacoby's response to fatherhood. I recently enlarged a snapshot of the two of us, taken when I was about four months old. I am already posing, looking head-on into the camera, but Dad, holding me in his arms, is in three-quarter profile because he can't take his eyes off me. In the tiny snapshot, I couldn't see the expression on his face, but in the enlarged photograph, I see a mesmerized look of undiluted love that takes my breath away. If a woman is lucky, she sees something evocative of that look, something that makes her feel safe and cherished, on the face of a man who loves her as an adult.

Right from the start, my father assumed child-care duties—changing diapers, heating bottles, bathing me—that were performed by few other fathers of his generation. "I don't think your grandfather, in his entire life, ever changed a diaper," my grandmother Broderick said. "Not that he didn't love his children, but it never would have occurred to him to be the one to get up when they cried. I never saw anyone as crazy about his kids as your dad was about you and Robbie." Needless to say, my mother received no special praise for doing the things that mothers are expected to do for their children.

More important than what my father did was the way he understood the mind of a child. My earliest memories date from age three, when my brother was born and my mother later returned to the hospital with severe anemia and, I suspect, with what would be called depression today. My brother was born in October, and Mom, who had not really regained her strength after the difficult birth of a baby weighing nearly eleven pounds, collapsed and was readmitted to the hospital a few months later. I was terrified because I was sure my mother was going to die; my grandmother's attempts to convince me otherwise were unavailing, because I had not been allowed to *see* my mommy. In those days, hospitals never permitted small children to visit, but my father was resourceful, and he understood that nothing but the sight of my mother would assuage my anguish. One day, Dad came home early and led me by the hand to a vacant lot strewn with broken bottles and dog droppings but with a clear view of Mom's room in the small Harvey hospital where she was being treated. He positioned me on his shoulders, and then my mother stuck her head out the window and waved and blew kisses. She couldn't keep the window open long, but my dad stood there holding me until dusk fell and the lights went on, enabling us to see my mother appear once more behind the glass. That night, I slept without nightmares. For the rest of my mom's hospital stay, Dad took me every day to wave good night to her from our position in the vacant lot.

I am still not certain how my father, starved for affection and attention throughout his childhood, learned how to love and how to show love. "There was a natural goodness about your dad" was my grandmother Broderick's explanation. "Some people, when they don't get what they need as children, keep back the same things from their own children. Bob wanted you kids to have what he didn't. I don't think he ever deliberately did a mean thing to anyone in his life."

MOM WAS the disciplinarian in our family. I remember only one incident during my entire childhood that prompted my mother to speak the words, dreaded in so many households, "Wait till your father gets home." At seven, I was allowed to walk to a small, family-owned grocery store about five blocks from our home in Hazel Crest, the Chicago suburb where we moved after my dad was fired from his job in the city. Such freedom would be unthinkable for any seven-year-old almost anywhere in the country today. The walk to the store was a much-anticipated treat, because there I would decide how to allot my allowance—fifty cents a week at the time—choosing among comic books, candy, and sets of prominent wax teeth (which we put in our mouths in order to "scare" our friends). The only drawback was that my four-year-old brother always wanted to tag along, and my mother almost always insisted that I take him with me. Robbie and I got along well most of the time—his unqualified adoration of me went a long way toward reconciling me to his existence—but I deeply resented having to take him along on these walks, which I relished because of the absence of adult supervision for the ten or fifteen minutes it took to get to the store. I would run far ahead of Robbie and torment him by pretending that I was going to leave him behind. One day, I had an inspiration. As we passed a creek that lay between our house and the store—needless to say, we were strictly forbidden to go near the water by ourselves—I ducked behind a tree and yelled, "I'm going to jump into the creek and drown myself now. You'll never see me again." Letting out a bloodcurdling yell, I produced a scream that faded away on the last notes, "Here I go-o-o-o." Robbie ran home, crying and telling my mother that I had jumped into the creek and drowned myself. Mom came running, dragged me out from behind the tree, and ordered me home. Her face paled and her lips tightened—both signs that she was furious—but she didn't raise her voice. "I just don't know what your punishment should be," she said. "I've never heard of a child scaring her little brother that way. We'll wait till your father gets home to talk about it." When Dad got home—there was no happy greeting, because the exhausted Robbie was still napping and I was confined to my room—I heard my mother telling him what had happened in a tone of controlled anger. My father, as usual, lost his temper and raised his voice when he ticked off the possible punishments. No allowance for a month, he told my mother, wouldn't be nearly enough. Being sent to my room was no punishment at all, because I would just amuse myself by reading. Ditto for not being allowed to go outside and play. Finally—I knew the penalty would be something unusual—Dad came into the room and asked me if I understood why he was so upset about my behavior and why I deserved a serious punishment. Then he delivered an admonition of such gravity—and absent his usual hyperbole—that I have never forgotten either his tone or his precise words. "Your brother loves you, he worships the ground you walk on," Dad said, "and that's why he makes a pest of himself. I know you don't like it when he follows you everywhere, but that's no excuse for what you did. You knew he was too little not to believe you when you said you were going to drown yourself, and you deliberately frightened him. You used his love for you against him. That's a terrible, terrible thing to do no matter how old you are." *You used his love for you against him.* Both the concept, and the way my father articulated it, were new to me—among several firsts that would embed the day's events in my memory.

By the end of my father's speech, I certainly did understand the weight of my offense. I was experiencing, for the first time (perhaps for the only time in my life), what the Catholic Church calls "perfect contrition": remorse prompted not by fear of punishment but by a genuine sense of the wrongfulness and hurtfulness of one's acts. In the Act of Contrition recited in the confessional during my childhood, the distinction between imperfect and perfect contrition was expressed in the lines, "And I detest all my sins because I dread the loss of heaven and the pains of hell, but most of all, because they have offended thee, my God, who art all good and deserving of all my love." Needless to say, imperfect contrition was the more common form of regret. If you were unlucky enough to meet with a fatal accident in a state of mortal sin—without any opportunity to go to confession—only perfect contrition could save you from the pains of hell. Imperfect contrition, however, was good enough for the confessional.

No confessor could have been a sterner judge than my father, who was unmoved by my tears (another first!) and said that "feeling bad" wasn't enough. "I've never spanked you, but I'm going to now," he declared purposefully. Then he turned me over his knee and gave me several halfhearted spanks on my bottom. When I looked up, he was crying too. "Don't ever make me spank you again," he said. While I don't, as a rule, believe in corporal punishment, I disagree with psychologists who say it's *always* bad to spank a child. Since I had never been spanked before, I knew that my father had gone against his own nature by imposing the humiliation of corporal punishment upon me; I knew, in the language of adults, that this was a symbolic punishment appropriate to the seriousness of my crime. Words could never have made the same impression on me. (Needless to say, the spanking would not have made an indelible impression if physical discipline had been a common occurrence in our home. I had already noticed that children whose parents did spank them—and most of my friends' parents did—seemed utterly indifferent to the humiliation and ran away laughing as soon as the spanking was over.) After my father left the room—he had kissed me good night with the reassuring words that his being mad at me didn't mean he had stopped loving me—my little brother, who had already deepened my remorse by wailing piteously as he heard me being spanked, completed the moral lesson of the day by presenting me with a mutilated slab of fudge cake. Having decided that being deprived of dessert was too great a penalty on top of the other punishments I had already received, Robbie concealed the cake in his fist upon leaving the dinner table and stored it under his bed (he had the bottom bunk) until lights-out.

That my mother turned over the disciplinarian's role to my father on that occasion was a measure of her emotional astuteness as a parent. Because she was usually the one who set the limits, and because she had a more clear-eyed view of my character than my soft touch of a father did, she knew that his disapproval would leave a deeper imprint than hers.

The years between 1948, when Dad lost his job, and the summer of 1953, when he got his second chance and we moved to Lansing, were the most difficult time in my parents' marriage. But I didn't know—or, at any rate, I didn't know much. Sometimes at night I could hear them fighting about money, mainly because my father could never keep his voice down in an argument, but when morning came, I would tell myself it had just been a bad dream. I didn't know anything about my father's struggles with gambling, or about his futile search for another job (it seemed perfectly natural to me that he would work for my grandfather Broderick). During this period, I am sure that my dad's lingering shame about his Jewish origins took second place to his remorse for his own behavior (though his conversion to Catholicism addressed both issues).

I have only one memory of my father saying anything about Jews during these years. In the spring and early summer of 1953, Julius and Ethel Rosenberg were tried, convicted, sentenced to death, and executed as atomic spies. Nearing age eight, I was very much aware of the case, not only because my parents and grandparents talked about it frequently but because I was already a newspaper reader. My father was extremely upset about the Rosenbergs, and I'm quite sure this was the first time I ever heard him single out anyone as "Jewish." He would tell my mother that he was afraid Americans would blame "all of the Jewish people" for the treason of those two (like everyone in my world, he took it for granted that both Rosenbergs were guilty). My mother would try to calm him down by telling him that America wasn't Europe, that it wasn't "the American way" to blame all of the people in a group for what one person had done. This may not have been the most persuasive argument in a country only a decade away from the wartime internment of Japanese-Americans on the West Coast, but it seemed to satisfy my father—until the next news break in the Rosenberg story, when he would erupt again. When the Rosenbergs were executed that June, Dad was relieved, commenting that "maybe now we won't be hearing the names *Rosenberg, Greenglass* every night on the news." My grandmother Broderick, characteristically, could think only about the two boys who had been orphaned by the executions. "I don't know whether she [Ethel] was guilty or not, I don't know about these things," Granny would say, "but I think the judge should have been thinking about those two children before he sent their mother to the electric chair." When other members of the family would say that the judge had no choice if the Rosenbergs had really "helped give Russia the bomb," Granny would reply, "Well, I'm not so sure it's so terrible if they do have the bomb. If both countries have the bomb, then it would be stupid for either of them to drop it."

My grandmother's belief that no country would be stupid enough to deliberately use atomic weapons was shared by all of the adults in my family. Many of my classmates at the Ascension School, where I attended first and second grades, were very scared of being killed by "the bomb," but my parents' and grandparents' convictions had insulated me from what was then a widely held childhood fear. Like all school authorities at the time, the nuns at Ascension had a plan for what to do in the event of an atomic attack. If fire broke out, we were, of course, to file outside as quickly as possible— but if an air raid alarm sounded, we were to head for the school basement. The nuns advised us to make sure that our basements at home were stocked with canned goods so that we could survive until the radiation had "gone away." Radiation, we were told, could kill us even if we couldn't see it or smell it. This did worry me, because our house in Hazel Crest had no basement. If the bomb was on its way, I wasn't sure we would have time to make it to my grandparents' house in Harvey, which did have a basement but was a ten-minute drive away. When I brought the nuns' advice home to my parents, they told me, in no uncertain terms, that the Russians were not going to drop the bomb because they didn't want the Americans to drop the bomb on them. "The Russians don't want their people to be hurt any more than we want our people to be hurt" was the gist of what Mom and Dad had to say—and that made perfect sense to me. Russians had families just like ours, I was told, and Russian parents didn't want to see their children suffer any more than American parents did. Because we said a prayer every day in school for "the conversion of Russia," I had a vague idea that Russians didn't believe in God and might therefore be more likely to start a war. My parents skipped over the whole issue of godlessness and told me that regardless of what religion the Russians practiced, it didn't mean they weren't good people. (My parents never suggested that the Russian leaders might not be as good as the Russian people. By the time I started thinking about such matters, Stalin was dead—and I had never really pictured him in my mind. Adolf Hitler, whose image still appeared in countless newsreels, was the bogeyman of my childhood.)

Looking back, I see that the tenor of these discussions about the bomb set my family apart from our neighbors. They also marked the beginning of my parents' (especially my mother's) sabotage of the Catholic education they insisted I receive. Yes, the Church was the final authority on faith and morals. But a lot of what the nuns and priests said wasn't really concerned with "faith and morals"— even though they might suggest otherwise—but was merely a matter of opinion. The godlessness and perfidy of the Russians was one of those matters of opinion. On such subjects, I was told, one's own conscience and brain were more reliable guides than the pronouncements of the Church. There could hardly have been a more subversive message in the Catholic world of the fifties.

MY MEMORIES of this early period of my childhood, before we left for Lansing, are almost entirely happy, and they remain much more vivid than my recollections of the first few years after our move to Michigan. I am certain that I would be a very different person today had I spent my entire childhood in Lansing and Okemos—not only because I would have been separated from my Broderick grandparents at a younger age but because I would not have been so thoroughly exposed to Chicago itself. The city, epitomizing excitement, achievement, and glamour, became a potent presence in my imagination during those formative years.

The relationship between cities and suburbs was very different during my early childhood from what it would become by the time I was a teenager. My parents had moved to suburban Hazel Crest in pursuit of a backyard and better schools, but we still looked to Chicago for shopping, restaurants, culture, and baseball. It was understood that only the city could supply such amenities, and we would have been incredulous had we been told that in only ten years, people like us would take our business to suburban shopping malls (the term *mall* didn't even exist during my early childhood) instead of downtown.

To me, baseball meant Comiskey Park, where my beloved White Sox played; culture meant the Museum of Science and Industry; and "going shopping" meant only one thing—a trip to Marshall Field's (whose founder coined the slogan "The customer is always right") on State Street in Chicago's Loop. My grandmother, mother, and I would all dress up in the good clothes (including gloves and, for the adults, hats) that all women wore to go downtown in those days. We nearly always took the elevated train into the city, which was part of the fun. As the familiar skyline came into view, I would become so excited that my stomach started to hurt. The greatest treat of all was just ahead—disembarking a block from Field's into an artificial darkness created by the network of overhead tracks and the tall, densely packed buildings in the heart of the Loop. As many times as we made the trip, I never ceased to be enchanted by the way the bright lights of the stores dispelled the gloom; this quintessential city image, of lights fighting the darkness, appeared in my dreams and helped form my dreams of the future.

I had already decided that I wanted to become a newspaper reporter when I grew up, and that was another dream generated during the Chicago phase of my childhood. The city still had many competing papers when I was small. I started reading the ultraconservative *Tribune* for the baseball box scores and wound up reading the *Sun-Times* and the *Daily News* as well, for my grandfather pointed out that these papers provided different interpretations of the news of the day. Gramps took me on a tour of Tribune Tower, where I stared wide-eyed at the huge presses and carefully wrote down one of the slogans engraved on the building, Thomas Jefferson's: "Our liberty depends on the freedom of the press that can not be limited without being lost."

CLOSER TO home, there was a neigborhood institution that was as enticing to me as anything in the city. Bowl Center, my grandfather's bar and bowling alley in Harvey, was the most enjoyable spot in my universe. My mother did not consider Bowl Center an appropriate environment for her children, but she usually yielded to my pleas that I be allowed to watch the ball game there on Saturday afternoons during the stifling Chicago summers. The bar didn't have air-conditioning—only movie theaters had air-conditioning in those days—but it was cooler than anywhere else because it was dark, illuminated only by neon beer signs (Schlitz: The Beer That Made Milwaukee Famous) and the flickering light from the television. Gramps had seen the possibilities of television early on, and each year, the newest model appeared over the bar. Bowl Center had the first TV, the first large-screen TV (large meaning larger than nine inches), and, finally, the first color TV in the neighborhood. By game time at 1:30 on Saturdays, there would be standing room only around the bar. The crowd would remain until the last out, when wives would drift in to tell their husbands, with commanding rather than neutral inflections, that there was still time to wash cars or mow lawns before dinner was ready. It was a family bar, even though the drinking crowd consisted almost entirely of men. They always made a big fuss over me, as the bartender (often Gramps himself, who tended bar only on Saturdays now that his real estate business was flourishing) made me one Shirley Temple after another. I became a true baseball fan during those long, somnolent afternoons, tutored by men who were old enough to remember the Black Sox scandal of 1919 and the legendary Yankee teams of the 1920s. Most of them, like Gramps, were of Irish descent and were gifted storytellers who never tired of talking. They argued endlessly about which team was better, the "Murderers' Row" Yankees of Ruth and Gehrig, or the fifties' Yankees of Mantle and Berra. To me, there was only one important point: the arrogant Yankees almost always won. They beat us ("us" being the White Sox rather than the Cubs, because Harvey adjoined the South Side of Chicago) year after year. When the World Series came around, the Yanks proceeded to beat the Brooklyn Dodgers. During the Series, the Bowl Center crowd always rooted for the Dodgers on "the enemy of my enemy is my friend" principle, and we sympathized with the perennially disappointed fans of Dem Bums. My father, of course, had been a Dodger fan as a child, something that surprised the men in the bar, who didn't know that Dad had grown up in Brooklyn because he didn't have a Brooklyn accent. (The popular television series titled *The Goldbergs* fostered a widespread identification of Brooklyn with "Jewish" accents in the fifties—just as the movie *Saturday Night Fever* would produce an equally stereo-typical equation of Brooklyn and working-class Italian-American accents in the seventies.)

One of my mother's main objections to my presence at Bowl Center was that I was bound to be exposed to bad grammar and vulgar language—what she called "lower-class" speech. In spite of (or perhaps because of) his having been raised in a much better-educated home than my mother's, Dad had no such objections. Robbie and I would imitate what we heard at home, he told my mother firmly (one of the few times he overruled her on a child-rearing issue), and, in any case, the men in the bar hardly ever cursed when I was around. This was so. Whenever one of them started to use "Jesus . . ." as a prelude to a curse in my presence, he would quickly turn the curse into a pious utterance by adding the Catholic formula ". . . Mary, and Joseph." Once, as my grandfather let out a "God-dammit," it came out, "Goddammit, Jesus, Mary, and Joseph." The strongest epithet I ever heard in that bar was "horseshit," a word I did use quite frequently on the playground when the nuns weren't listening (contrary to my father's prediction).

Those Saturday afternoons were, I now realize, a running

history lesson of a particular kind—history from the vantage point of working-class men, then in their forties, fifties, and early sixties, who had grown up in near-poverty, survived the Depression, and lived into an era of prosperity they could never have envisaged when they were young. Nearly all of the men had been born at home (as, indeed, my mother was in 1921), because their parents would never have considered spending hard-earned money on a hospital birth. I heard of mothers who died giving birth because, by the time the family realized something was wrong and a doctor was called, it was too late to do anything. I heard of children who had suffered from scurvy and rickets during the Depression, of frantic efforts to borrow the money for a new drug—sulfa—that was said to save people in danger of death from pneumonia. These men revered Franklin D. Roosevelt, whom they gave full credit for bringing the country through the Depression and the war. None of my grandfather's customers had been out of a job since 1940, when the economy began gearing up for war. They owned homes and cars, and many of them (like my grandfather himself) could point with pride by the early fifties to the first child in their families ever to get a college education. Although they venerated the memory of FDR, nearly all of them voted for Dwight D. Eisenhower in 1952. Adlai Stevenson, they said, knew nothing about "the common man." He was no FDR. He was not even Harry Truman. He was also divorced, and these men subscribed to the notion that "a man who can't run his own family can't run the country." Gramps had known many of his customers since childhood, and he was the most successful among them. Though he and my grandmother had lost their house after the stock market crash, he had enough resources in 1932, when real estate prices hit rock bottom, to borrow money from a bank in order to buy Bowl Center. When Prohibition was repealed, the profits from the ever-reliable bar would enable Gramps to start his own real estate firm. By the early fifties, he didn't really need Bowl Center (which he eventually sold), but he liked being there, and he enjoyed his position as the most enterprising among a group of men who had all done better than they ever imagined they could. I would often see Gramps take a twenty-dollar bill out of the cash register and slip it to one of his cronies, "to tide you over till payday."

What I remember most about those years is spending a great deal of time with adults. They were all interesting to me, and they were all interested *in* me. My granny, the most purely decent person I have ever known, was the tender heart of the Broderick family. My grammar school was about eight blocks from my grandparents' house, and, although I was strictly forbidden to walk over there from school by myself, I ignored the prohibition one day when I got into a fight with two boys on the playground. There was a lone Negro girl in my second-grade class, and I had punched one of the boys in the face when I heard him calling her "tar baby" and "nigger." He responded by knocking me to the ground, and I ran off howling toward Granny's, without asking anyone for permission to leave. My frantic grandmother met me about a block from her house: the boys had tattled to the nun in charge of the second grade, and she had phoned ahead. By then I was as scared (because I wasn't quite sure whether I had taken the right street to get to Granny's house) as I was furious at the boys. I was unable to repeat the terrible word; it came out "nig . . ." when I tried to say it to Granny. I had already heard that word at Comiskey Park when my favorite player, Orestes ("Minnie") Minoso, befuddled yet another opposing pitcher with his aggressive baserunning. Minoso, a coal black Dominican who eventually became one of the most popular players in the history of the White Sox franchise, was a provocative baserunner very much in the style of the young Jackie Robinson. Although the home fans generally called out "nigger" to *praise* Minoso (as in "Look at that nigger fly!"), my father and grandfather instantly informed me that the word was used only by ignorant and uneducated people, and that it was an insult to Negroes (or, as Gramps called them, "the colored"—the polite term for Negroes during his childhood). That was why, I explained to my grandmother, I had pushed the boy in the face.

There had been no doubt that the word *nigger*, used on the playground, was intended to wound and insult the only Negro girl in our class. Granny took me into her backyard, which was filled with vivid tulips of every hue. Granny pointed to her garden and said, "It would be plain silly to say that red tulips are good and yellow tulips are bad. They're just different colors, that's all, both of them beautiful. That's the way it is with colored people and white people. Humans come in different colors, just like flowers. The color of their skin doesn't tell you anything about what's inside." Instead of fighting the next time, Granny suggested, I should explain why the boys were wrong by telling them about the tulips. My mother, when she learned what had happened on the playground, also thought the tulip analogy was a fine way to convince bullies that they shouldn't use racial slurs. My father, however, declared that "people like that only understand a punch in the face." "*Bob*," my mother said sharply, "she was the one who got hurt and knocked down." I didn't know then that my father had been victimized during his boyhood by the same kind of apprentice bigots. Looking back on this incident, I am struck most forcefully by the realization that none of the adults in my life told me that I should have minded my own business and done nothing.

IF WE HAD lived in New York rather than in Chicago, the human landscape of my childhood would have been completely different. In 1912, my Broderick grandmother had to quit school after eighth grade so that she could contribute to her family's household expenses by picking onions for twenty-five cents a day in the farmland still surrounding Chicago. In that same year, with their father's legal career still flourishing, Aunt Edith and Uncle Ozzie were attending Manhattan private schools and being groomed for Ivy League universities. And although Ozzie and Edith eventually had to make their own way after their father gambled away his legacy, they never lost the aura of entitlement engendered by their privileged upbringing.

By the fifties, Granny Jacoby and Aunt Edith had both relegated the memory of the family's downward mobility to the unpleasant past. By the time I came to know them, they seemed to regard their prosperous lives (courtesy of Uncle Ted) as nothing more than their due. Only rarely and vaguely did they talk about the Depression or the twenties, when Ozzie stepped in to support the family while his father's life disintegrated. The occasional allusions to a wealthy past—the unimaginable time when Granny Jacoby was young and Aunt Edith a little girl—sounded like a remote fairy tale, unconnected either to the specific history of the Jacoby family or to any larger social history.

From my father's family, I could never have absorbed the lessons I learned from my maternal grandparents—that people could not always make it on their own; that life and society could hand out unexpected and undeserved blows; that intelligence and hard work did not always lead to success for those born without educational and economic advantages. As far as Granny Jacoby was concerned, only moral turpitude (her husband's) could have caused the family's financial reverses. Otherwise, the Jacobys would have remained where they belonged—on top.

Before meeting my mother, my father had halfhearted intentions of returning to New York when he was discharged from the army at the end of the war. But there was no chance of that after my mother met Granny Jacoby and Aunt Edith: she immediately sized up both women as born meddlers and realized that my father was much better off living a half-continent away from them. My mom was appalled by Granny Jacoby's constant criticism of my father, who, although he disliked being around his mother, nevertheless still longed for her approval.

Uncle Ozzie was the only member of my father's family whom I liked when I was a child, but I did not come to know him well until I was an adult and turned to him for help in reconstructing the family's past. I didn't really know Aunt Edith or Granny Jacoby either, but what I saw and heard on our trips to New York was enough to convince me that I didn't want to spend much time with either of them. In my thirties, I would begin to revise this judgment of my aunt as she told me more about her own relations with her difficult mother, but my view of Granny Jacoby is, if anything, harsher than it was when I last laid eyes on her as a teenager.

When we first started visiting Dad's family in New York, Aunt Edith and Uncle Ted lived in their own house on Staten Island, and Granny Jacoby had a separate apartment. In the fifties, before the opening of the Verrazano Bridge, Staten Island seemed even less a part of New York City than it does now. With its large tracts of still-undeveloped wooded land, the island seemed far less urban to me than the Chicago suburbs. Neither Aunt Edith nor Uncle Ted seemed to have any interest in Manhattan (though Ted still went into "the city," as everyone called it, to work at Macy's). They lived in an insular, largely Irish Catholic world—most of Ted's family lived on Staten Island—and the Church was the center of their lives. We always stayed with Edith and Ted, because my parents couldn't afford a New York hotel, but Mom and Dad naturally took us into the city on the Staten Island ferry so that we could see the famous sights of Manhattan. Edith and Granny Jacoby never came along. The city was too noisy. Too dirty. Too dangerous. Too expensive. The last point was always made by Granny Jacoby in a tone implying that my father could not possibly afford a carriage ride through Central Park or a lunch in one of the Rockefeller Center restaurants. This attitude toward Manhattan—a place I found even more intoxicating than Chicago because it was less familiar—seemed to me a natural extension of Aunt Edith's and Granny Jacoby's killjoy attitude toward everything. In view of the cultural sophistication of several generations of Sondheims and Jacobys, this antiurban posture was weirder than I knew. Edith was a passionate music lover; as a young working woman, charged with the responsibility of supporting her widowed mother, she had scrimped on food in order to buy tickets to the Metropolitan Opera and concerts at Carnegie Hall. Yet she secluded herself in the only part of New York City then sepa-

rated from the concert halls of Manhattan by a two-hour combination of bus, ferry, and subway rides. She was also an art lover (something I did not know at the time), but she only visited museums en
route to or from the Catholic shrines of Europe. As far as Edith was
concerned, the great collections of the Manhattan museums might
as well have been an ocean away. When Uncle Ted, who did like
restaurants and good food, would suggest that they get dressed up
and have "a night on the town," Edith would usually agree in order
to please him. But it was easy to see that she would have been happier eating one of her own bland and horrible dinners, reading some
inspirational article or book connected with Catholicism (especially
the sufferings of Catholic leaders, like Josef Cardinal Mindszenty,
under the Communist regimes in Eastern Europe), and going to bed
early in order to be up in time for the 8 A.M. Mass she attended every
day at St. Christopher's Church.

On our summer trips to New York, I always begged to see pictures of my dad, and the rest of his family, when he was a little boy.
At first, I expected Granny Jacoby to bring out boxes of snapshots
and photo albums, because that's what my granny in Chicago did
whenever I wanted to see pictures of my mom when she was a little
girl. But Granny Jacoby always said that most of the old photographs
had been misplaced, left behind during a move from one house to
another, or (backing up my father) destroyed in a fire. The only picture of my father that I remember seeing during my girlhood was a
handsome formal portrait photograph, taken during his freshman
year at Dartmouth. The dearth of family snapshots struck me as just
one more incomprehensible peculiarity of my Jacoby relatives.

But there *was* a family album, covering the period from, roughly,
1895 to 1917. At some point, Granny Jacoby had passed it on to
Uncle Ozzie. When Uncle Ozzie and Aunt Mary died, the album
wound up in the home of their younger son, Jon, a prominent businessman and financier in Little Rock, Arkansas. It is absolutely typical of the Jacoby style that no one had kept track of this treasure
trove of pictures: if Aunt Mary had not been a packrat who saved

everything, the album, and the light it sheds on my family's history, would probably have disappeared decades ago. I first heard about the pictures from Judy Jacoby, the widow of Ozzie's elder son, Jim, who had been his father's bridge partner for many years and died of lung cancer in his fifties. (I have always wondered whether Jim's lung cancer was caused by immense amounts of secondhand smoke—for he, like Ozzie, was a nonsmoker—inhaled at bridge tournaments.) I had never met Jim as a child, but I knew him slightly as an adult because, like his father, he sometimes passed through New York on the way to tournaments. And I had never met Jon at all, though I naturally knew who he was—the only male Jacoby for two generations, as my dad once remarked, who had been smart enough to hang on to the money he made instead of gambling it away. Ozzie's two sons, and my brother and I, were the only grandchildren of Oswald Nathaniel and Edith Sondheim Jacoby, yet we never met as children. This too strikes me as distinctly odd—a mark not of estrangement but of the carelessness that seems to me both a cause and effect of the Jacobys' collective memory loss. It simply never occurred to my father or my uncle that their children, first cousins, might benefit from getting to know one another, or that they ought to go out of their way to facilitate such family contacts. When Judy Jacoby told me about the photo album in 1995, I immediately called Jon in Little Rock—the first time I had ever spoken to him—and asked about the pictures. Yes, he said, there was an album filled with turn-of-the-century snapshots. He wasn't sure who all of the people in the pictures were, but I was welcome to come down and take a look.

IN THE ALBUM of yellowing photographs in Little Rock, I finally discover the family images I so wanted to see as a little girl. I already know what my grandfather looked like from the snapshot Aunt Edith gave me after my father's funeral, but I have never seen pictures of my Jacoby and Sondheim great-grandparents or my grandfather's siblings, Harold and Geppy. Here is the patriarch, Max, a white-haired man with a bowler hat and trim beard, slim and dapper in his seventies, holding Ozzie and the newborn Edith in 1907. And Sarah Sondheim, Granny Jacoby's beautiful mother, her still-dark hair piled atop her head, using a cane and walking a ridiculously tiny dog along a river promenade. One of the biggest surprises is Granny Jacoby herself, a young mother with long, dark hair flowing down her back, playing with Ozzie in the middle of a meadow. I never saw her with her hair down or with anything remotely resembling a playful expression on her face. In another picture with her brother and sisters, she smiles even more brightly. I have no trouble connecting the vibrant, youthful Si, Carrie, Mabel, and Adele with the jolly aunts and uncle I met fifty years after this picture was taken, but I find it virtually impossible to reconcile the unbending grandmother I knew with the approachable young woman in the snapshot. Why would she never show me these pictures when I was growing up? Did she, too, have trouble reconciling the images of the young wife and mother with the crabbed old woman she became? Perhaps it was unbearable for her to recall a time in her life when the future still stretched out endlessly, and hopefully, before her—a time when she expected to raise a family whose members would remain as devoted to one another as her own brothers and sisters did throughout their lives. Would I feel differently about her today if she had ever taken out this album and shared it with me when I was a little girl? Would I be more willing to forgive her for the way she treated my father?

Finally, Jon shows me our Jackson great-grandmother's silver tea service, a testament to the early-nineteenth-century wealth of Eve Jackson Jacoby's family. Granny Jacoby had been absolutely determined to hang on to the family heirlooms, even when she needed money desperately in the 1930s, and she succeeded in passing them on to her children and grandchildren. But she failed to pass on the memories, and the history, embodied in the photo album. She could have turned those pages with me when I was seven, eight, nine, ten, and told me the stories connected with each image, each person. That's what grandparents do. Or are supposed to do.

· · ·

IT WAS ALWAYS with a most profound sense of relief that we packed the car and headed for the ferry that would take us back across the Verrazano Narrows. Aunt Edith would promise to say a special prayer every day at Mass to St. Christopher, the patron saint of travelers, until she knew we were safely home. This was not merely an indication of her intense religiosity: my father needed all the help he could get. He was, quite simply, the world's worst driver—a deficiency attributable not only to his blindness in one eye but to his chronic (and on the road, dangerous) distractibility. He was one of those drivers unable to carry on a conversation with anyone in the backseat without turning his head around. On the way home—the trip always took three days in the pre-superhighway era—I would think about the puzzling behavior of my father's family for an hour or two, until my fascination with the Burma Shave signs put an end to the questions raised by both my aunt's and grandmother's behavior. When we got home, I would invariably drag out our own family snapshots, which included pictures of my mom's parents when they were young. Their images formed my image of where I came from. I wouldn't think about the missing faces on my father's side of the family until it was time for our next trip to New York. But I knew, all along, that something important was missing from my image of both my father and myself.

VIII

Elementary Education

I LEARNED TO READ when I was five years old, in 1950, before there was a television in my home. This precedence of literacy shaped my tastes and interests in a way that set me apart from many of my contemporaries in childhood and drew me as an adult toward friends born ten to twenty years before me. I began to think and to learn in a quieter, more contemplative world than the one my brother entered only three years after me. I entertained myself as a small child—there was no choice—instead of being entertained by video images. In that crucial aspect, my early childhood resembled that of my parents' generation more than it did the experience of the baby boomers.

The adults who shaped my childhood were not intellectuals, but they were all passionate readers of books, newspapers, and magazines. We subscribed to at least two newspapers (more when we still lived in Chicago) and all of the mass-circulation, general-information magazines of the era—*Collier's, The Saturday Evening Post, Look, Life, Time*, plus a half dozen women's magazines. Aunt Edith also sent us an annual Christmas subscription to *The New Yorker*; in spite of her piety, she had not abandoned the witty secular publication she began to read as a New York "career girl" in her twenties. *The New Yorker* was to play an important role in my intellectual development; when I began reading the articles instead of just flipping through the pages for cartoons, I soon realized that there were very different ways of looking at the world from the conventional wisdom I encountered in the other publications we received. In spite of their shortcomings, nearly all of the general-interest magazines of the fifties offered, to readers of all ages, a staggering amount of serious information, especially when compared to the celebrity-mad publications of the nineties.

Both of my parents, as well as my Broderick grandparents (especially my grandfather), were always arguing about history and politics—a stream of talk, coupled with my reading, that fostered preoccupations somewhat out of sync with my contemporaries in the neighborhoods where I grew up. In a recent conversation with a much older friend, a woman of my parents' generation, I made some reference to "the war." She looked at me curiously and said, "You're the only baby boomer I know who means World War Two when she says 'the war.' " I take her point, even though I know others of my generation who call the Vietnam War "Vietnam" and reserve "the war" for the worldwide conflict that was over before they were born. But my friend is basically right: my parents' war does occupy a large and unusually vivid space in my consciousness, given that I was born after the fighting and dying were over in Europe. Growing up, I felt that the catastrophes of 1939 through 1945, and the ominous events leading to war during the preceding decade, were very close to me. I became attached, at a young age, to a past that wasn't quite mine.

One explanation for my fascination with the war was the procession of tenth anniversaries, guaranteed to generate discussion within my family, that unfolded when I was in the first through fifth grades. Pearl Harbor, the Bataan Death March, D-Day, the Battle of the Bulge, FDR's death, V-E Day, the dropping of the atomic bomb on Hiroshima: one after another, they became real to me through the memories of my parents and the accounts of journalists for whom World War II had been the defining experience of their lives and the making of their careers. I believe I first saw photographs of concentration camp survivors—and of the corpses of those who did not survive—in the spring of 1955, which marked the tenth anniversary of the liberation of the camps by the advancing Allied armies.

In the mid-fifties, when we acquired our first hi-fi set capable of playing 33 rpm records, my parents bought a series of albums, narrated by Edward R. Murrow, titled "I Can Hear It Now." The records strung together memorable speeches by just about everyone who shaped the world in the thirties and forties—Franklin Roosevelt, Winston Churchill, Adolf Hitler—as well as famous curios such as King Edward VIII's renunciation of the British throne for "the woman I love." I listened to these recordings over and over, driving everyone in the house crazy with repeated renditions of Churchill offering nothing but "blood, toil, tears, and sweat," of Hitler raving away in a language I could not understand but in a tone I understood very well, of FDR twitting political opponents for making an issue of his having allegedly wasted the taxpayers' money by sending a destroyer to pick up his dog, Fala. All of the Roosevelt charm came across on the record. I can hear his teasing irony now: "These Republican leaders have not been content with attacks on me, or my wife, or on my sons. No, not content with that, they now include my little dog, Fala. Well, of course, I don't resent attacks, and my family doesn't resent attacks, but Fala does resent them."

I also heard excerpts from Murrow's famous 1945 broadcast upon the liberation of Buchenwald, in which he described what he found there in graphic—especially for that more reticent era—fashion. With the liberation of Bergen-Belsen, Buchenwald, and Dachau, millions of Americans had been informed, for the first time, of the tortures the Nazis had inflicted on concentration camp victims (though the fuller horror of the mass extermination camps on Polish soil, then being liberated by the Red Army, was not yet known).

Although the word *Jew* was never used in Murrow's broadcast from Buchenwald, I was well aware, as a ten-year-old listening to the recording in 1955, that Jews, unlike most other people victimized by the Nazis, had been targeted for total destruction. This I learned at home, not in school, for recent history received short shrift in the American elementary and secondary school curriculum of the 1950s. In world history, teachers usually made it up to the French Revolution by the beginning of May, leaving the entire nineteenth and twentieth centuries for the last four weeks of school. In American history, everything after the Civil War was compressed into the same end-of-term rush. Even when the teachers did get around to World War II, the destruction of European Jewry was treated as a secondary topic, worthy of only the briefest note. In the public high school I attended, the curriculum was even more cursory in its discussion of the camps than my parochial elementary schools had been. While the nuns were primarily interested in Hitler's treatment of Catholics—a lesson that naturally never touched on what the Vatican did, and did not do, to aid Jews during the Holocaust—my teachers did say the Nazis *also* aimed their persecutions at the "children of Israel." Like my father, the sisters never used the word *Jew*.

My mother was the one who told me that the Jews had been put to death in gas chambers, and she was the parent who handled most of my questions about why people had hated Jews enough to kill them. My ideas about Jews were still hazy; I had heard about them only in connection with concentration camps, the crucifixion, and Old Testament prophecies foretelling the coming of the Messiah. My mother explained Jew hating to me not in religious terms but in terms of ignorance and fear, comparable to the hatred of some whites for Negroes, of small-minded people for anyone who looked or thought differently. Why were the Jews different? Well, my mother attempted to explain, the Jews didn't believe in Jesus—but that couldn't be the real reason for the Nazis' hatred, because there were some Jews who *did* believe in Jesus and who had converted to the Christian religion, just the way my father had converted from the Episcopal to the Catholic Church. . . . And those "Christian

Jews," as Mom called them, were killed anyway, just because they had Jewish parents. Small wonder that my father usually turned over these questions—how agonizing they must have been for him!—to my mother. Ignorance, fear, and prejudice were like contagious diseases, Mom told me. Most of the time, she added, it was pointless to look for a reason. On one occasion, my father did point out that the very structure of the word *prejudice*—*pre*-judge—meant there was no rational explanation for the phenomenon. Before fifth or sixth grade, my interest in the camps, and the people who had been killed in them, was mainly an outgrowth of my fixation on the war. That would change, however, when I turned eleven and read Anne Frank's diary for the first time.

MY PAPERBACK copy of the diary, a twenty-five-cent Pocket Book, is yellowed and crumbling, falling apart page by page. I bought it in 1956 from the newly installed paperback book rack in Grettenberger's drugstore in Okemos. This was the first book I ever bought with my own money, and it is the only book I have kept from my childhood. Anne's diary went along with me to my college dormitory at Michigan State University, to Washington, and then to Moscow, where I loaned it to a Russian friend but took care to retrieve it before I returned to the United States in 1971. I was unaware, until I was in my late thirties, that there were Jewish cultural commentators who thought the widespread public interest in the diary may actually have done more harm than good as far as American knowledge of the Holocaust was concerned. (In fact, negative critiques of the diary hardly existed before the early 1980s, when the movement toward Holocaust memorialization recast an old question—who has the right to speak for and represent victims?—in an increasingly politicized light.)

The debate over the sentimentalizing, de-Judaizing presentation of Anne's diary, reinvigorated by a 1997 Broadway revival of the play, has been conducted primarily by literary critics and Holocaust scholars, many of whom genuinely believe that the average American reading the diary forty-five years ago (and perhaps even today) would have somehow overlooked the family's Jewishness and failed to understand that the lives of the Franks' were imperiled only because they were Jews. This is a patronizing assumption that not only refuses to credit the intelligence of ordinary readers but also fails to acknowledge that Anne's diary would not have been published (certainly not in its original adolescent form) if the author had survived. Philip Roth had the latter reality in mind when, in his novel *The Ghost Writer*, he created an Anne who *does* survive, without her father's knowledge, and who learns that Otto Frank himself is alive only when she reads about the Dutch publication of her diary in a newspaper. Instead of contacting her father and telling him that she too has come through the ordeal, the fictional Anne decides to remain dead to the world so that the power of her testimony will be enhanced by her martyrdom.

It is now well known that Otto Frank withheld certain portions of his daughter's diary that he considered "too Jewish," too pessimistic, too critical of his wife, or too candid about Anne's emerging sexuality. Fortunately, Otto was too conscientious a man and a father to destroy the offending passages, which he turned over to the appropriate authorities for publication in a definitive edition after his death. The Broadway revival incorporated a good deal of the material that had been excised from the original edition of the diary; consequently, the 1997 theatrical production had a darker tone than the original. This version of Anne Frank's story could no longer be summed up in the famous line, "I still believe that people are really good at heart." Still, the changes and restorations did not change many minds; the public enthusiasm for the diary remains a sore point with a number of high-profile Jewish intellectuals. Their animus cannot be attributed to the contents of the diary itself, in either its formerly bowdlerized or currently available uncensored version, for there is no dispute about Anne's precocious writing talent and powers of observation.

For some Jews, the real problem with the diary is the kind of

Jews the Franks were. Otto Frank, in addition to being a grieving survivor wanting to put the best face on every member of his murdered family, was an acculturated, nonobservant Jew who, before the Nazi era, had considered himself a German like any other and who retained his attachment to German culture after the Holocaust. He was the kind of Jew my grandfather would surely have become if he had been raised, as Otto Frank was, in imperial Germany. Otto's connection to Judaism as a religion was so tenuous that it is easy to imagine, had Hitler not come along, a late-twentieth-century Frank family with as many Christian converts in Germany as the Jacoby family produced in America. The subliminal (and in many cases overt) critique of the diary boils down to the conviction that if one person is going to stand for the murdered millions in the eyes of the goyim, it should not be the child of a man whose idea of a Hanukkah present for his daughter was a Christian Bible.

Otto, like many of my own ancestors, represents a Jewish possibility that arouses deep emotions, ranging from pity to disdain—with various nuances of anxiety and ambivalence in between—on the part of many contemporary American Jews (secular and observant). Among those most repelled by this Jewish possibility, the public response to Anne's diary is seen as the product of a concerted and highly manipulative attempt to deemphasize the Jewish particularity of the Holocaust in favor of a universalized view of the extermination camps as just another example of the terrible things human beings are capable of doing to other human beings.

While the critics of the "Anne Frank industry" are right about the intentions of the publisher, the original Broadway producers, and (to some extent) Otto Frank himself, they are dead wrong in their contention that the bland, universalized approach succeeded in wiping out Anne's Jewish identity for average readers—many of whom, like me, were children. The Holocaust scholar Lawrence Langer has written that "an audience coming to [the] play in 1955 . . . would find little to threaten its psychological or emotional security. No one dies, and the inhabitants of the annex endure minimal suffering." These are the words of an historian who already knows most of what can be known about the Holocaust (except by those who lived through it). What is left out of this analysis is the impact of a first encounter with the diary (and later, the movie based on the play) on someone like me in the mid-fifties. From reading critiques by pompous Holocaust gatekeepers, one might conclude that the lesson drawn from Anne's diary by young American readers amounts to nothing more than "There's so much good in the worst of us / And so much bad in the best of us / That it ill behooves any of us / To talk about the rest of us."

It is true that when I bought the paperback edition, with a fore-word by Eleanor Roosevelt, of *Anne Frank: The Diary of a Young Girl*, I could not have known less about what a Jew was. I am sure that the main attraction for me was Anne's picture on the cover and a blurb calling the book "a deeply moving story of adolescence." At eleven, I knew that Anne and her family had joined the masses of skeletal victims, in striped uniforms, whom I had seen in newsreel photographs. What I did not know was anything about their lives before the abyss.

In the opening pages, I learned that people called Jews, on another continent, to be sure, but only a few years before I was born, were kept out of public schools, banned from parks and movie the-aters, and required to turn in their bicycles. Anne, at twelve, had been forbidden to do all of the things I liked to do. These measures, I understood, were the prelude to the extermination camps. Roth was right: the diary, though it is also the work of a gifted young writer, derives its moral power from our knowledge of what hap-pened to the inhabitants of the secret annex and to millions of oth-ers. What Anne's diary did for me as a child (and I daresay for many of my elders) was to make the connection between a faceless group of victims and individual lives. I was seized by the realization—and it definitely *did* threaten my sense of security—that people could be killed for nothing, nothing at all, other than having been born into a despised racial or religious group. A year after reading Anne's diary, I immediately linked her story with the photographs of hate-filled whites jeering at the "Little Rock Nine," the embattled black students who desegregated Little Rock Central High School in 1957. And if this was universalization, it did not impel me to disregard the singularity of what had happened to the Jews but instead enabled me to understand that laws and practices depriving people of the right to go to school, to movies, to public parks, could lead—*had* led, only fifteen years earlier—to the denial of the very right to live. No, this teenage writer's diary wasn't the film *Shoah* or Primo Levi's *The Drowned and the Saved*. As a child, I was infused by Anne Frank's diary with an awareness of evil that would one day lead me to other chapters in the book of genocide. The diary inspired me to learn more: this is not the worst thing to be said on behalf of a small work of art that has entered popular consciousness around the world. And if there were and are many readers who took in the story simply as the tragic tale of one life cut short—well, the Holocaust was that too, six million times over, experienced separately by each person as well as collectively by a people. For me, Anne's diary became one of those books a reader looks back on for the rest of her life and says, "Yes, that changed me forever."

It would be foolishly reductive of me to conclude that I became unusually interested in Jews primarily because some sensor mechanism had been triggered by my father's silences and evasions about his family's past. Still, *something* set me off, for the concentration camps and the Jews were subjects that simply did not come up in my everyday life. I was still attending Catholic school when I read the diary, and I remember making a conscious decision to avoid using the chronicle of life in the secret annex for a book report—not only because my sixth-grade nun would have disapproved of the subject but also because I didn't want to reveal, to a roomful of eleven-year-olds, how deeply I had been affected by Anne's story. Around that time I began having the recurring concentration camp nightmare in which Hitler himself turned up to inform me that "you're no better than anyone else here." The diary had set off a depth charge that forced previously submerged contradictions to the surface of my mind. Like Anne herself, I could no longer reconcile the idea of an all-knowing, all-caring God with the evil that human beings, said to be divine creations, were capable of inflicting on one another. I could no longer accept what I was being taught in Catholic classrooms.

IN ALL memoirs, there is an ever-present temptation to project current preoccupations onto a past self, to rewrite private history in a fashion that minimizes anything inconsistent with the person one has become and exaggerates the importance of anything that is clearly a precursor of the adult self. My father, whenever I would bring up some aspect of "this Jewish business" in my twenties, would remind me of my onetime infatuation with the political philosophy expounded by Senator Barry Goldwater in *The Conscience of a Conservative* (fifty cents at Grettenberger's in 1960). I was convinced that the graduated income tax was one of the worst things ever to happen to Americans, and Dad's arguments on behalf of social justice (not to mention that his accounting firm would have gone out of business without progressive taxation as administered by the Internal Revenue Service) fell on deaf ears for a time. I had forgotten about my brief passion for Goldwater—and my opinion, in 1960, that both Nixon and Kennedy were too liberal—until Dad reminded me years later. When I moved on politically, I obviously eradicated the conservative hero from my intellectual résumé. My father was right to remind me of the selectivity of memory, but he was wrong to imply (as he surely intended) that I was retrospectively exaggerating the degree of my youthful alienation from Catholic certitudes and the intensity of my interest in everything to do with Jews. Resistance to religious authority and a desire to learn more about Jews were two themes, though they were not connected in my mind at the time, that emerged in childhood and grew even more important during my adolescence; while the former could be explained by the force-feeding of religion in parochial school, the latter seemed to come, as my father insisted, "out of nowhere."

·   ·   ·

MY CATHOLIC education ended at fourteen, when my parents transferred me from St. Thomas to Okemos High School. There is no question that I was influenced profoundly by those years of parochial school, which left a deeper impression than any subsequent part of my formal education. Thorough indoctrination in pre–Vatican II Catholicism gave me a firm idea of what I did *not* believe—a point of intellectual and spiritual departure. For this I have always been grateful. Even the most retrograde aspects of parochial school religiosity served the useful purpose of stimulating doubt. In class, we were all embarrassed, and would snicker uneasily behind our hands, when we were forced to listen to a bloodcurdling record dramatizing the death of twelve-year-old Maria Goretti, who had only recently been canonized by Pope Pius XII for resisting her rapist unto death. "No, no, it is a sin—God forbids it!" screamed the Maria stand-in as her attacker stabbed her over and over. Why, I asked myself, should a girl have to prove her virtue by resisting a man until he murders her? I knew I would have given in so I could go on living—and this certainty didn't make me feel guilty at all. This is not (as my dad might suggest if he were alive) a piece of feminist revisionism, exaggerating the depth of my preteen repulsion at the idea that it was better to die a virgin than to survive a rape. If dying was what it took for a girl to become a saint, I didn't want any part of sainthood. "Unjust! Unjust!" (I had just read *Jane Eyre*) was my visceral reaction.

Chastity, which had not been emphasized in the early grades, became the focal point of religious instruction as Catholic schoolchildren approached puberty. Lust (barely comprehensible to me at that point) was treated as the deadliest of the deadly sins—and it was clear that girls were responsible for provoking it in boys. Those who began to "develop" in sixth or seventh grades were subjected to merciless scrutiny by the nuns, who seemed to regard uncontrollable hormonal changes as outward signs of inward moral turpitude. The early developers were not even allowed to wear unbuttoned sweaters outside their uniforms on cold days, because a sweater, even with a cotton blouse and serge jumper underneath, might outline breasts and provoke lustful thoughts. On the two days each month when we were allowed to wear regular clothes while our uniforms were being dry-cleaned, pullover sweaters (for girls) were forbidden altogether. The rules changed constantly, as the nuns vigilantly rooted out new attempts by the fashion industry to draw attention to the female form. In the spring of 1957, my grandmother Broderick had bought me a dress in a new style—the no-waist chemise. The shapeless, green-and-white striped dress definitely did not emphasize my nonexistent figure, but the school principal, Sister Mary Aurelia, scrutinized the garment carefully because it was *different*. After this inspection, she gave her approval (while reminding me not to add a belt). This emphasis on the practice of chastity and the subjugation of lust bothered me not only because of its disproportionate nature (what about covetousness and sloth, which seemed much more common in children my own age?) but also because of the intrusive insistence on the necessity of controlling thoughts as well as deeds. Exactly how were you supposed to control your thoughts? And why? How could "coveting" a friend's Mickey Mouse watch belong to the same universe of sin as actually stealing the watch? The explanation offered by the nuns was that covetous and impure thoughts could easily lead to covetous and impure acts. But what if the thoughts *didn't* lead to deeds? What if they stayed thoughts? That was still sinful, we were told, because God knew our thoughts. The essence of what I was being taught, it seemed to me at the time, was that the Church—God's representative on earth—spelled out right from wrong, in both thought and deed. The duty of the individual was not to make moral decisions, in spite of all the talk we heard about "free will," but to let the Church decide for him. Or her. This ran counter not only to my own nature but to much of what I learned at home from my parents. My dad didn't know it when he was baptized, but he would have made a better Episcopalian, given the Anglican Church's origins in rebellion against pontifical authority, than a Catholic.

Had I gone to public elementary school, I might have accepted the less obtrusive role Catholicism played in the lives of children who received religious instruction only once a week in the evening. My parents told me to think for myself but at the same time turned me over to an institution that insisted it had all the answers. When we moved to Okemos, which had a small but excellent library, Mom and Dad were among the rare parents who readily signed a permission slip enabling me to take out any adult book I chose—yet they sent me to a school where I was taught that it was a mortal sin to read any books on the Vatican Index.

I was not avid to crack the Index, in spite of the lure of the forbidden, because it included a wide range of works, from the writings of Voltaire to Vladimir Nabokov's *Lolita*, that sounded boring to me at the time. Like most children who become omnivorous readers, my reading as I entered adolescence was a hodgepodge of classics and trash, including comic books, contemporary best-sellers, historical novels, children's books I had already reread dozens of times, and serious novels that did appeal to me even though they were way over my head. On any given day, the array of books under my bed (a mess that infuriated my mom, because it often led to library fines) might include *Gone with the Wind*, Howard Fast's *Spartacus*, Lloyd Douglas's *Magnificent Obsession* (a treacly tale of a dissolute young man who blinds a woman in a car accident and is redeemed by faith in God), Nevil Shute's *On the Beach* (which scared me to death with its scenario of total atomic destruction brought about by human error), *Jane Eyre*, *A Tale of Two Cities*, *The Red and the Black*, *Emma*, *The Hunchback of Notre Dame*, the short stories of John O'Hara, and the preteen novels of Maud Hart Lovelace, who chronicled the childhood and adolescence of three turn-of-the-century Minneapolis girls named Betsy, Tacy, and Tib. My parents almost never interfered with my reading; the only time I remember my father posing an objection was when I brought *The Man in the Gray Flannel Suit* home from the library. The best-selling novel by Sloan Wilson (later made into a movie starring Gregory Peck) has as its main character a married veteran who fathers an illegitimate child with an Italian woman during the war. My father wasn't sure that this was an appropriate theme for a twelve-year-old, but, after a brief discussion, he agreed with my mother that it was too late for them to start trying to censor my reading. My mother and father set different standards from the ones preached in school, and this dichotomy set me apart from my Catholic friends in ways my parents surely did not intend. Or did they?

Catholic school, in addition to engendering a lifelong interest in religion (albeit in a form quite different from what the nuns envisaged), gave me a secular education far more rigorous than the one I would have received in the public schools of our area and era. Most of the Dominican sisters at St. Thomas, which I attended from the sixth through the eighth grades, were great and dedicated teachers. Beginning in the seventh grade, we took Latin, which the public schools were already beginning to jettison in a reaction against stuffy, old-fashioned academic requirements. I can still hear Sister Aurelia speaking eloquently on the value of Latin and its relationship to all modern languages, including English. "If you learn Latin," she would tell us, "you will not only understand your own language better but you will find it much easier to learn any other language." (Twelve years later, when I found myself in Moscow and was able to make rapid progress in Russian, I understood how right she had been. A number of the American journalists in Russia, never having been exposed to declensions, were defeated by case endings and found it nearly impossible to make themselves understood, or to profit from the expensive lessons financed by their respective newspapers and magazines.) The nuns, like my father (and unlike most of the teachers I encountered in more "progressive" public schools), believed in memorization, and not only of prayers, hymns, and catechism answers. You simply did not get out of the eighth grade at St. Thomas without having your brain permanently imprinted with large chunks of the Declaration of Independence and the Constitution, the entire Gettysburg Address, and nineteenth-century lyric poems (Samuel Taylor Coleridge, Sir Walter Scott, and, surprisingly, Edgar Allan Poe, were among the nuns' favorites). Most of my teachers had a deep feeling for language; I remember Sister Aurelia, who taught seventh- and eighth-grade English as well as Latin, pointing out that the Gettysburg Address was profoundly moving not only because of its ideas but because of the way in which those ideas were expressed. She gave us an exercise—to translate Lincoln's speech into what she called "less elevated" language, and to see whether it would have had the same effect. It was a wonderful assignment by a genius of a teacher, and I could never understand how the chastity-obsessed sweater monitors could also be such gifted educators. Only when the feminist movement engendered a reevaluation of all women's lives did I consider the possibility that the convent might have been seen as the only real alternative to marriage by devout Catholic women born, as my teachers were, between 1900 and 1930. While there were many aging Irish Catholic bachelors in the early decades of the century, there were few aging spinsters, and those few were viewed by their families as pitiable burdens. The honorable maiden aunt, a staple in old New England Protestant families, did not have a respectable place in American Irish Catholic society; if a woman did not wish to marry, for whatever reason, she could find security and community only in the convent. And it was easy, even for children, to tell the difference between the warped, sour women who had probably entered the convent because no man would have them and the vibrant and unforgettable nuns, like Sister Aurelia, who had chosen to pursue their genuine vocation for teaching instead of taking on the responsibilities of Catholic wifehood and motherhood. For anyone who benefited from the work of such dedicated women in the Catholic schools of the fifties and early sixties, it came as no surprise when, in the mid-seventies, the good female soldiers began to push for more recognition, responsibility, and equality in the running of the Church to which they had devoted their lives.

To these women, it was always a sin not to do your best. We were frequently assigned compositions, and I usually got A's, so I was shocked to receive a C on one assignment. Sister Aurelia asked me to stay after class, and she wanted to know how long it had taken me to write the composition. I confessed that I had completed the work by flashlight in fifteen minutes, after lights-out, because I had stayed up late to listen to a night baseball game on the radio. (My White Sox were in contention that fall.) "It showed," she said. "You didn't develop your ideas logically. I gave you a C because for you, this wasn't an effort at all. Without trying, you can do C work. To get an A, it has to be an A *for you*—the best you're capable of doing. What you did is like cheating, but it's worse than copying someone else's paper because you're *cheating yourself.*" This was a teaching I could accept, and if the nuns failed to make a Catholic out of me, they succeeded in turning me into a person who regarded learning as an ethical imperative. In that sense, I have never stopped being Sister Aurelia's student.

In 1959, when I entered public school, I also began reading the Bible from cover to cover. No one familiar with the history of the Reformation will be surprised to hear that reading and interpreting the Bible on one's own were definitely not activities encouraged by parochial schools. In public school, we were assigned *Romeo and Juliet* for ninth-grade English (with its dangerous emphasis on teenage passion, the play would never have passed muster with the nuns), and I soon realized that it was impossible to fully appreciate and understand Shakespeare without having read the Bible. I had never really looked at the Old Testament, although I was more or less familiar with the New Testament because so many passages from the Gospels and the apostolic epistles were included in the liturgy of the Mass (which we were required to attend every day at St. Thomas). I soon fell under the spell of the King James Bible. The Douay version, used in the Catholic liturgy of that era, was all but identical in content (with the exception of a few hairsplitting changes), but the majestic language of the King James version made the "Catholic Bible" sound, at times, like a tin-eared imitation.

As I became familiar with the Bible, I began to suspect that my father, who did not know even the most famous psalms by heart, could not possibly have had *any* religious education as a child. He knew only the Catholic prayers he had learned in religious instruction as an adult. With his prodigious memory for verse, it was inconceivable that he would have failed to memorize passages like the Twenty-third Psalm if he had really gone to Episcopal Sunday school (as he claimed at the time of his conversion). This was yet another piece of my father's official version of his life that didn't make sense.

I half hoped that through reading the Bible, I would discover a set of religious beliefs that I could substitute for the Catholic teachings that seemed so illogical to me. But as far as I could see (and my ideas about the differences among Protestant denominations were hazy), the Bible conferred no more—or less—legitimacy on Presbyterians, Methodists, Baptists, and Episcopalians than it did on Catholics. Moreover, after reading the Old Testament, I found the God of the Jews just as irrational as (and even more intractable than) the God of the Christians. When I came to the slaying of the Egyptian firstborn, I shuddered as I had when I first heard of Herod's Slaughter of the Innocents, a story that has started more than one "fallen-away" Catholic on the road to agnosticism or atheism. The Catholic educators of my youth (and the sixteenth-century Church hierarchy) were quite right in their assumption that independent Bible reading posed a danger to faith. As a child, I told myself—and, with what I am certain was insufferable frequency, my parents—that even if God existed, I wanted no part of a Supreme Being who would slaughter innocent babies. My mother would usually ignore my professions of agnosticism (I wasn't quite prepared to go so far as to declare myself an atheist), saying that was all very well, but I was still going to Mass on Sunday with the rest of the family.

My father, however, would go wild. "Honor student!" he would say contemptuously. "You look at the intricate design of each leaf—of each and every leaf—and you say it 'just happened.' Just came out of nowhere. The millions of brain cells in your head came out of nowhere. Well, maybe yours did. That's brilliant. The universe came

out of nowhere. An A student! Where do those A's come from?"
"Bob, there's no need to get overwrought," my mother would say.
"She's just going through a phase. You're egging her on by rising to
the bait." Eight years later, I laughed out loud, thinking of my dad,
when I came across a diatribe by the furious father of young Alex
Portnoy in *Portnoy's Complaint:* "Do you know men study their whole
lives in the Jewish religion, and when they die they still haven't finished? Tell me, now that you are all finished at fourteen being a Jew,
do you know a single thing about the wonderful history and heritage
and saga of your people? . . . A's in school, but in life he's as ignorant
as the day he was born."

By the standards of most of the people around me, my dad's style
of communication was as overwrought as that of Portnoy père. Dad's
contentiousness, my mother would explain, had been nurtured not
only by his chronically argumentative family but by his having been
born and raised in New York, where people were in the habit of
shouting at one another instead of speaking politely. I knew this was
true from our summer visits to the city. Furthermore, most New
Yorkers (like my dad) "talked with their hands"—another habit my
mother was always trying to break me of. That my father's style of
communication was not only typical of New Yorkers but also stereotypically associated with Jews was something I didn't know.

IX

Out of Somewhere

⌇

As I ENTERED MY teens, the subject of Jews—who they were, why so many of them had been murdered in the camps, what they believed, and what they represented to non-Jews—began to impinge more and more on my consciousness. At fourteen, in a 1959 issue of *The New Yorker*, I came across a story that led me to consider what it might mean to be a Jew in an America I could recognize, just as Anne Frank's diary had once forced me to think about what it meant to have been a Jew threatened by the Nazis in a Europe I could not recognize. I began reading Philip Roth's "Defender of the Faith" under the amusing misapprehension, engendered by the title, that this must have something to do with Catholics. I soon became involved in the story (it seems that I started growing up as a reader as Roth came of age as a writer), set during the last summer of World War II, between the end of combat in Europe and the bombing of Hiroshima and Nagasaki, which finally ended the fighting in Asia.

The hero of the story, Sergeant Nathan Marx, is a Jewish veteran forced into a complicated conflict of loyalties as a result of his relationship with Sheldon Grossbart, a draftee in his stateside training platoon and a smarmy operator who attempts to gain special favors from his sergeant by appealing to their bond as Jews. Marx goes along for a time, asking his commanding officer to release the Jewish soldiers who want to go to *shul* on Friday night; sympathizing with their distaste for the *treyf* in the army mess hall; giving Grossbart the benefit of the doubt whenever he asks to be excused from army duties on religious grounds. But when Marx learns that all of the other draftees in the platoon are being shipped to the Pacific—all but Grossbart, who has somehow managed to pull strings to get sent to New Jersey—he goes out of his way to obtain a reversal of the order. The story ends:

> I stood outside the orderly room, and I heard Grossbart
> weeping behind me. Over in the barracks, in the lighted win-
> dows, I could see the boys in their T shirts sitting on their
> bunks talking about their orders, as they'd been doing for
> the past two days. With a kind of quiet nervousness, they
> polished shoes, shined belt buckles, squared away their
> underwear, trying as best they could to accept their fate.
> Behind me, Grossbart swallowed hard, accepting his. And
> then, resisting with all my will an impulse to turn and seek
> pardon for my vindictiveness, I accepted my own.

At fourteen, I certainly did not understand all (or even most) of the nuances of this story. The Jewish critics who attacked Roth at the time—mainly because they regarded the character of Grossbart as an anti-Semite's dream—would have been utterly bewildered by my Catholic schoolgirl's analysis. Grossbart, in my interpretation, became all of the prissy, hypocritically pious girls who curried favor with the nuns by spending extra time in church, who informed on less pious classmates, who went around proclaiming "I am a Catholic" at every conceivable opportunity. And Marx—well, who else would Marx be but me? Wouldn't I just love to get even with the girls who went around trading "holy cards" with pictures of saints instead of baseball cards? If I were their drill sergeant, I'd cheerfully make them eat meat on Friday if that was the will of the U.S. Army. I did not understand what kind of Jew Nathan Marx considered himself to be (as opposed to what kind of Jew Sheldon Grossbart was), but I did grasp the pull of competing loyalties at the heart of the story. Marx, after all, had not been insensible to the pull of group loyalty. What Jewish veteran of the war in Europe, only months after the liberation of the death camps, could have dismissed the claims of loyalty made by another Jew? The character of Nathan Marx struck me deeply and forcefully, and the sorting out of loyalties seemed to me all the more impressive because I understood by then—Anne Frank's diary had helped me to understand—that being a Jew wasn't a choice in the same way that being a Catholic was. To be a Jew meant more than to be a member of a church. My father, I knew, had become a Catholic by an act of will, and I was beginning to believe that for me, religion could be undone by an act of will. But I understood that Nathan Marx was a Jew whether he ate pork sausage or not, whether he observed the Sabbath or not.

I did not talk about "Defender of the Faith," or my reaction to it, with either of my parents. By then I knew what I had not known when I read Anne's diary at the age of eleven—that the subject of Jews was definitely not something my father wished to discuss. Only a year later, though, we heard news of import for Jews that even my dad could not ignore: on May 23, 1960, the Israeli prime minister, David Ben-Gurion, announced that Adolf Eichmann, the man in charge of the practical strategy for implementing the Final Solution, had been captured by Israeli agents in Argentina. Eichmann had been living there since 1950 under the name Ricardo Klement, an identity he assumed with the help of one of the underground organizations dedicated to helping prominent Nazis escape punishment.

The Eichmann trial, which began a year later in Israel, opened a new chapter in public consciousness of what would come to be called the Holocaust. The horror that had greeted the disclosures of mass murder at the end of the war, bolstered by the vast amount of evidence presented at the Nuremberg trials, had faded in fifteen years. Moreover, the trial provided the first opportunity for anyone under roughly age twenty-five (many of the details were new to most Americans, whatever their age) to absorb the magnitude of what had happened. The news media, including television, covered the Eichmann trial extensively. In the basement "rec room," containing our new twenty-inch TV, my father would watch, tight-lipped, as "the man in the glass booth" appeared on the evening news. There had been considerable dispute in the press over whether Israel had the right to try Eichmann, but the controversy dissipated as the grave statistics poured forth in the courtroom. (I was unaware of this dispute at the time; none of the adults I knew ever suggested that Eichmann should be tried anywhere but in Israel.) "He's in a courtroom, he has a lawyer," my father would say. "Did he give any of his victims a trial?"

In *New Lives*, an account of the experiences of Holocaust survivors in America, Dorothy Rabinowitz observes that "for a great many American Jews, the Eichmann trial was a galvanizing force, bringing them face to face with emotions theretofore repressed, with events whose full scope and reverberations had been kept, rumbling, beneath the surface of consciousness." This was true even for a Jew as detached from his origins as my father had been for so long. His mask began to slip, and if he did not come face to face with his emotions, he did allow some of them to escape from the place where they had been buried, submerged in the persona of a Catholic convert. Only five years later, he would be able to face his daughter's knowledge that he was a Jew without running away, and he would enter into a dialogue—however anxious and acerbic—about the reasons for his family's long denial.

The Eichmann trial was definitely a turning point for me. My concentration camp nightmares were reinforced by my reading in the public library, where I sought out everything that was available (though there wasn't much) about the camps. I became obsessed (and this is not too strong a word) with learning more about the tortured history of the Jews. The pull of this obsession was strengthened by my unwillingness to share it with others; my friends weren't interested and knew almost nothing about the subject, and I understood, without being told, that my father would not like it if he knew how many books I was reading about Nazi Germany and the camps and how much time I spent thinking about what it meant to be a Jewish victim. In addition to my nighttime terrors, I daydreamed about what it would be like, at my age, to have my head shaved (a particularly horrifying detail for a teenage girl), to be hungry, to be deprived of everything and everyone I had ever known. I reread Anne's diary, feeling happy that she had at least kissed a boy before she was taken away into the darkness. I also read Elie Wiesel's autobiographical *Night*, an account of his experiences, and survival, as a fifteen-year-old in Auschwitz. If Anne's story impressed me with an ordinariness that encouraged identification, *Night* made its mark for precisely the opposite reason: nothing in my experience had prepared me for the knowledge of exactly what went on in a facility designed expressly for the purpose of murdering human beings. I was fifteen when I read *Night*; Wiesel was fifteen when he descended into hell: that was enough.

It must be remembered that the Holocaust, even after the Eichmann trial, had not become an integral element of public consciousness by the early sixties; scholars had not yet focused on Hitler's attempt to exterminate the Jews, and written accounts by survivors were rare. The majority of survivors in America were still in their thirties or early forties, occupied with raising their families, looking to the future rather than the past, and disinclined to talk publicly about an experience that could only elicit pity and horror, setting them apart from their fellow Americans in a land that had given them the opportunity to rebuild their lives. The infrequent survivor's account, like *Night*, caused not a ripple among gentiles in a town like Lansing; I found out about the book only because the Okemos librarian, Hope Borbas, who knew I was interested in the camps, recommended it to me. She also recommended John Hersey's novel *The Wall*, based on the uprising in the Warsaw ghetto. I wasn't nearly as impressed by *The Wall* as I was by *Night*, because the author, unlike Wiesel, hadn't lived through the events he was describing. Little did I know that Hersey's novel, which was quite faithful to the historical facts, would eventually be eclipsed by *Mila 18*, a florid and distorted popular novel on the same theme by Leon Uris, the author of the best-selling novel *Exodus*. Uris, as he did in *Exodus*, gave his Jewish hero a shiksa lover. They moved easily back and forth through the ghetto wall (somehow the Nazis never caught either of them), enjoying romantic assignations even as the last ghetto defenders were being burned and buried alive.

If one is interested in postwar American images of Jews (as distinct from images of the Holocaust), there is no better place to start than Leon Uris. My father loved the book *Exodus* and the 1960 movie starring Paul Newman, Eva Marie Saint, and Sal Mineo. In this, he reacted like the millions of Americans, Jews and non-Jews alike (including his daughter), who were enthralled by the sexy Newman as Ari Ben Canaan, the Israeli independence fighter, and by Saint as his American girlfriend. Uris could conjure up a Jewish lover neither for his Israeli hero nor for a Jewish fighter in the Warsaw ghetto. Ari's shiksa is a nurse, who finally overcomes her initial discomfort at the combative behavior of the Jews she meets in Israel, decides to stay there with her lover, and allies herself with the cause of the new Jewish state. He, in turn, overcomes his initial fear that a woman who looks like she could have flown in the day before from Darien might not fit in on a kibbutz. This was truly a romance fit for the fantasies of a fifteen-year-old. For several years, Paul Newman was my idea of what a Jewish man looked like (though I didn't know that he, like me, had a Jewish father). And oh, how I wanted such a man for myself! Strong but sensitive, he might even recite the Song of Solomon while making love to me.

Dad's enthusiasm for Israel (the real state as well as the sentimental fantasy portrayed in *Exodus*) was boundless; he approved of everything about Israel, including—and especially—the incomparable courage and effectiveness of its army. This bellicose enthusiasm was uncharacteristic of my father, who was leery of everything to do with the military and military actions (with the exception of his generation's war). My father's boredom with military matters was so great that he blew his chance at a fat army pension by failing to keep up his reserve status as an officer after the war. As soon as the Nazis were defeated, he lost all interest in putting on a uniform.

Israel's army, however, was quite another matter. The Arabs, Dad said, would never be able to do to the Israelis what the Nazis had done to the Jews in Europe. The Jews would not go quietly again. This was something that Jewish parents were saying to Jewish children across America and around the world, but I was not a Jewish child and my father was not . . . well, perhaps in this instance he *was* behaving like any other American Jewish parent. The birth of Israel, and the new image of the Jew as a fierce and effective warrior, must have touched a deep chord within my dad. The boy who ran away when he was attacked and called "baby Jew-boy" was thrilled by the spectacle of an entire country of Jews who stood up to their enemies. He was happy that I had read the book and seen the movie of *Exodus* (in contrast to his indifferent reaction when he looked at the jacket of my library copy of *Night*) and more than happy to go with me himself when I begged (longing for another look at my idol Newman/Ari) to see the film a second time. *Exodus* was released around the same time as the capture of Eichmann, so it is not surprising that images from the trial and scenes from the movie were fused in my head for many years. *Life* magazine's cover story on the arrest of the most prominent war criminal to evade the dock in Nuremberg was followed, only a few weeks afterward, with a cover on *Exodus*, the movie, featuring a still photo of the young Sal Mineo playing a former *Sonderkommando*—a concentration camp inmate who had once performed the terrible task of hauling corpses out of the gas chambers and shoving them into the crematoria—reborn as a fighter for Israel. It is a tribute to the overwhelming imaginative hold of Hollywood that I never questioned the historical authenticity of Uris's *Exodus*; to me, his tale was every bit as true as the testimony against

Eichmann. I would have been surprised at the time had I been informed that Uris's epic was not received nearly as favorably in Israel as it was in America and that the real Israeli captain of the real blockade-running ship had said the book was filled with inaccurate stereotypes and outright errors.

There is no question that the effect of the movie, at least in the portion of Middle America where I lived, was to suggest that one good thing had arisen from the ashes of European Jewry. To my father, the rebirth of Israel was another proof that God existed. As we were coming out of the movie, he told me the existence of Israel was a "miracle" that proved God always had a plan for everything, even if it took a long time for his aims to be recognized by men. The Israelis were a free people, he pointed out, while Eichmann would surely never see the outside of a prison again, even if he didn't receive a death sentence. "You mean, six million people had to die so there could be an Israel," I said angrily. "If God had such a good plan, why can't there still be an Israel without killing six million people?" "Miss Has-to-Know-It-All" was his reply.

By the 1970s, when I began talking with my father about his and his family's attitudes toward Jews, he remembered nothing of our conversations about Israel in 1960 and 1961. He had also forgotten that we had watched any portion of the Eichmann trial together, though he had a vague recollection of having been pleased at the sight of the war criminal confined within a glass booth. What my dad did remember was having read Hannah Arendt's *Eichmann in Jerusalem* when it originally appeared in *The New Yorker* in 1963. He had disagreed with Arendt's phrase, "the banality of evil," and he remarked that nothing truly evil could ever be banal. "I guess what she meant," he said, "was that Eichmann looked like your average ordinary accountant. But she mixed up the doer and the deed." Then my father added, "I'm not a New York intellectual, I probably don't know anything." I told him, with absolute honesty, that if I had been writing book reviews in 1963, I would have begun my review with his words. He flushed with pleasure and said, "Well, you may be an intellectual but at least you've got some common sense."

In retrospect, it is easy to see that my father, for all of his intense desire to leave the baby Jew-boy behind, and to conceal that part of himself from his children, was a pretty poor liar. To put it another way, he lacked the essential attribute of all effective con men—the capacity to believe in his own fictions. Growing up in an environment free of Jewish cultural influences, I could not possibly have developed such an intense interest in Jews and things Jewish without the subtle cues I received at home. Furthermore, I received as many of these cues from my non-Jewish mother as from my father—if only because she encouraged me to read anything I wanted about Jews even as she suggested, without ever coming right out and saying so, that there was no reason to become embroiled in arguments about these books (or their appropriateness for a young teenager) with my dad. I cannot imagine what my life would have been like if my mother had been as devout and single-minded a Catholic as the man Aunt Edith married. At one point during my childhood, Aunt Edith offered to pay for my college education, on the condition that I be sent to the Roman Catholic Trinity College in Washington. My parents turned her down without giving the offer a second thought.

Throughout our childhood, my brother was as indifferent to as I was interested in everything to do with Jews and religion. I believe this was partly a matter of the age difference between us—Rob was too young to have been impressed by all of the somber war anniversaries that made such an impression on me—but mainly a matter of temperament. My brother was not, at that time, an avid reader. He was more outgoing, more athletic, more popular, more in tune (at least outwardly) with our suburban environment. Rob and I were teen allies: we talked not about the Bomb or the Jews or the fate of the nation but about tactics to get our own way with our parents. My little brother had toughened up considerably since the days when he saved me chocolate cake in spite of my cruel pretend-suicide. He had become a hardened negotiator who demanded $5 cash when I begged him to fake being desperately sick so that my mother would have to stay home and take care of him instead of embarrassing me by attending a high school basketball game. At the game, I planned to meet a boyfriend of whom Mom vehemently disapproved, and I just knew she would ruin the evening for me. Of course, we both got caught, but Rob somehow contrived to keep my money. How could I share my lofty thoughts on history with someone who would do that to his loving sister? Nearly two decades would pass before my brother, after he became a father himself, began to share my interest in the hidden history of our father's family.

DURING MY senior year in high school, I began practicing the craft of journalism, which would become my life's work. My entry into the newspaper world stimulated my curiosity about Jews still further, because many of my editors and colleagues at my first job, on the Michigan State University college newspaper, were Jewish. They were the first openly Jewish Jews (apart from my high school French teacher, "Madame" Betty Goldstein, whose last name was identifiably Jewish even in Okemos) I had ever known.

I started working on the *State News*, which was no ordinary student newspaper but a profitmaking enterprise run on a professional basis with salaried student editors, while I was still in high school. After I attended a summer journalism seminar on Michigan State's East Lansing campus, about a fifteen-minute drive from our home in Okemos, the *State News* editors asked me if I would like to continue working there after school during my senior year. Would I ever! The job offered me an escape from the boredom of the obligatory but superfluous final year of high school, which I regarded as an infuriating obstacle in the way of my plan to finish college as quickly as possible so that I could go to work on a big-city newspaper.

Michigan State had a substantial number of Jewish students, most of them from New York. MSU's archrival, the University of Michigan at Ann Arbor, had long been a magnet for New York students whose parents could not afford pricier private institutions but were unwilling to consign their children to the then unimpressive New York State university system. MSU, still known disdainfully as "Moo U" because of its huge agricultural school, was a second choice but had managed to attract a growing number of out-of-state students by the early sixties. President John Hannah, determined to improve the academic standing of his school and achieve the national reputation enjoyed by his Ann Arbor rival, had made a concerted effort to attract top students from other states. In 1962, Hannah inaugurated a program offering a $100 bonus to any National Merit Scholar who chose MSU. This small carrot, combined with an intensive public relations campaign informing high school seniors and their parents about the advantages of the university's Honors College for top-ranking students, was hugely successful and soon brought more Merit Scholars to MSU than to any other university in the country. By the time I began working on the *State News* in the fall of 1962, Moo U was rapidly being transformed from a parochial backwater into a cosmopolitan institution with an increasingly distinguished faculty (Hannah also offered huge salary inducements to lure big-name professors away from better-known universities) and a more heterogeneous student body. The Jews on the student newspaper, nearly all of them from New York, were part of the change occurring in every aspect of campus life. The newspaper's faculty adviser, and my first professional mentor, was Lou Berman (who was not a New Yorker but the Jewish owner of a small-town newspaper in Whitehall, Michigan). The advertising manager was Leo Goldberg (not his real name), a swarthy, wisecracking Jew who bore a slight resemblance to Lenny Bruce and who fascinated me with his brashness, his open pride in being a Jew, and his sexual charisma. I knew I was much too young for Leo, but that didn't stop me from dreaming. I must have talked a little bit too much about him at home, because my dad dropped by the offices of the *State News* one day and insisted, in a highly unsubtle and mortifying (to me) fashion, on meeting "that smart ad manager I've been hearing about." His comment was succinct: "That's a Sammy Glick if I ever saw one." I had no idea who Sammy Glick was, and Dad told me he was a character in a novel. When I read Budd Schulberg's *What Makes Sammy Run?*, I accused my dad of being an anti-Semite. "Oh, don't be ridiculous," he said. "Hustlers come in all races and religions. This just happens to be a Jewish hustler."

My father need not have worried about Leo, who was certainly interested in blondes but definitely not interested in seventeen-year-olds. He had two girlfriends (that I knew of), an adoring shiksa named Mary Ann, and the stunningly beautiful (and Jewish) Debbie. Mary Ann was always hanging around the office, hoping for a last-minute date with Leo, while Debbie was a self-possessed young woman who would never have thrown herself at a man. Poor Mary Ann. Leo never called her in advance for a date, frequently failed to show up when they had agreed to meet, and generally treated her like dirt. The sexual dynamic of their relationship—her yearning, his callousness—was obvious even to someone as inexperienced with men as I was.

I didn't connect any of this with his being a Jew and her being a snub-nosed shiksa until I met Debbie at the annual party Mr. Berman (whom I never called by his first name) threw for the *State News* staff. Leo's respectful attitude toward Debbie stunned me: I had assumed he treated all girls the way he treated Mary Ann. Debbie and Leo, Mr. Berman told me, planned to be married after graduation. He had tried to warn Mary Ann that she was wasting her time (Mr. Berman was a real *yenta* who knew everything that was going on with his student editors), but Mary Ann wouldn't listen when he told her there was no chance that Leo would ever marry a gentile. I don't know whether this was true or whether Mr. Berman wanted it to be true. By then, I had begun to feel as sorry for Debbie as I did for Mary Ann. I had already heard the conventional wisdom that Jewish men make the best husbands, but I had ample reason for doubting the applicability of the generalization to Leo. When he told me my first JAP joke, I wondered why, if he wouldn't consider marrying a Christian, he was telling jokes with Jewish women as the targets. Of course I laughed, as we all did in those days to show that we were one of the boys. A decade would pass before Jewish feminists pointed out that JAP humor was the creation of Jewish men projecting anti-Semitic stereotypes onto Jewish women. Greedy. Pushy. Manipulative.

My father must have realized, from the moment I entered the world of journalism—a world in which I was bound to meet a great many Jews—that it was only a matter of time until I put the pieces together and figured out that he too was a Jew. Even so, he was still trying to keep the secret from me. Mr. Berman, who took one look at my father and knew he must be Jewish, told me years later that my dad had specifically asked him not to tell me that Jacoby was a Jewish name. After assuring my father that he would not be the one to break the news, Mr. Berman remarked that I was sure to find out any-way—that I must already suspect the truth. "You should be the one to tell her," he advised my dad. "I'm sure this is not going to upset her." My father, according to Mr. Berman, became extremely angry and told him to mind his own business.

I DID SUSPECT—deep down, I knew—the truth by the time I fin-ished college in 1965, but I hadn't really allowed the knowledge to penetrate because I was engaged in an unusually turbulent transition from adolescence to young adulthood. That passage included a head-long rush to earn my bachelor's degree in just two years, by taking double credit loads and going to summer school. If I regret one thing about my youth, it is the pell-mell nature of my formal education at MSU. I was a National Merit Scholar and could have gone to school anywhere—my dad hoped I would choose Radcliffe, my mother wanted me to go to Northwestern—but I insisted on going no far-ther than East Lansing. It wasn't as capricious a decision as it appeared to my parents (though a boyfriend did play a role). I knew myself fairly well, and I knew I had just about *had it* with classes, financial dependence on parents, and the nonadult status of college students during that era before the youth revolt of the sixties (the end of *in loco parentis* policies in academia was still a half-decade away). But I also knew that no newspaper was ever going to hire me without a college degree, and I feared that if I went to a rigorous institution, like Radcliffe, that would force me to spend four years earning a B.A., I would become a dropout and ruin my future. My father's disappointment in my college choice went deeper than I realized at the time, for I had deprived him of the chance to give me what he had been denied—a first-rate higher education, free of financial worry.

Still, I found a variety of brilliant mentors at Michigan State. They were all men; like so many women of my generation who attended coeducational universities, I never had a female professor. The late Alfred G. Meyer, a Slavist, professor of political science, and refugee from Nazi Germany who would become a lifelong friend, stimulated my lasting interest in both communist and fascist governments. Al, who made it out of Hitler's Germany at the last minute—in 1939, at age nineteen—was the first person I had ever known who grew up under the Nazis. Fluent in German and Russian, he was assigned by the army to interrogate suspected Nazi war criminals in 1945. He told me how he had imagined, literally thousands of times, the vindictive triumph he would feel when he returned to Germany, with the U.S. troops, as a conqueror rather than a victim. And he talked about how the long-anticipated sense of triumph quickly metamorphosed into "a futile sense of sorrow and waste"— a recognition that even if just punishment should be meted out to individual Nazis, there could be no recompense adequate to the scale of the crimes. What I recall most vividly from these conversations is my sense of relief at being able, for the first time, to ask direct questions about subjects that had troubled me for so long. Here was a man who would not be upset to know that I had been reading *Night*. Here was a father figure I did not have to protect (though I suspect Al's children might have held quite a different view of him). In those almost involuntary flashes of comparison, the knowledge of who my own father really was—and why so much remained unspoken between us—began to seep into my conscious heart.

A mentor of a very different kind was George Hough III, my favorite journalism teacher. A nephew of Henry Beetle Hough, the longtime owner of the *Vineyard Gazette* on Martha's Vineyard, George himself had owned a small-town newspaper in Wisconsin. To his students at Michigan State, he passed on not only his practical experience as a reporter and editor but his deep civil libertarian convictions, honed during the McCarthy era in the senator's home state.

Above all, I was indebted to George for his shrewd advice on how to get a job. He was the first person to point out to me that my being a woman would make it tougher to land the newspaper reporting job I wanted so badly. In the prefeminist era, the reality of sex discrimination had not yet dawned on me: my parents had always told me I could do and become anything I wanted, and I am not certain that I knew, at eighteen, about the reluctance of newspapers to assign women to anything other than the society beat. It was George who told me that I would have to prove myself far more thoroughly than any man, George who recommended me for a part-time job as a campus stringer for *The Detroit Free Press*. He felt it would make a great difference, when I began interviewing for jobs, to have a collection of articles printed not in a student publication but in a professional newspaper. And he was right. Although my clippings did me no good at the *Free Press* itself (where the managing editor told me I would never be assigned to general news because the paper couldn't guarantee my safety at night), they did impress *The Washington Post*. Within a week of receiving my clips, a *Post* editor called and asked me to fly to Washington for an interview.

Eager to prove my self-sufficiency, I had held down not one but two newspaper jobs in addition to my college course load. I had also found the time to enter a marriage (following in Mom's footsteps) that never had a chance in view of the ages of the bride and groom—nineteen and twenty-three, respectively. Looking back on this frantic period, I wonder how I ever found time to go to class. My husband and I, behaving like the ill-matched and immature college roommates we were, split up after fifteen months of fighting and chasing cockroaches in our filthy off-campus apartment. Receiving my degree at twenty, in 1965, I realized my first professional dream when the *Post* hired me as a cub reporter assigned to the city desk. I was a young woman in a hurry, far too much of a hurry for a backward glance at Okemos or my immediate family—much less the generations that had gone before. I assumed that there was still plenty of time for me to address the foremost unsolved riddle of my youth—my father and his family's real identity. My dad, at fifty-one, looked and acted like a much younger man, and his older brother and sister, who knew a great deal more than he did about the family history, were in equally robust health.

In Washington, the few remaining scales fell from my eyes (to borrow another metaphor from the conversion of Saul) quickly and painlessly. Surrounded by people who generally assumed I was Jewish because of my last name, I acknowledged my father's origins—*so that's the deep dark secret!*—with a sense of genuine pleasure and release. Dad's Jewishness explained all of the inconsistencies and half-truths, as well as the powerful mixed signals he had been sending, and I had been receiving, throughout my teenage years. The late Alan Barth, a fervent civil libertarian and an eminent editorial writer for the *Post* when I began working there, was the first person who suggested to me that I might someday want to find out what had happened in previous generations to produce such a radical rejection of both Judaism and Jewishness by my father's generation. Alan, a man of great kindness, formidable erudition, and fierce principles, was one of the older journalists who took the twenty-year-old hotshot under their wings at the *Post* and forced her to expand her utilitarian view of knowledge and education. To understand what had happened to the Jacobys in America, he admonished me, I would have to acquaint myself with the history of German Jewry. But that would first require me to fill in what Alan charitably described as the "gaps" in my general knowledge of European history before the twentieth century. Only then, he told me, could I hope to unpack the baggage my father's ancestors had undoubtedly brought with them to the New World.

X

Holocaust, Holocaust, Holocaust

~⌒~

I left Judaism in 1911. I know that this is in fact impossible.
—*Kurt Tucholsky to Arnold Zweig, 1935*

I AM CERTAIN THAT IT was a relief to my father, though he initially responded by becoming extremely upset, to know that he no longer had to hide his Jewish origins from his children. My eighteen-year-old brother, in spite of his general lack of interest in the subject, was neither upset nor particularly surprised to learn that Dad was a Jew. He did suggest that I might be smart to refrain from pressing our father for more details about a part of his life that was obviously a source of great pain.

Of course, I couldn't stop. In my early twenties, I did not know how to ask Dad questions about his boyhood without distressing and angering him, and he was not quite ready to talk. I still had no real comprehension of the nature of American anti-Semitism in the first four decades of the century, so I could not possibly understand how my father's view of himself had been affected, and distorted, by attitudes like those expressed in the Dartmouth administrators' correspondence on the subject of Jewish enrollment. That this ignorance was due, in large measure, to my father's own omissions and fabrications did not make it easier to talk; on the contrary, the long history of silence and evasion heightened both my combativeness and my father's defensiveness. Nevertheless, Dad's attitude began to shift subtly in the late sixties, and only in part because he had already been found out and found blameless by the people who mattered most to him—his children. Of considerable, albeit lesser, importance were the cultural changes taking place in every area of American society, among them the ascendancy of Jewish writers and intellectuals who did not feel obliged to conceal their origins. Even my father could see that a Jew no longer had to put down a phony Washington Square address to increase his chances of being admitted to an Ivy League college—that Jews were beginning to be *in charge of* college admissions offices. And he knew that I regarded my "Jewish" byline as an asset rather than a liability, that by the late sixties, being a Jew made you more rather than less a member of the journalistic club. One of his most insightful observations during this period— and how I resented my dad for saying it!—was that identifying oneself as a Jew simply because Jewishness had acquired a certain social and professional cachet was just as opportunistic as denying one's Jewishness to escape social or professional stigmatization.

This dialogue was interrupted in 1969, when I married Anthony Astrachan, who had just become the Moscow correspondent of *The Washington Post*. I took a leave of absence from the paper to accompany him to the Soviet Union and began writing my first book, which focused on everyday Russian life. I did, however, make a careful record of my conversation with Felix Frankfurter's sister during my honeymoon in Florence, with notes to myself to follow up on the leads she had given me concerning my paternal grandfather. But that would have to wait until I returned to the United States.

My Moscow experience—we lived there from mid-1969 until the end of 1971—left a permanent imprint on me, as it did on every western journalist who worked there during the repressive era following the 1968 Soviet invasion of Czechoslovakia. Thanks to Al Meyer, who had encouraged me to study Russian in college, I soon felt at ease speaking the language. Without the ability to speak and understand Russian, I doubt that I would have learned anything about the country in an era when the political climate inhibited all contacts between Russians and foreigners. The Brezhnev gerontocracy was cracking down on all political dissidents, including the first wave of Jews who wished to emigrate, and it was impossible for anyone living in the Soviet Union at the time, whether Russian or foreigner, to imagine that, only fifteen years later, a Soviet leader would embrace many of the basic principles espoused by the dissidents of the sixties—freedom of speech, freedom of religion, and the freedom to leave.

An eye-opener for me was my first exposure to good old-fashioned Eastern European and Russian anti-Semitism. Whether a foreign correspondent was a Jew or not mattered greatly to Russians of widely varying political views. If you ran afoul of the press department of the Foreign Ministry, which monitored all articles by western correspondents, you could often expect some allusion to your Jewish origins. My husband was actually called a "cosmopolitan"—a code word for Jews that had heralded anti-Semitic campaigns throughout the Stalin era—in an article in the newspaper *Trud*.

Nonofficial Russians would question me endlessly about my family background when they learned that my maiden name, which I always used professionally, was Jacoby (*Yakobi*, in Russian, is invariably a Jewish name). What "nationality" (the word Soviets used for what Americans call ethnicity) was my mother? Why had my father converted to Christianity? Was it true that in America there were no barriers to the practice of the Jewish religion? Did a *Yakobi* have any trouble getting into a university? Quotas in higher education were not a memory but a living reality, and a major impediment to their ambitions, for young Soviet Jews. Sometimes, Russians who did not know I was a *Yakobi*—who assumed, because of my blond hair (only my hairdresser knew for sure) and blue-gray eyes, that I was a full-blooded gentile—would express their conviction that the American press, banks, and political establishment were controlled by Jews. More important than these stereotypes was what I came to think of as the Flicker—an expression that said "gotcha"—when I would dispute the assertions and add, "I'd be telling you this even if my father weren't Jewish." The Flicker said, "Ah, so that explains why you care so much about dissidents and Jews who want to leave their motherland. Of course. You're one too. And you're all troublemakers." Jewishness mattered as much to the Russian philo-Semites we knew (and we knew many in Moscow) as it did to the anti-Semites. The difference between living in Moscow and living in Washington was that nothing to do with Jews was ever treated matter-of-factly in Russia, as a subject requiring neither defense nor attack. Russian Jews, including those who were party members with good jobs and a secure place in the old Soviet system, also behaved differently toward western journalists who were known to be Jews. I remember one long interview with a school principal, Isak Borisovich Piratsky, a creative educator who demonstrated that it was possible, even within a centralized bureaucratic system, to work with initiative and integrity. Piratsky made a point of walking Tony and me out to our car, so that no one could possibly overhear (or record) what we were talking about. "*Nu, tovarishchi,*" he said (giving the word for "comrades" a meaning very different from its usual political connotation), "you should know that not all Russian Jews want to leave their country. What I would wish is to change my country so Jews wouldn't want to leave it." Then he suggested that we go to Moscow's central synagogue to observe the celebration of Simchat Torah, the Jewish holiday that marks the end of one annual cycle of reading the Torah and the beginning of the next. On that day, secular Jews (joined by the tiny community of observant Jews remaining in Moscow at that time) gathered in the street outside to sing, dance, and proclaim their cultural, if not religious, affiliation. Piratsky's mention of the celebration was in itself a significant statement of his political orientation, signifying that he was what Russians then called an *inakomis-lyashchi* (one who thinks differently). On Simchat Torah, the street outside the synagogue would be filled with people who, though few of them had crossed the dangerous line into open political dissent, were willing to let their presence register their alienation from the official system. The crowds, which grew larger every year, also included many non-Jews with dissident political views. During this period, there was a great deal of overlap between the emerging Jewish emigration movement and the dissidents who were committed to remaining in and changing their native land; both groups agreed that the freedom to emigrate (and to return without penalty) was a crucial right that all Soviet citizens had long been denied by their government. Outside the synagogue on Archipov Street, the number of KGB agents observing the crowd also increased every year. It was on Simchat Torah that Tony and I first heard a song lampooning the folk belief that Jews control everything. "The Jews, the Jews, the Jews encircle us everywhere" was the refrain of the song written by Vladimir Vysotsky, whose satirical verses were known to everyone even though they were never officially published or recorded. My favorite verse, which scans both in English and Russian, went, "Even Khrushchev, glory to God, used to run to the synagogue." Had he not been a party member and a school principal, Piratsky undoubtedly would have been among those celebrating a Jewish holiday they had never observed in a religious sense. "Shalom," he said as he waved good-bye to us in front of his school.

In Moscow, I also met Jews born in Poland, Lithuania, Latvia, Ukraine, and Byelorussia, who had survived the Holocaust because they managed to flee eastward just ahead of the invading Nazi armies in June 1941. After the war, they remained in Moscow because most of them had married Russians—and because they had nothing to go back to: The once-vibrant Jewish communities of Lvov, Riga, Vilna, Minsk, Bialystok, Lodz, and Warsaw had been reduced to human ashes. These Jews were, on the one hand, grateful to the Soviet Union for saving their lives, but they were also bitter because the Soviet government had never acknowledged the special nature of Jewish suffering under the Nazis. At the time, the official Soviet posture was not to distinguish between the Jewish victims of the Nazis and the other Soviet citizens who perished. The result of this policy was the imposition of a public silence about the Holocaust: In a country filled with conspicuous memorials in tribute to the immense sacrifices and suffering of the Soviet people during World War II, there were no monuments, as the poet Yevgeny Yevtushenko wrote in his famous poem, at places like Babi Yar. In that infamous ravine outside Kiev, more than 100,000 Soviet citizens, most of them Jews, were shot, their corpses falling over the edge and piling atop one another until the earth could hold no more. At the beginning of the massacre, more than 33,000 Jews were marched out of Kiev and murdered in just two days. Germans did the shooting, and Ukrainian collaborators (according to many firsthand accounts) helped keep the Jews in line while they awaited their fate. During my years in the Soviet Union, it was nearly impossible to persuade an official guide to stop at Babi Yar. Visiting Kiev, we had to elude our official chaperones, who reported to the KGB, in order to drive out to the ravine with a dissident friend. (Babi Yar does have a memorial today; Mikhail Gorbachev's *glasnost* put an end to the long official silence concerning the fate of Jews in Nazi-occupied portions of the Soviet Union.)

From time to time, Russian friends (many of them survivors of Stalin's gulag) would take me to meet non-Russian Jewish survivors who had, through odd combinations of circumstance, moved eastward instead of westward after their liberation by the Red Army. One of these Jews, who became a good friend in spite of the constrictions on relationships between foreigners and Soviet citizens, had what was, for me, the most resonant story. I tell it now, as she once asked me to, because she and her family are finally beyond the reach of any adverse official "consequences" (as she put it) from the now-defunct Soviet government.

•   •   •

KATYA STEIN MOROZOVA (her name has been changed) was born in Budapest in 1924 into a nonobservant, assimilated German-speaking Jewish family. Her father was a doctor, her mother a secondary-school teacher of German and English. When I met her, in 1969, she looked extraordinarily young for a woman who had spent her entire adult life in the Soviet Union, where women in their forties generally bore the marks of having lived through hard times and looked like American women in their sixties. This was all the more remarkable in view of the suffering that had preceded Katya's life in Moscow.

Until 1944, under the independent Hungarian government of the fascist Nicholas Horthy, Katya and her family, like most Hungarian Jews, remained relatively unharmed, a small island in a sea of Nazi mass murder. During this period, Katya's father had the foresight to obtain forged papers for her, including a baptismal certificate bearing a non-Jewish name. Should the Nazis ever occupy Hungary, he thought, his blond, blue-eyed daughter would be protected by the documents. In March 1944, with the Russians advancing from the East, the Nazi army finally occupied Hungary. But the forged papers did Katya no good; she became prey for the Nazis not because she was a Jew but because she was a young woman. The beautiful twenty-year-old was scooped up by a German military police patrol while she was walking down the street and was then forced into service in a brothel for troops on leave from the front. This lovely, sheltered daughter of cultivated parents was sterilized without anesthesia.

"I thought constantly of suicide, and I am sure it would have come to pass were it not for one young German soldier. They were each allowed fifteen minutes, and your worst fear was that a soldier would make a bad report about you, that you had not been enthusi-astic enough. This young man came to me—he could not have been more than sixteen or seventeen, by then the Germans were throwing babies at the Russian troops—unzipped his pants, and climbed on. But he didn't do anything. '*Fräulein*,' he said, 'please be quiet.' Can you understand what that meant, being called *Fräulein*, told 'please' in a civilized way, in that place? He said that he could not do this thing, he was sure he was going to be killed in battle, and he could not go to be judged by God with such a sin on his conscience. But it had to look to the others as if he were taking his pleasure with me, or it might go badly for both of us. I understood, of course. In his mouth he had chocolates, and he passed them to me when he pretended to kiss me. This, too, was a miracle for the starving. He told me his name was Kurt, that he came from Stuttgart, and that I must try to live, to survive the war to tell people what the Nazis had done. No German could ever expect forgiveness in this world, he said, but he hoped for forgiveness in the next. I told him, 'Your God'—this was a slip that could have revealed I was a Jew, saying *your* God rather than simply *God*—'will surely have mercy on you.' He thanked me— *he* thanked *me*—he left, and that was the end of it, but this moment of kindness gave me the courage to go on living. I tried to keep myself clean, so as not to catch a disease from the soldiers, and be shot or deported to the gas, if the weekly test showed I was infected. When people say that all Germans are monsters, as many people in Russia do, I know this is not so. At least one German was not a monster."

Katya served as a *Feldhüre*, as the Germans branded the women they forced into prostitution, until she was liberated by the advancing Red Army in October 1944. Almost unimaginably to the tormented women left behind by their Nazi captors, the Russian soldiers took up where the Germans left off and began a new orgy of rape. "Just when it looks like we are all going to die a second time," Katya said, "I saw Misha for the first time." Misha was a Red Army captain, and he soon put an end to the rampaging of his troops by ordering summary public executions for all soldiers who raped, assaulted, or robbed civilians. When he saw Katya, who by then weighed less than eighty pounds, it was apparently love at first sight. Standing six feet tall, he picked her up in his arms and carried her to a field hospital behind the Soviet lines. He must have had high-level connections, because he somehow managed to acquire sulfa (virtually unobtainable anywhere in war-torn Europe, much less Russia) to treat her pneumonia. When the war ended, Misha (who was not Jewish, Katya informed me at our first meeting) tracked Katya down in a makeshift displaced persons' camp and they were married. He was twenty-two years older than Katya and had retired, by the time I met them, as a full colonel.

In 1948, the couple adopted two Jewish children from an orphanage in Moscow. Katya's parents and the rest of her relatives had all been deported to Auschwitz and gassed in Adolf Eichmann's eleventh-hour roundup of Hungarian Jews, the last large surviving Jewish community in Europe, in the spring of 1944. "My husband and children reconciled me to life again," Katya said. In Moscow, Katya learned Russian and followed in her father's footsteps by studying medicine and becoming an obstetrician. It was the best profession she could have chosen, though her husband had worried that bringing babies into the world would be a painful reminder of her inability to have her own.

"Just the opposite," she said. "With each baby I helped into this life, I felt that I was repairing the ruined world. And if it was a Jewish baby, I felt this twice over. This was why I specifically chose Jewish children to adopt." It took only a few minutes with Katya to realize that here was a great soul, one whose experiences had only served to magnify her compassion and empathy. "When Misha asked me to marry him, I at first said no because I was uncertain that I could ever be a normal, loving wife—you understand, after what had happened I was not certain I could ever happily be with a man again. He said he would take his chances, he had enough love for both of us. His wife had died of starvation during the siege of Leningrad, and their only son had been killed in the first year of the war. What I remember is the first time Misha and I were together, I wept when I realized, yes, I could still be with a man and feel happiness, and give happiness. I knew then that I had not just survived, I was still alive, and the Germans had not killed the thing inside that makes a *chelovek* (human)."

Katya saw nothing ironic about the fact that her particular fate had been determined not by her Jewishness but by her womanhood. "*Vsyo ravno* (it's all the same)," she said. "Once someone made the remark to me, 'Well, your father made quite a mistake, didn't he. You never would have been taken to the German soldiers if they had known you were a Jew.' Such ignorance! What mistake? My family all went to the gas. I am here, having *pirozhki* with you, with a husband who has cared for me all my life, two beautiful children, and some-day, maybe grandchildren. My father chose from the many bad choices available to a Jew in those days."

Katya's husband, who had of course always known about every-thing that happened to her, was not happy that she had broken her silence of many years and felt what he saw as a mysterious "compul-sion" to tell her story to carefully selected people. This was an understandable fear on his part. Katya's account had many elements (not the least of them the behavior of certain Soviet soldiers during the liberation) that could do a Soviet citizen no good if the authori-ties somehow learned what she was saying. But Misha never tried to stop Katya from doing anything she really wanted to do, and he bowed to her wishes even though he was baffled by her need to dig up the past. Finally, Katya told me something I already suspected: the blond (now silver-haired) Red Army officer had a Jewish mother. Even though he was a graduate of the prestigious Frunze Military Academy and a much-decorated war hero, Misha would not have risen to the rank of colonel had he not used his father's Russian "nationality" on his internal passport. (Soviet citizens of "mixed" backgrounds were allowed to choose the nationality of either parent for registration on their internal passports, mandatory identity cards used for everything from travel within the country to school enrollment. Most Russian half-Jews, mindful of official and unofficial anti-Semitism, chose to be registered as Russians.) Half-Jews with Russian names and Slavic features, like Misha, were extremely care-ful about disclosing the Jewish side of their backgrounds. They needed time to gauge the attitudes of foreigners (and, for that matter, other Soviet citizens), to decide whether they could be trusted, before revealing their true heritage.

Katya was well aware of the emerging Jewish emigration movement in the Soviet Union. She herself would never wish to leave, she said, but she hoped that one day it might be possible for her children to emigrate. Although they bore the Russian name of their adoptive father, they looked Jewish and had been subjected to anti-Semitic comments, and physical assaults by "hooligans" (as Russians used to call teenage toughs), throughout their lives. Katya was extremely interested in my family story (what I knew of it at the time), for her own family in Hungary had been filled with Catholic converts. The intermarriage rate for non-Orthodox Jews in prewar Hungary was quite high; Katya's father had four sisters, and three of them married gentiles. None, however, had escaped the Holocaust. Katya urged me, on my return to the United States, to try to find out more about what had happened to the Jacobys in the nineteenth century. "There are always consequences, consequences that can never be anticipated, for pretending that you are someone you aren't, or you aren't someone you are," she observed when we met for the last time before I left the Soviet Union. Her own family's attachment to German culture, and her aunts' belief that they would be protected by their marriages to Christians, had led them to underestimate the nature of the threat from Hitler's Germany. Katya herself had come to feel that Jews must never again be deluded into thinking that they could conceal their Jewishness through conversion or complete assimilation. This deepening conviction played an important role in Katya's refusal to abide by her husband's wishes that she keep her story to herself. What had happened to her as a woman, she emphasized repeatedly, had happened within the context of Jewish extermination. "Even in that place," she said, "I knew things would go far, far worse for me if they ever found out I was a Jew. I tell my children, 'You can't write yourself out of Jewish history.'"

Soon after I left Moscow, Katya's husband died of a heart attack. She died of breast cancer in 1983, at the age of fifty-nine, but lived long enough to enjoy the company of her four grandchildren. In 1987, taking advantage of the looser emigration policies under Mikhail Gorbachev, her sons fulfilled their mother's dream by emigrating with their children to the United States. I carried Katya's story inside me for many years, mindful that in the absence of her protective and well-connected husband, Katya and her family might still be harmed by Soviet officialdom.

I HAVE THOUGHT often of Katya while sifting through the layers of conversion and assimilation that make up the Jacoby family's history. I find it easy to imagine German or Czech or Hungarian versions of my father, aunt, and uncle embarking on their adult lives in the early 1930s in Berlin or Prague or Budapest. I see them marrying Christians and identifying themselves with the same cosmopolitan culture as their non-Jewish contemporaries. What would Uncle Ozzie have done in Berlin in 1935, had he already been married to a Catholic and fathered a son classified as a first-degree *Mischling* under the Nuremberg Laws? Would he have gotten out, right away, with his Catholic wife and son? Or would he have told himself, as Katya's father and aunts did in neighboring Hungary, that this was the twentieth century and that it was quite impossible to imagine the repeal of Jewish emancipation—not to mention civilization itself?

I asked Uncle Ozzie, after my return from Moscow, whether he had ever considered any of these questions during the period around the end of the war, when the full horror of what the Nazis had done to the Jews of Europe was being revealed. He cocked his head and looked at me as if I were asking him whether he had ever considered what it would be like to live on Mars. "I'm not sure what you mean," he replied. "Like everyone, I found it hard to believe when the first news of the camps came out, how human beings were capable of doing what the Nazis did. But if you mean did I ever think, 'That could have been me,' or asked myself what I would have done if I'd been a Jew in Germany, the answer is no, it never really occurred to me. It didn't really have anything to do with me, because my grandfather got out of Europe in the 1840s." Uncle Ozzie may well have been the least introspective person I have ever known, but this conversation, which took place in 1975, suggests a degree of emotional obtuseness that still baffles me when I look at my notes. In some respects, Ozzie's relationship to his own Jewishness was much more complex than my father's, because he lived in two worlds and my father lived in one. Ozzie's professional life on the tournament bridge circuit was spent among sophisticated and generally liberal people, who simply assumed that he (like many of them) was Jewish, while his family life in Dallas unfolded in a far more conservative environment than my father's life in Michigan. Dad's cronies at the Sip'n Snack in Okemos, who breakfasted together once a week after their early-morning golf game, were (like my father himself) middle-of-the-road small businessmen bemused by the social upheavals of the sixties but flexible enough to try to figure out what was going on with their children. Most were lukewarm postwar Republicans who had voted for Eisenhower in the fifties and for Richard Nixon in 1960 (though my father voted for Kennedy) but had found Barry Goldwater far too conservative for their taste in 1964. If they voted for Nixon again in 1968, it was not because they were opposed to the Democratic social programs of the era but because Hubert Humphrey was too closely identified with the Vietnam War. The main concern of these men was to keep their draft-age sons out of a war that disturbed them deeply—not least because, as veterans of what they all considered an entirely just war, they had never imagined a time when they would encourage their boys to avoid military service. If any of my dad's friends suspected that he was Jewish, they regarded this as a matter of little consequence. He was one of them.

The denizens of the Dallas Country Club, where Ozzie twitted his cardplaying cronies about their enthusiasm for Goldwater, were another matter altogether. Many of the club members were ultra-conservatives who, as Ozzie himself told me, "were only sorry that Kennedy was shot because it gave Dallas a bad name." Fifty years ago, they would certainly not have allowed a Jew into their club—

and these were men who paid the closest attention to race, ethnicity, and religion—unless he was as famous and as fond of high-stakes gambling as my uncle. One thing I never understood about Ozzie was his ability to sit around a table and joke with men to whom words like *wetback*, *nigger*, and *sheeny* came as naturally as a taste for barbecue and neat bourbon. Ozzie was simply a master of compartmentalization: he took what he wanted from people (in this case, the free-and-easy Good Old Boy love of gambling) and ignored what didn't suit him. My father would have flown into a rage—I saw him do it often enough when people made racist comments—if anyone had joked about the Kennedy assassination in his presence.

Ozzie's home environment, as a result of Aunt Mary's devoutness, was also more Catholic than my father's. It was always understood, for instance, that my cousins Jon and Jim would go to a Catholic college (they both did their undergraduate work at Notre Dame). I once asked Jim, who was thirteen at the time of the Nuremberg trials, whether he remembered having any of the kinds of conversations about the Holocaust that I had with my father while I was growing up. Although Jim remembered many discussions of battles, he could not recall anything special having been said about the concentration camps. "I knew that the Nazis had murdered millions of people in those camps," he told me, "and I knew they were mostly Jews. But I didn't connect it in any way with my father's family. I never had any sense that you say you did, of something being left out of my father's stories about growing up. But that may be because he wasn't around as much as your dad was. I never thought of myself as anything other than a Catholic, because that was the way my mom brought me up. And it was very clear that she was the one in charge of raising the children."

My father, too, said he never gave any thought to the juxtaposition of his own conversion with the still-recent revelation of Hitler's genocidal war against the Jews. "If I had thought about it at all," he said, "I would have thought that it [the Holocaust] proved my father was right, that no good could come from identifying yourself with a

people that had been so victimized, had suffered so much." Unlike
Ozzie, my father began to have second thoughts (not about his conversion but about his assumption that conversion could eradicate his
Jewishness) around the time of the Eichmann trial. It still puzzles me
that it took him so long to accept what had been clear since the history of Hitler's war against the Jews began to unfold during the
Nuremberg trials—that "race" and "blood," not religion, had been
the determining factor in the targeting of Jews for extermination.
Conversions and intermarriages had only served to delay the closing
of the vise around most members of the Jewish "race." In the end, to
stand my dad's observation on its head, little good came to the Jews
who did *not* identify with their own people. By the mid-seventies,
though, my father had altered his thinking and come to the conclusion that his father had been badly mistaken in his belief that assimilation, and abandonment of any connection to religious Judaism,
would eventually rule out the possibility that his family would ever
be identified as Jews. "You're proof of that," he said tartly. "I'd say
you're carrying a Jewish gene if it didn't make me sound like a Nazi."

My dad continued to be a reasonably observant (much more so
than my mother), if hardly devout, Catholic until the end of his life.
He believed in God, and in his view, Catholicism was as good as any
other religion. Twenty-five years ago, when I was in my late twenties, it drove me wild when Dad would talk that way. Holocaust
scholars were beginning to uncover the record of all that the Roman
Catholic Church had not done to protest the Nazis' treatment of
Jews. I felt an unquenchable anger at the Church in which I was
raised as the unfolding historical record showed that Roman Catholic
officialdom throughout Europe had reserved its concern primarily
for Jewish converts to Catholicism. Hearing about the noble exceptions—such as the shelter offered by individual convents and monas-
teries throughout Europe, or the unremitting efforts of many Italian
clergymen outside the Vatican (from cardinals on down) to rescue
Jews from deportation—only made me angrier. What if the Church
hierarchy in Poland and France had demonstrated as much concern

for all Jews as the Catholic clergy did after the Nazis occupied north-
ern Italy? My distress about the role of the Church was not based on
the mistaken notion that Protestants in Europe had treated Jews
with great benevolence during the war; I cared more about the
Catholic record because I was still struggling to come to terms with
my own religious upbringing and with my father's decision to convert. This concern was, perhaps, an ironic remnant of the pride-filled
"I-am-a-Catholic" training in parochial school; Catholics, the nuns
always said, must judge and be judged according to a higher standard
than that applied to people of other faiths.

The more I learned about the role of the Church in most of Nazi-
occupied Europe, the more trouble I had comprehending how a Jew,
any Jew, of whatever degree of deracination, could have converted to
Catholicism in the aftermath of the Holocaust. And yet it happened
often enough—and even among camp survivors themselves—to
have produced a growing body of memoirs by children of Holocaust
survivors for whom the subject of conversion is fraught with far
more pain and danger than the American-born Jacoby converts could
ever have imagined.

To this day, however, I still do not understand how my father,
while taking instruction in the Faith, could have accepted his priest's
flippant rationalization of the deicide charge against Jews with the
remark that if Jesus had been born in America instead of Jerusalem,
he would have been denounced and crucified by Indians. Relations
between Jews and Catholics (as well as other Christian denominations) have improved immeasurably during the past forty years, and
the change would never have taken place without the Church's
explicit repudiation of the teaching that Jews, as a people, bore
responsibility for the crucifixion of Christ. But the alteration in the
Church's attitude toward Jews was part of the spirit of *aggiornamento*
fostered by Pope John XXIII in the early sixties; the transition had not
even begun during the period when my aunt, father, and uncle converted to Catholicism. The deicide accusation was not, as my father
implied, some irrelevant theological formality but the very heart of

the historical Christian (not only Catholic) animus toward Jews. At
the time my father and I were watching the Eichmann trial on television, various Protestant and Catholic publications, arguing against
the death penalty for the defendant, brazenly compared the proceedings to the condemnation of Jesus. "The difference in the two trials,"
declared an article in a prominent Episcopal publication, *The Witness*,
"is that Eichmann's condemnation does not save a single man from
bondage and service to death, while the condemnation of the other
defendant [Jesus] set men free from death and from the power of
death in their own sin." Attitudes informed by this view of Jews—
and of their historical responsibility for the murder of Christ—were
not universal, but neither were they rare among Christian clergymen
during the era when my father and his siblings first embraced
Catholicism.

I have always disliked the term "self-hating Jew," and I dislike
it even more today because it most commonly appears as a label
applied by right-wing Jewish fundamentalists to anyone who does
not share their narrow and repressive view of what one must do to
live honorably as a Jew. (*Fundamentalist* is a better term for these people than *ultra-Orthodox*, because the latter term—even with an
"ultra" in front—does not apply to the millions of Orthodox Jewish
believers who would not presume to use their own standards of
observance as a measure of who is, and is not, a Jew.) In any event,
"self-hatred" is far too gross a term to describe my father's motivation. Shame, not self-hatred, was the emotion that enveloped my dad
when, out of nowhere (as he saw it), he was beaten and called a kike
in the schoolyard. It is a particularly shaming, and confusing, experience for a child to be persecuted for belonging to a group, a religion,
a cultural tradition that he has been raised to regard as utterly alien.
What was remarkable about my father, in view of his upbringing, is
that he made a real attempt, at a stage in life when it is difficult to
reexamine anything, to understand and come to terms with the profound self-doubt generated by the vacuum in which he was raised.
My dad often expressed the conviction that a preoccupation with the

Holocaust was not the best way for me to honor the Jewish side of my heritage. "I'm not sure exactly what I'm talking about," he said with uncharacteristic hesitancy, "but I think it's . . . well, kind of a dead end to consider yourself a Jew because Hitler would have sent you to the ovens along with all of the full-blooded Jews. It's . . . it's like letting Hitler define the terms. Holocaust, Holocaust, Holocaust—well, it seems to me that being a Jew has to mean something more."

This conversation took place at some point in the late 1970s, when my father was in his early sixties and I was in my early thirties. I was old enough to listen, and he was old enough to talk in ways that he—and we—had never talked before.

XI

Principles

⌒

"AND SO, WHAT DO YOU consider yourself now?" The question was posed in 1984 by a rabbi who had invited me to speak about my recently published book, *Wild Justice: The Evolution of Revenge*, at a current events forum sponsored by his Reform congregation in Scranton, Pennsylvania. In *Wild Justice*, I had discussed the pejorative Christian identification of Judaism with "Old Testament vengeance," an identification based largely on a superficial and selective reading of the famous "eye for eye" passage in Exodus. The rabbi—an expansive man whom I remember fondly because he paid his speakers not by check but in cash, pulling out $100 bills from the safe in his office— was interested in my family story because his own congregation included many descendants of assimilated German Jews like Max Jacoby. A few had returned to Judaism after generations of conversions in their own families (though not, the rabbi hastened to add, conversions to Catholicism). Most of his sheep had returned from Episcopalian or Unitarian folds. He asked, with some hesitation, whether I had ever thought of converting to Judaism, a step that would be required under *Halachah* (Jewish law) to gather a half-Jew with a gentile mother into the embrace of Judaism. Hating to disappoint the rabbi, I gently told him no, that I was an atheist who would be as out of place at Shabbas services as I had long been at Mass. I believe this was the first time I ever used the uncompromising "atheist" rather than the less certain (by definition) "agnostic" or the wishy-washier "skeptic."

Make no mistake about it: to most Americans, *atheist* is an epithet, rather than a reasonable and honorable self-description. It is impossible to imagine anyone running successfully for the American presidency after declaring that he or she does not believe in God. Unlike Europeans, Americans generally view atheists as disturbers of the peace on the one hand (those grinches who want to spoil everyone's Christmas by keeping carols out of the schools), or pitiable crackpots on the other. More than once, newspaper editors have suggested that I strike the word *atheist* from personal essays because "it makes you sound like an extremist."

A significant number of my contemporaries, mindful of the American cultural injunction to believe in some Higher Power but unwilling to subject themselves to the demands of a traditional religion with an internal logic, have embraced New Age mush. With its prattle about a "Universal Spirit," New Age religion—which bears the same relationship to traditional religion as New Age music does to a Bach fugue—offers the befuddled a comforting set of associations requiring no intellectual consistency. This bland form of "spirituality" is far more acceptable in American culture than atheism, which does have an internal logic and, above all, demands consistency. I do not share the doctrinaire and self-congratulatory view of atheism as externally and objectively verifiable, à la "scientific communism" as defined by the onetime priests of the Soviet Union; I am quite willing to concede that mine is a theology like any other. I often try to dodge the so-what-are-you-now question, because any reference to atheism is frequently greeted by, "Oh, you mean you're nothing."

The rabbi, however, deserved an honest reply. And being a man of both secular and sacred Jewish tradition, he was not taken aback by the A-word. "Well, you can be a Jewish atheist," he said cheerfully. "It's certainly not outside Jewish history." "Half-Jewish," I reminded him. He countered: "Don't you think it's your Jewish half that made you an atheist?"

IT WOULD be much easier to write an ending to the story of my family if mine were one of the "return-to-religion" odysseys so characteristic of my generation. I have friends who, after at least two decades of nonobservance, can now be found at Mass on a fair number of Sundays or in temple not only on the High Holy Days but on ordinary Sabbaths. Whether this new observance will metamorphose into a permanent and fundamental change of heart and habit, to be passed on to the next generation, or whether it is merely another hyped, evanescent stage in the baby boom generation's progression from cradle to grave, remains to be seen.

"Reverse converts"—those who have returned to a faith originally held by their ancestors but obliterated by accident or by design—occupy a much smaller and special place among the rediscoverers of religion. Their stories have a powerful symmetry and a powerful emotional appeal, especially for American Jews, as a minority threatened not by persecution but by generations of assimilation and intermarriage. Such journeys suggest a continuity and permanence in which most of us want to believe. They also imply that nothing is ever really lost—that a family like mine, so careless of its heritage and its gifts, can reconnect with its past if only someone has the will to do so.

Christian conversions *to* Judaism, virtually nonexistent in the history of European Jewry, have also become a small but significant factor in the current mix of American Jews. Most of these new converts to Judaism are formerly Christian women married to Jewish men, and a few are half-Jews, with gentile mothers, who were required by Jewish law, as I would be, to undergo formal conversion in order to return to the faith their fathers (or grandfathers) had abandoned.

When children are involved, such conversions represent a real alternative to the confusing arrangement described by a couple interviewed for a 1997 *Newsweek* cover story on mixed marriages. "We're going to position this as 'Daddy likes this and Mommy likes that,' " declared a Wisconsin management consultant, raised a Methodist and married to a Jewish woman. *Newsweek* reported that the couple's four-month-old son had undergone neither a ritual circumcision nor a baptism but an ecumenical "dedication" at a Chicago church. "He'll get exposed to both [religions]," the father declared, "and won't be overdosed in either." O my America! In this brave new nation, religion is not an organic way of being in the world but something, to use the language of marketing, that a parent must "position."

If I believed in any god, it would be the God of the Jews. If I could be consoled by any prayer, the Kaddish would be my first choice. But the possibility of religious consolation was closed to me long ago—not by my parents' mixed marriage but by my own nature. Had I grown up in a somewhat observant Jewish home (I can so easily see my father as either a Conservative or a Reform Jew) and been exposed to a good dose of Hebrew school, I am quite certain that I would still have turned out to be a nonbeliever. I would have choked on the *El Mole Rachamim—God, full of mercy*—as I used to choke on Catholic prayers when I was old enough to comprehend the meaning of evil. As a Jewish child raised by Jewish parents, I may have been even less disposed than I was as a Catholic child to believe in the mercy of a God who was allowing other Jewish babies to be murdered while I was thriving in my mother's womb. I cannot honor the Jewish side of me by embracing Judaism as a religion, but my father was right when he suggested that "Jewish identity" cannot be based solely on remembering the Holocaust. "Never again" is a noble admonition, but it does not provide an intricate, authentic pattern for a life. By the early 1980s, when I was working on *Wild Justice*, which drew heavily on my Catholic background as well as on my newer interest in Jewish law and philosophy, my pattern was emerging more clearly. But my search, and my dialogue with my father, had been delayed for some years by the marriage that began with a busman's honeymoon in Russia.

THE FORM OF my wedding to Tony Astrachan, on June 22, 1969, was one manifestation of the confusion engendered by my (and, in a very different way, his) upbringing. I was the first Jacoby in two generations to marry a Jew, but the wedding was celebrated in the inner-city Episcopal church of St. Stephen's and the Incarnation, by a close friend who was also an Episcopal minister. It was the kind of half-baked ecumenical service, with the outward form but none of the inner substance of religion, that began to proliferate in the sixties. Such services were made to order for couples disinclined to confront sticky questions of exactly what they believed and what the ceremony represented. Tony's parents, Irving and Manley Aaron Astrachan, were not merely secularists but committed atheists; they had nothing but disdain for the sort of German Jews, like my great-grandfather, who had opted for Ethical Culture as an easy way out of traditional Jewish observance. But Tony, unlike his parents, did believe in God. In 1945, he had insisted on a bar mitzvah—much to the dismay of Manley and Irv, who had to join a temple so that their son could make his formal entry into Jewish manhood. Astonishingly (in retrospect), Tony and I never really discussed the decision to be married in a Protestant church. He was emphatic about not wanting to be married by a judge—his first marriage, which, like mine, ended in divorce, had been a hastily arranged civil ceremony—and he wanted a "real" wedding this time. In Washington during the sixties, it would have been difficult (though certainly not impossible) to find a rabbi willing to violate *Halachah* by marrying a Jew to the daughter of a non-Jewish mother. Our apostate Christian service satisfied Tony's desire for ceremony and acknowledgment of a Supreme Being. I was so much in love, at twenty-four, that I would probably have married Tony (to paraphrase Uncle Ozzie's description of his wedding) in front of a Druid altar. That my acquiescence in this ceremony represented a denial of some of my deepest convictions, and was therefore a poor way to begin a marriage, was a harbinger of trouble that I did not see at the time.

My Washington wedding had brought together both sides of my family for the first time in many years. My brother and parents made the trip to Washington from Michigan; my still-vigorous Broderick grandparents flew in from Chicago; Uncle Ozzie dropped by en route from Dallas to yet another bridge tournament; and Aunt Edith and Uncle Ted tore themselves away from Staten Island for the day. This would turn out to be the last family occasion to bring my father, aunt, and uncle together under the same roof.

The Jacobys, Brodericks, and Astrachans voiced no reservations about this wedding. My in-laws, who were married by a judge in 1926, had already seen their son through one broken marriage to a shiksa. What was one more non-Jewish wedding in the scheme of things? My Broderick grandparents saw nothing strange about the service; they had, after all, watched my mother marry my father in a Lutheran church. Even Aunt Edith and Uncle Ted, the most devout Catholics on hand, seemed content. After all, the semi-Episcopal service sounded something like a Catholic marriage ceremony without the Mass. (Ted's only comment on the wedding and the reception was that he had never seen so many black people together at one time except in the news photographs of the crowd listening to Martin Luther King's "I have a dream" speech. Tony and I probably did have an unusually large number of African-American friends, because we both belonged to Washington's integrated Capital Press Club. The organization had been founded as an alternative to the National Press Club, because the latter institution had a virtually all-white membership at the time and was also closed to women.) My father-in-law's best friend took my hand outside the church and said, "I'd give anything to have a woman look at me just once in my lifetime the way you looked at Tony in there." Who would have been churlish enough to spoil such a joyful and promising day with talk or thoughts of religious and nonreligious principles?

. . .

THE SEVENTIES, during which the feminist movement forced a continuous reconsideration and renegotiation of privileges and obligations between men and women, were hard on all marriages. Settling in New York after our return from Moscow in 1972, Tony and I lived in a world in which unions of much longer duration than ours—marriages with children to be considered—were collapsing all around us. An additional problem was our shared profession, even though our journalistic interests and experiences also created a powerful bond between us. While we were never in direct competition for the same job or the same writing assignment, we were engaged in a fierce indirect contest in which we measured our work, and our professional selves, against each other. This was an abrasive, corrosive, and ultimately exhausting process that made it necessary for us to divorce in order to save a remnant of the love, respect, and common enthusiasms we had brought to our marriage. The zeitgeist of the Me Decade was, to be sure, the main factor in our divorce, but the huge blank spaces in my father's and his family's history—and the persistent sense of insecurity he had communicated to me—also played a role. Many years would pass before I began to understand that I had been raised on the unspoken (and all the more powerful for being unspoken) message that malleability in the pursuit of social mobility is no vice. Had I not been my father's daughter, I would not have entered a marriage in which my husband and I had failed to discuss something as important as the reasons why we were pledging ourselves to each other in a Christian sanctuary where neither of us truly belonged. While Tony and I were in the process of a sorrowful but nonrancorous divorce in the late seventies, I told a friend that I hadn't wanted to veto a church wedding, and spoil everyone's pleasure in the occasion, by taking an antireligious stance that was, after all, based on an abstract principle that had little to do with everyday life. "But people *are* their principles," she replied. That is an overstatement, but I cannot deny that my views on religion, while they have little to do with quotidian matters, have had a great deal to do with what I hold most dear in life—with the people I love and the passions that engage me as a writer. It is now difficult for me to recapture the state of mind that allowed me to begin a marriage by setting aside one of my most deeply held—yes, sacred—convictions. People are more (and frequently less) than the sum of their principles, but some principles matter more than others.

DURING MY thirties, while my marriage unraveled and I moved from straightforward journalism to more analytical historical writing, I began to comprehend, bit by bit, the impact of the unfinished business in my father's family on my own life. This was due in part to living in New York City, the first place where I had ever felt completely at home. In an environment with the thrillingly high human decibel level I remembered from my childhood visits, I fitted in in a way I never had anywhere else. And I saw that my dad, after more than thirty-five years in the Midwest, had remained a New Yorker in many respects. When my parents visited me in Manhattan, my mother would become anxious when two strangers started arguing with each other on the street. Only recently, when I fell into a mild dispute with a fellow bus passenger about Mayor Rudolph Giuliani's pedestrian barricades and attitude toward political demonstrations—all right, so I might have compared His Honor to "the little man on the balcony"—my mother turned to me and said, *sotto voce*, "That's a total stranger, why are you opening your mouth? What if he had a gun? Why do you care what he thinks?" "He doesn't have a gun, Mom." "How do you know?"

My dad, by contrast, relished the abrasiveness of New York discourse and easily slipped back into the rhythms of city life—disappearing into the subway, where he remembered all of the stops; shaking his fist at errant (more errant than in his youth) taxi drivers; racing off to the deli on Sunday morning for bagels and lox. He used the word *salmon*, though, instead of the customary New York *lox*. He remembered his mother telling him that salmon was the correct term for what they were eating and that lox was a "vulgar colloquialism." Way too Jewish. My dad told me this with considerable amusement in his voice; by his late sixties, he had begun to view his mother and his upbringing with greater detachment.

During these years, my father, Uncle Ozzie, and Aunt Edith all began to open up more about their childhoods. The idea of writing a book about my father's family began to crystallize during the second half of the seventies. I never explicitly told Dad that I was gathering material for a book, but Uncle Ozzie did know—or rather, he guessed. And his help was invaluable, because he was the only one of the three siblings old enough to have known his grandfather, Max, and to possess such basic information as our common ancestor's first name. Over lunch at the 21 Club—Ozzie's favorite New York restaurant—he cocked his head and skewered me with the intense gray eyes he, my dad, and I had inherited from Eve Jackson Jacoby. "Of course you're writing a book about all this," he said. "I'll help you all I can, ask me anything you want, just make sure to present me in a favorable light for the ages." In his late seventies, Ozzie, having announced and rescinded his "retirement" from bridge on several occasions, had scarcely slowed down at all. Still standing over six feet and boasting a mane of curly white hair, still tripping over his own sentences because his mind moved faster than his tongue, still bubbling with the manic energy he and my father shared, Ozzie always turned up with no warning. He had a constitutional aversion to calling and making plans in advance: if I didn't happen to be home when he was making one of his whirlwind passages through town, he was always surprised and aggrieved. He never came to my apartment and always took me out to eat; his refusals of my invitations for a home-cooked meal were, I suspect, born of his suspicion that I might not satisfy his demands for "white" food. (The only other person I have ever heard of who shared this preoccupation with the color of his food was the Broadway producer Leland Hayward.) Restaurants like 21, where Ozzie had been a customer since the 1930s, catered to his taste for what was essentially baby food—the only exception being his insistence on very rare steak. On the day Ozzie got me to confess that yes, I was writing a book, he was tucking into a repast consisting of chicken hash smothered in cream sauce, creamed corn, and mashed potatoes, followed by a coconut-covered dessert called a snowball. All of this was accompanied by milk. Ozzie shunned alcohol, an abstemiousness attributable not to any drinking problem but to a conditioning regimen he considered necessary to maintain the alertness and stamina required of him during marathon card tournaments. He was also—unusually for a man of his generation—a committed nonsmoker.

My eccentric, and egocentric, uncle really tried to help me. Sometimes the phone would ring because an old memory, usually of something his father told him, had just bobbed to the surface. He called me excitedly one night in the early eighties because he had just recalled his father's bitterness about the exclusion of Jews from social fraternities at Columbia during the 1880s. "Does that help you?" he asked. "I still don't really understand why anyone would care about fraternities, but maybe you can make sense of it." I have absolutely no way of knowing whether Ozzie had been hurt in any way by anti-Semitism; if he had, the experience was buried beneath a monumental self-regard that armed him with a shell of indifference to the opinions of others.

Ozzie demonstrated his thick skin in 1969, when the Internal Revenue Service went after him for more than $250,000 in back taxes on what the IRS claimed were gambling winnings and Ozzie claimed as gambling losses. He promptly filed a lawsuit disputing the IRS's findings. The widely publicized trial, reported in *Time* magazine and *The New York Times* as well as in the Dallas papers, did not involve Ozzie's income from professional bridge tournaments or writing but from his extracurricular gambling activities. (The IRS basically took the position that anyone as successful as my uncle was at professional cardplaying must have been equally successful at after-hours games and must therefore have underreported his income.) One newspaper observed that "the white-haired Jacoby listened with an amused expression" as his wife, Mary Zita, testified that he had lost hundreds of thousands of dollars because he was "like an alcoholic who is drunk. He can't control himself." Aunt Mary testified that Ozzie had cashed in his own life insurance policy, and sold most of her stocks, to make good on his gambling debts. Ozzie had paid off his bookies with checks made out to cash, which the IRS did not regard as sufficient proof of losses. Ozzie told the tax court judge that many of his creditors, who wanted to hide their identity as gamblers, had endorsed his checks with other names or signed their own names in illegible scrawls. Many of his poker losses, he testified, came in high-stakes games—for at least $5 a chip—at the Texas, Petroleum, Cipango, and Dallas country clubs in his home town. Small wonder that his cronies at the Dallas Country Club didn't care that Ozzie was a Jew! Eventually, as is the case with most such disputes, Ozzie and the IRS reached an out-of-court settlement. At the time (and to the end of his life) Ozzie was unrepentant and unashamed. The case had one important domestic outcome, however: Ozzie ceded (or was forced to cede) complete control of the family finances to his wife, whom he dubbed the Boss. He accepted this with equanimity, and although he did not die a wealthy man (which he surely would have had he not been a compulsive gambler), he did die a solvent one.

For my father, as the owner of an accounting business in a small town, the national disclosure of Ozzie's tax problems in *Time* was more than a trifle embarrassing. It is not unreasonable for people to assume that a man's brother might also be his tax preparer (though this was emphatically not the case). Dad had reason to be relieved when Ozzie's real accountant, the unfortunate Harold S. Sparks, was called to testify at the trial. I was living in Moscow at the time of Ozzie's tax travails, but my father told me years later that his chief reaction had not been one of embarrassment but of relief that he was not the one forced to account for gambling losses. "That could have been me—would have been me if I hadn't gotten control of my gambling," he said. "And I wouldn't ever have been able to make enough money to pay off what I owed." I asked Dad if he didn't envy Ozzie because his legitimate earning capacity was large enough for him to eventually make good on his debts. My father looked at me with unfeigned astonishment. "You mean, do I think that if only I were a bridge champion and not an accountant, I could have had the fun of gambling on the side and gotten away with it? Are you serious? That's the kind of thinking that gets people into the hole in the first place. I may have thought that way at thirty, but it wouldn't even occur to me today. Which, come to think of it, shows how far I've come in my life."

I repeated these remarks to Ozzie, and he nodded. "That just proves what I'm telling you," he said. "Your father has grown up to be a hell of a man. A *good* man. Which, considering what our father was like, is a huge achievement. Not huge. Colossal." I never told my dad about this conversation—an omission I deeply regret, because I know that praise from his older brother would have meant a great deal to him. I can only explain my behavior in terms of the inchoate sense of disloyalty I felt whenever I talked about my father with my uncle—a feeling rooted in my knowledge that Ozzie had always been his mother's favorite and that my father had been deeply wounded as a result. Even though my dad and Ozzie became much closer during what turned out to be the last decade of both of their lives, I suppose I didn't really want my father to know how much I had come to love my uncle, in spite of his faults, as I began to know him better. I wasn't giving my dad enough credit, for he never considered love a finite commodity, in which any tenderness directed toward one must be subtracted from the total available to another. When my book tour for *Wild Justice* brought me to Dallas in the autumn of 1983, my father was deeply gratified that Ozzie insisted I stay in his home. Ozzie had already been stricken by the cancer that would kill him nine months later, and he was battling chemotherapy-induced nausea, but he wouldn't hear of my staying in a hotel. He had a special reason for wanting to see me: he had gone through as many old papers as he could unearth from the boxes of unsorted memorabilia in his house, and he had prepared a list of birth and death dates that might help me find out more about his father's, and his grandfather's, generation of Jacobys.

It was my good fortune that most of my Jacoby relatives lived into their ninth decade with intact minds and memories. In my father's generation, he was the only sibling who died before age eighty. Moreover, the Jacoby men—beginning with my great-grandfather—were all over thirty when they married and started having children. Max Jacoby, born in 1831, had three grandchildren—my father, aunt, and uncle—who were alive and well 150 years later.

Because Ozzie never lived at home for any length of time after 1918, he was unfamiliar with the day-to-day details of his family's life (apart from its need for his financial contributions) during the period of progressive paternal withdrawal and marital disintegration that scarred my father's childhood. But he told me one story, during our final meeting in Dallas, that certainly goes a long way toward explaining why my father disliked talking or thinking about his boyhood.

After a visit to the Bronx Zoo when he was about five years old, my father somehow got the idea that his stuffed teddy bears had once been alive, and he refused to play with them. His easily annoyed mother boxed up the bears and took them to his school, suggesting—no doubt out of a sense of noblesse oblige—that the kindergarten teacher distribute them among her son's less fortunate classmates. My father was thus forced to endure the double pain of seeing his beloved toys given away to other children while being reminded of his anguish at the thought that his teddies had once been alive and had been killed for use as playthings. He told his classmates that the bears should be given a proper burial, and most of the children scoffed at him. Only one boy took my father's worries to heart, and the two buried the bear in a vacant lot. That pal was my father's schoolyard defender, Fred Groff. Ozzie, who was seventeen at the time and still in the army, heard the story secondhand from his mother, who caught the boys burying the bear and promptly sent her son to bed without his supper. "Mother's point was how could I have left home, when Bobbie needed a 'brotherly influence' to make him grow up and stop clinging to these childish ideas. Father had been no use at all, she said, because he told Mother he didn't see any reason, no, no reason at all, why Bobbie shouldn't bury the bears if it would make him happier. So you see, though your aunt Edith would never admit it, Father also had his side when it came to the story of that marriage. Mother's view was that Bobbie was just too tender-hearted for his own good, and he needed to grow out of that. Well, he never did grow out of that, did he? A good thing for you and your brother."

UNCLE OZZIE's story about the teddy bears offered a different, more sympathetic prism through which my grandfather might be viewed. He was a man who, whatever his failings, was able to understand the emotions of an imaginative and sensitive child. That he allowed his wife to inflict so much emotional damage on that child is another black mark on his record, but my father might have suffered more acutely had his father physically left home. Many years would pass, and both my uncle and my father would be dead, before I would begin to think of Oswald Jacoby more as a tragic than as an evil character. The cache of articles about my grandfather's witty 1909 defense of the feckless literary agent Broughton Brandenburg, which I unearthed only recently, reinforced this shift in perspective: for a man of such immense ability to have become his own worst enemy is surely the essence of tragedy. I would not have wanted this Shake-spearean character for a father, but I cannot deny that both of his sons—who had much better luck with wives than their father did—inherited many of Oswald's character failings (albeit in attenuated form) along with his charm and formidable intelligence. I loved my father and my uncle, so, at a merciful remove, a part of me loves a part of the self-destructive grandfather I never met.

I HOPE THAT my dad forgot the maternal cruelty expressed in the teddy bear episode—but somehow I doubt it. Dad could never stand to be around the stuffed hunting trophies that so many of his neigh-bors had mounted in their basement recreation rooms. I have an indelible image of my dad disrupting a party when one neighbor unveiled his newly acquired glass-eyed buck with antlers. "It takes a real man to bring that home," he said. "Was it a fair fight? Did the deer have a gun?" The neighbors didn't hold it against Dad: most of the women agreed with him anyway, and the men accepted his disdain for hunting as yet another eccentricity over which my father had no control. Dad's contempt for hunting had been inculcated in him by his father, who told him that "Jewish people don't hunt other living creatures." Dad told me this only a month before he died of lung cancer, when he allowed many elusive memories of childhood to come flooding back. When Dad asked why Jewish people didn't hunt, his father replied, "It's simple. We know how it feels to be hunted." This was the only time my father recalled his father using a first-person pronoun when he talked, as he rarely did, about the heritage he had abandoned.

DURING THESE years, I also brought up the subject of the family's rejection of Judaism with Aunt Edith, whom I approached with considerable trepidation not only because she was the only truly devout Catholic in the family but also because she was a thorny, critical personality (in some respects very like her mother). Neither my father nor Ozzie had much to do with their sister, who talked unendingly about religion, treated her brothers like two-year-olds, and (perhaps the most important factor) rubbed both of their wives the wrong way. While I never came to know or to love my aunt as I loved my uncle, I found, as I became better acquainted with her during the eighties, that she was a far more complex, and a much warmer, person than she had seemed to me when I was younger. I never made any real attempt to get to know my aunt until after my father's death in 1986. She had flown out to Michigan for my father's funeral, and I had told her of my desire to find out more about what had made the Jacoby family turn away from Judaism so decisively. She remarked, in the prickly fashion that pushed away the very people she most wanted to draw close, that she supposed I was finally asking for her help only because both of her brothers were dead. Yet she responded with surprising (to me) good humor when I conceded that she was absolutely right and asked, "Is that such a bad reason for me to be coming to you now?" Edith half barked and half laughed in a fashion that reminded me of Uncle Ozzie, and she said that the question of why the Jacobys were so ashamed of being Jews had always interested her too. A few weeks later, she sent me several nineteenth-century photographs of both the Sondheim and Jacoby families.

When she was young, Edith was the only member of her family who was attracted to religion, who noticed or felt deprived by the absence of religious observance in the Jacoby home. And Edith was the only one of the three siblings who took note of the confusion in the household over the relationship between Judaism as a religion and Jewishness as cultural tradition. For her, as for many nonobservant Jews today, the confusion was embodied in the way the family celebrated—and did not celebrate—Christmas.

Ozzie, Edith, and my father had longed for a Christmas tree as children. As an adult, no one loved the holidays more than my dad; I still remember the entranced look on his face as he held my hand tightly while we looked down from a balcony upon a magnificent fifty-foot tree rising through the central atrium of Marshall Field's landmark Walnut Room. (That tree, in the 1879 building replacing the store that burned down in the great Chicago fire of 1871, was as much a Chicago Christmas tradition as the Rockefeller Center Christmas tree is in New York.) Decades later, long after I had discovered the secret of his Jewish birth, Dad made a poignant comment about the difference between his childhood memories of Christmas and mine. "I didn't look forward to Christmas when I was a boy," he said, "because we didn't make any fuss about it at home. I would have been ashamed to invite anyone home during the holidays—not that I ever invited many friends to our house—because there weren't any decorations. I used to make up stories for my schoolmates about our tree, and what we had for Christmas dinner. But you have all of those memories that I only wanted to have. So you see, I never could have imagined that you would think I was depriving you of something because I didn't tell you my parents were Jewish. The way I saw it, I was giving you what I hadn't been given."

Aunt Edith, seven years older than my dad, had a more complex view of her family's childhood Christmases—or non-Christmases. That she had given an immense amount of thought to the subject, and had worked hard to unearth her memories, was evident to me when, over a long lunch, she suggested that I take notes. There was plenty for me to write down, as Edith recalled yet another source of serious conflict in her upbringing.

> Naturally, we kids wanted a tree. Like your father, I didn't
> want to bring friends home from school around the holidays
> because our house looked so bare and odd, when everyone
> else's was beautifully decorated. Father explained—if you
> can call it an explanation—that we didn't have a tree because
> it wasn't a Jewish thing to do. This was very, very confusing
> to me and to Ozzie—Bobby hadn't been born yet. We didn't
> understand what a tree had to do with being Jewish, or not
> being Jewish, because we didn't know what being Jewish
> meant. My mother's brother, Simon, went to something
> called a temple, which was where Jews went, but none of us,
> including Mother, ever went there. Father wouldn't have
> allowed it. We didn't go to any church either, though there
> were Christian prayers in the private schools Ozzie and I
> attended. The holidays were a tense time. Mother would tell
> Father that we might as well have a Christmas tree, since the
> Jewish religion wasn't practiced in our home, and they
> hadn't told their children anything about what the religion
> meant. She was being sarcastic; I think this was her way of
> saying she disagreed with Father and would have liked us to
> know more about Judaism. But she never did anything about
> it, just sniped. I can only assume that even though Father
> had no respect for any religion, something in him was still

Jewish enough that he didn't want to do something as Christian as having a tree in his house. After all, Christmas does mean "Christ's Mass"—even though no one pays much attention to that these days. Uncle Harold and his family did have a tree, and we envied our cousins. Father said his brother had become "very very High Church"—we didn't know what that meant either—since he had married Aunt Annie. He would put on an English accent and purse up his lips when he said that, the way your father and your uncle used to do when they were making fun of someone.

By that point, in the late 1980s, I had discovered that Uncle Harold's real first name was Levi. This fascinated Edith almost as much as it did my long-lost cousin, Maclear Jacoby Jr. This piece of information jogged Edith's memory, and she recalled that her mother had wanted to call her Rachel, but her father had insisted on a first name that did not sound Jewish. "Mother told me this in the 1920s, after she and Father had become completely estranged. Her Sondheim grandmother, whom she never knew, had been named Rachel. My name was just one of the many things she held against Father— and probably against me too. Which was ironic, since Mother's first name was also Edith." My grandparents' decision to name two of their three children after living relatives—themselves—was also a measure of their detachment from Jewish naming practices. Uncle Ozzie, with his full name of Oswald Nathaniel, was a "Junior," though no one ever called him that, and he conceded that his name was a reflection of his father's aspirations to WASP status.

Aunt Edith said she felt an inner "spiritual hunger" from early childhood. In her teens, she read a great deal about various religions—she was surprised to hear that I had embarked upon the same quest forty years later—and tried out Protestant and Catholic church services. But Edith had never entered a synagogue, even though she knew her uncle Simon had once been an observant Jew and a member of a temple. "I think I knew this would have been intolerable to Father," she said. "And if he found out, he might have blamed Simon, whom we all loved dearly."

IN A STRANGE twist of fate, Uncle Si, the last observant Jew in either the Sondheim or Jacoby families, was buried in 1970 from a black Christian evangelical church in his neighborhood in the New York City borough of Queens. Since the 1930s, he and his sisters had lived together in the same house in an area (not far from their child-hood home in Brooklyn) that was once largely Jewish but became predominantly black during the sixties. After Mabel, Carrie, and Adele died during the first half of that decade, Aunt Edith and Uncle Ted tried to persuade Si to move in with them. In his eighties, he refused to leave the home and the neighborhood where he had spent most of his adult life. Edith—aware that her uncle was proba-bly the most stubborn member of a stubborn family—eventually stopped trying to coax him into leaving for the literally greener pas-tures of Staten Island.

Si's African-American neighbors looked after the frail old white man in their midst, and when he died, they arranged to hold his funeral in their church. In addition to his neighbors, Uncle Si's funeral was attended by Uncle Ozzie and Aunt Mary; their son Jon and his wife, Caroline; and Aunt Edith and Uncle Ted. (If Ted thought there had been an extraordinary number of black people at my wedding, he must have felt truly surrounded at a service where his wife's uncle was eulogized by an African-American pastor and the hallelujahs were sung by a gospel choir.) I was in Moscow at the time, and I do not know why my father failed to make the trip to New York for the funeral of his much-loved uncle. This service in an African-American community church was a first for the Jacobys and the Sondheims; the only variety of funeral my family has never partici-pated in during the past hundred years is a Jewish funeral. I am cer-tainly sorry that I missed Si's farewell, which I only heard about recently from my cousin Jon. Neither Ozzie nor Edith, who told me subsequently about Si's having once been a religious Jew, ever mentioned the interesting circumstances surrounding his burial. I simply assumed—a terrible mistake in my family!—that Si had been buried as a Jew. My guess is that Si did not abandon Judaism but that Jewish institutions, including his temple, abandoned the neighborhood when most of the Jewish residents moved out. It would have been very much in character for Si to have become involved with the church (I have no way of knowing whether he was actually a member) attended by the neighbors who helped him maintain his independence in old age.

EVEN IN college, when her father could not possibly have known anything about her religious practices, Edith never gave Judaism a try. At Smith, her reluctance to identify with Jews in any way was reinforced by the social separation of Jews and gentiles at the Seven Sisters as well as the men's Ivy League schools, a separation encouraged by the institutions themselves through dormitory room assignments. Edith—although she, like my father, had declared "no religious preference" on her Smith application—was assigned another Jewish student as a roommate. (At many schools, the practice of assigning Jews and gentiles roommates of "their own kind" lasted into the early sixties.)

"My freshman-year roommate was a girl from a very wealthy German Jewish family," Edith remembered. "They lived somewhere on Fifth Avenue—I don't know exactly where, because we didn't get along very well and I was never invited to her home—and her family belonged to Temple Emmanu-El. She made it very clear that she resented having to room with me, a nobody from Brooklyn, instead of one of the gentile girls who had been her classmates at the Brearley School in Manhattan. And I resented it too. It was very clear that the only reason we had been assigned to room together was that we were both Jewish. All of the Jewish girls were paired off in the dorms with other Jewish girls. When there were mixers, and we went to the boys' colleges for weekends, there was no dating across Jewish-Christian lines. No official dating, that is. I gravitated to Catholic boys—not that there were so many of them in Ivy League schools in those days—and I think that was part of the attraction for me. They were outsiders too, in a way, and although their families wouldn't have been happy to know that their sons were going out with Jewish girls, there was more of an equality. Those boys named Lowell and Peabody and Cabot would never have gone out with an Edith Jacoby. And I thought, well, Father was right. There's really nothing good that can come of being identified as a persecuted minority."

After Edith graduated from Smith and began working as a sales-girl at B. Altman, she fell in love with the notorious Feeney. They were married by a justice of the peace because, Edith recalled, "he told me his parents would never accept his marrying a Jewish girl, so it would be better not to make a fuss and throw it in their faces. Of course, he never had any intention of staying married to me. He just wanted to get me into bed. Why would he want to celebrate a wed-ding to me with friends and family? Only when I met my Ted, and he waited and worked and prayed so that we could be married in the Church, did I realize what real love was."

I listened to this account on a long drive from New York to a Con-necticut convent where the widowed Edith was staying while she vis-ited her late husband's nieces and nephews. Edith's frugality and indifference to the comfort—or the lack thereof—of her surround-ings did not change after her husband's death. Other wealthy widows might have checked into the Plaza Hotel when they visited New York, but Edith was much happier in a room with a single bed, a cru-cifix on the wall, and a chapel where she could attend daily Mass with the nuns instead of having to travel to a church. That day, she did consent to go out for lunch at a lavish country inn, but she refused to order dessert because it wasn't included in the price of the entree.

Over our glasses of wine (which Edith, surprisingly, had sug-gested) she earnestly explained that her hasty, miserable first mar-riage was "all part of God's plan." Her eyes glowed as she described the "miracle" of finally being able to marry Ted before a priest. "God was watching over me from the beginning," she said, "because I never could have been happy with Feeney, who could not be faithful to any woman. When I married Ted, I not only found real love but I was also freed to live out the religious life I had always longed for with a man who had a deep spiritual side." I was doing my best to say nothing, so as not to interrupt Edith's stream of consciousness, but I must have betrayed my impatience by some physical gesture. She stopped in mid-sentence and said, "I can tell just from the way your chin is tilted that you think I'm a nut—loony Aunt Edith. Well, I can't explain faith—or the longing for faith—to someone who doesn't have it. But I can tell you this: if Ted and I had had children, I never would have concealed the fact that I was born Jewish from them the way your father and Ozzie did from you kids. I have too much respect for religion. And also, I am a Catholic who believes deeply in Judaism as the forerunner of Christianity. I was thrilled when Pope John the Twenty-third came along and reached out to the Jewish people in a way no pope ever had. I felt more Jewish after I became a Catholic—certainly more Jewish than Mother or Father ever did, teaching their children nothing about where they came from. And you know, I think it's wonderful if you write a book about that generation, and the one before, because my main view of our family is how confusing it is not to be able to stand up and be proud of who you are, to claim the past that belongs to you."

Perhaps it is not surprising, in view of the seriousness with which Edith approached religion, that she was the only one of the siblings who gave any thought to the Jewish covenant when she converted to Catholicism. "If Father had been around when God was choosing the Chosen People," Ozzie quipped, "he would have said, 'Thank you very much, you're too kind, but I'd rather you choose someone else as your favorite.'" For Edith, the Jewish covenant was no laughing matter. Like other Jews who made the extraordinary leap of faith into Catholicism, she regarded her new faith not as the negation but the fulfillment of Old Testament prophecy, an attitude that gave rise to her pious pronouncements, so mystifying to me as a child, about Our Lord having been born a Jew.

As an idealistic young woman, Edith was impressed (as the young Eleanor Roosevelt had been twenty-five years earlier) by the work of the settlement houses on New York's Lower East Side. She had hoped to become a social worker after graduating from Smith, but the settlement houses ran largely on the volunteer labor of socially conscious (and conscientious) wealthy women who did not need to earn a living wage. Edith, well aware that she would be required to contribute to her mother's support, established herself in retail sales and eventually worked her way up to an executive position in Macy's personnel department. One of the mysteries of Edith's life is how a young woman who admired Jane Addams and Dorothy Day not only fell in love with but stayed happily married to a man who was not only a religious but a political conservative. Ted regarded FDR as a dangerous left-winger, and, although an immensely charitable man in his private life, he believed that New Deal public health and welfare programs were the work of the devil.

Edith gave no hint that she did not fully share her husband's views until after his death, when she went through a metamorphosis that startled the rest of the family. As a widow, beginning in the mid-1970s, she became deeply involved with Catholic groups pushing for racial and economic justice in society as a whole and for reforms within the Church. Edith wanted a priesthood opened to women and to married men. She had gay friends and declared her disagreement with those who branded homosexuals as mortal sinners. Both my dad and Ozzie regarded her involvement in left-wing Catholic circles as yet another bizarre manifestation of the true-believer temperament that used to manifest itself in pilgrimages to Lourdes and Fatima. I was equally astonished, and initially baffled, by my aunt's change of heart in old age, because I would have expected her to ally herself with Catholic right-wingers who pined for the Latin Mass, conducted by a priest who kept his back turned to the congregation while celebrating mysteries deemed too sacred for the eyes of the ordinary faithful. After I became better acquainted with Edith in the late 1980s, I came to understand that her enthusiasms in old age were a throwback to her social concerns as a young woman, to a hunger for meaning that might have found an outlet in service to others but was channeled instead into a religious devotion bordering on fanaticism. The personality of the girl who once longed to help immigrants on the Lower East Side had not disappeared during decades as an afflu-ent Staten Island matron, the wife of a Papal Knight; after Ted's death, Edith's youthful self reasserted itself in the aging woman's desire for what she called a more "inclusive" Catholicism.

Edith (again, unlike her brothers) had agonized over the Church's historical role vis-à-vis Jews. On trips to Italy with her hus-band, who, as a Papal Knight, was granted private papal audiences, she met three popes—Pius XII, John XXIII, and Paul VI. In the late sixties and seventies, as historians dissected the Vatican's role during World War II, Edith became increasingly upset by the harsh assess-ments of Pius XII's actions with regard to Jews. She was distressed not because she rejected these assessments but because she feared there was a great deal of truth in them. "I had heard the same thing from priests in places like Assisi," Edith told me. "I couldn't dismiss their opinions as anti-Catholic propaganda; they were there during the war, and they knew that most of the help for Jews had come from priests and bishops who acted on their own." Edith sent me a book titled *The Assisi Underground*, which describes the activities of Father Ruffino Niccacci, a Franciscan who was instrumental in saving hun-dreds of Jews (for which he was honored by Israel in its Avenue of the Righteous, established in tribute to gentile rescuers). "You see," she wrote me, "the history of Jews and Catholics is not only the Inquisition."

Edith's admiration for the clergymen and nuns who acted on their own to save Italian Jews played an important role in her attraction to Catholic groups dedicated to the renewal of the Church from the bot-tom up rather than the top down. With her unshakable, albeit socially adaptable faith, Edith tried to convince me to give Catholi-cism another try. "Real religion, true religion, religion that feeds the hungry and rescues those who are persecuted, doesn't come from a small group of men in Rome but from the hearts of everyone," she said. "I wish you could see that."

One of the last things my aunt said to me before her mind clouded over was that she hoped I would someday realize "that you can be both a Jew and a Catholic—just as Jesus was." She pursed her lips—that Jacoby twitch of amusement—when she recalled Uncle Ozzie's response to her statement of dual loyalty: "But Sis, think about what happened to him."

XII

Loyalties

⟨⁓⟩

HALF-JEW. IT HAS A nasty sound, with its "half-breed" connotations, even if not intended nastily. When someone—Jew or gentile—calls you a half-Jew, don't expect an invitation to join his club. The Nazi definition of a *Mischling*, embodying the detested mating of Aryan and Jew, speaks for itself. The inevitable association with the Nuremberg Laws, and their life-and-death calibration based on the number and propinquity of one's Jewish ancestors, has rendered the term "half-Jew" especially suspect, especially unsettling, when applied by one Jew to another. The writer Cynthia Ozick once noted casually in a lecture—her observation presumably was intended not in a pejorative but in a descriptive sense—that the Diaspora has produced no major Jewish writers, "unless you insist on including two French half-Jews, Montaigne and Proust." Do I insist? I would like to. Actually, I would like to argue with both halves of the proposition.

What I hear, when Jews talk about half-Jews in this fashion, is an undertone of exclusion. Not quite kosher. Not quite One of Us. Ozick's remark reminds me of the first time I met my future mother-in-law (the same woman who once tried to talk her son out of a bar mitzvah), when she asked if it was true that I was a "half." I did not understand this odd dangling locution at first, but I soon realized that Manley (born Malka in Riga), who, unlike my father, had no problem using the word *Jew* by itself, considered "half-Jew" very rude indeed. When I answered that my mother was Irish, and my Jewish father a Catholic convert, she looked pensive for a moment and then brightened. "But I understand you don't go in for any of that stuff," she said. When I assured her that I didn't go in for any of that stuff, she seemed satisfied—though she did question me closely about whether I knew the difference between a *schlemiel* and a *schlimazel*. Oh yes, I told her, I was going to marry her son because he didn't fall into either category. We got along wonderfully after that, and she never subjected me to another Yiddish vocabulary quiz. Over the years, I have become largely—but never entirely—accustomed to such little tests, designed to determine whether a half-Jew has a right to consider herself "culturally Jewish." In my extended phase (which lasted into my mid-thirties) of yearning to be a whole Jew instead of a half-Jew, I leaped at every chance to demonstrate my Jewish credentials. I was not ready to subject my own behavior to the same scrutiny I had long applied to my father and the rest of the Jacobys, not yet able to acknowledge that I was exhibiting my own mutation of the family trait that impelled my ancestors to shed unwanted and inconvenient identities without looking back. Craving acceptance as a New York Jew, I actually felt obliged to answer when someone twitted me by asking, "Why is lobster Newburg doubly forbidden to those who observe the laws of *kashrut*?" Why either my inquisitor or I thought that knowing the answer to such a question might qualify me as a Jew is another question altogether. A Talmudic scholar told me his reply would have been, "Lobster Newburg is forbidden only once if you use nondairy creamer for the sauce." What I should have done was ask my interrogator if he could explain the Pauline Privilege.

As I moved through my thirties, I began to deal with the emotional fallout from my mixed heritage and from the long cover-up of that heritage within my family. For much of the 1980s, I wrote a column for the magazine *Present Tense*, a journal of liberal Jewish opinion—a sort of counter-*Commentary*—then published (and later abandoned) by the American Jewish Committee. An essay titled "I Am a Half-Jew, American-Born" brought me more mail than I have ever received in response to any article on any subject (including those published in general-interest magazines with a much larger circulation than the AJC's stepchild). I got a kick out of calling myself a half-Jew, without qualifications and explanations—a very different sensation from hearing the term applied to me in an exclusionary way by others. I suspect Alfred Kazin got a similar kick out of seeing the title of his 1978 memoir, *New York Jew*, in print. My father gasped, shook his head in bewilderment, and finally laughed out loud when he saw Kazin's title—which he found far more vulgar than the word *Jew* by itself—staring out at him from the window of a bookstore as we walked along Broadway during one of his visits to New York.

In my *Present Tense* essay I made the point (it is still valid) that the unprecedented American tolerance of marriages between Jews and Christians had not yet produced a literature reflecting the complexity and importance of a social experiment that used to be viewed as equally threatening by Christians and Jews. When Saul Bellow opened *The Adventures of Augie March* with the line, "I am an American, Chicago-born," he was asserting a specifically Jewish claim to everything America had to offer. Jewish readers in 1953 understood Bellow perfectly, and it is obvious that the line would have had no meaning (for Jews or gentiles) if its author had been Henry James. But what would readers have made of a sentence written by a man— let us call him Paul Bellow—declaring, "I am a half-Jewish American, Chicago-born"? Many of the readers who responded to my *Present Tense* essay were miffed, even angry, at my play on Bellow's line. "*Half-Jew*," scoffed one woman. "It means nothing. You are an American, that's it." Another correspondent said flatly, "You aren't any kind of Jew, and your writings don't belong in a Jewish magazine." A Conservative rabbi commented, "You write about half-Jewishness as if it were a special condition. But it is not a condition—not, at any rate, in a country with no Nuremberg Laws. What would be the attributes of this condition? What does a half-Jew believe? Eat? For that matter, where is a half-Jew buried?"

That rabbi really knew how to hurt a girl, and I was tempted to answer, "Hath not a half-Jew eyes . . . if you prick us, do we not bleed?" But these rhetorical questions only serve to underscore rather than to negate the specialness and ambiguity of the half-Jewish condition. It really boils down to the old question, "So what will the children be?"—the predecessor of the Scranton rabbi's "So, what are you now?" People would continue to ask me the latter question, and I would continue to ask it of myself, even if my father had not lied to his children about his and their origins. But this is not a fundamentally religious inquiry, although it is usually framed in religious terms when a Jew marries a Christian. At its heart, "So, what are you now?" really means, "Where do you belong?" It is a question of loyalty. To what and to whom, beyond ourselves and our immediate families, do we owe our deepest moral obligations?

It is one thing for a Jew to try to sort out the cultural legacy of an assimilationist upbringing burdened by shame and conflict, as my father's was, yet presided over by parents who at least acknowledged that they were Jews. It is quite another matter (though obviously a part of progressive deracination) for a half-Jew to sort out the loyalties attached to two separate heritages—especially when the Jewish portion of the heritage has been denigrated or, as was the case in my family, covered up altogether. Because my father and uncle pretended for so many years that the family's Jewish past did not exist, they made it far more difficult for my generation of half-Jews to know where or how to begin the sorting-out process. The slow fading of both the invidious and the ennobling distinctions that set peoples apart from one another is a nightmare undreamed of in the traditional Jewish parent's warning, delivered to a child contemplating marriage to one of the goyim, that the gentile partner will surely shout "kike" at the first hint of marital discord.

For the most part, America allows—indeed encourages—me and others like me to minimize the dissonances and accentuate the harmonies of a mixed heritage (a far more problematic stance for the children of racially mixed unions). Intermarriages of every sort are no longer viewed as marginal to the majority culture of America; they are rapidly becoming the majority culture. Few Jews sit *shiva* for a child who marries a gentile, and few Christians go to their family Bible (if they have a family Bible) to strike out the name of a child who marries out of the faith. Even in the days when there were more *shiva* sitters and name strikers, the proverbial reconciliation upon the birth of a grandchild was, like so many clichés, more fact than fiction. Putative offspring—the source of fierce parental arguments against mixed marriages—became, when they actually appeared, ex post facto justification for the betrayal of tribal loyalty. The grandchildren were redeemers, infant messiahs to both Jews and gentiles.

Four basic patterns of child-rearing are commonly practiced by mixed couples, and each fosters a different kind of ambiguity. The first ignores the whole issue of religion. If the practice of religion holds little importance for either the Jewish or Christian partner, symbols like Christmas trees lose all nonsecular content. As long as there is no Baby Jesus among the gaily wrapped packages, everyone can have a good time. The second pattern, touted by the Jewish-Methodist couple in *Newsweek*, relies on the utopian (or hellish, depending on your point of view) notion of educating children in both religions and allowing them to make their own choices. This relatively recent, quintessentially American experiment is based on the notion of faith as a "lifestyle choice" roughly equivalent to vegetarianism vs. meat-eating. Happy little children, with a crèche under the tree and a menorah on the table. In a third and somewhat more unusual pattern, neither parent converts to the other's faith, but the children are raised in the religion of the parent to whom religion matters most.

The conversion of one spouse—the course taken by my family for generations—was (and for all I know, may still be) the most popular strategy for child-rearing within mixed marriages. Through centuries of intermarriage between Jews and Christians, the Jewish partner was almost always the one who converted. Few Jews of my father's generation—observant or not, proud of their heritage or not—could have imagined a time when certain Christians, upon marrying Jews, would find it not only spiritually fulfilling but socially expedient to convert. If my dad was startled by the words *New York Jew* on the cover of a book, he would have been utterly baffled by the greeting cards proclaiming, "Congratulations on Your Conversion," now sold next to bar and bat mitzvah cards in Judaica shops. American children now being raised as Jews, after the conversion of a Christian parent, may prove to be a unique and unprecedented group of *Mischlinge*—bound to the Jewish covenant by a parent's genuine choice instead of to the New Testament covenant by the subtle-to-blatant coercion that runs through the history of Jewish conversions to Christianity.

Such conversions, however joyfully they may have been celebrated by unusual, spiritually motivated converts like my aunt Edith, have never been occasions on which one Jew offered congratulations to another. Conversions by Jews have, for the most part, been tainted by shame, self-loathing, fear of persecution, and jockeying for social advantage—in varying proportions and accompanied by varying degrees of coerciveness. No cause for celebration there. In some instances, conversion has nothing to do with mixed marriages but instead represents a collaboration between two Jewish parents, like Madeleine Albright's mother and father, united in their determination to rewrite the past for the next generation. But when the denial of Jewishness plays out within a mixed marriage, the children inherit a double whammy: the Jewish parent's heritage is not only hidden but abandoned in favor of, and therefore presumed to be inferior to, the other parent's lineage. This might not matter in a psychological sense to the next generation if a family's true past could be completely and permanently erased, but there is almost always a chink in the wall of suppression. Yet Jews who try to pass as gentiles, whether or not they marry non-Jews, usually manage to convince themselves (even in the face of direct evidence to the contrary) that no one will ever find out. How else can one explain the behavior of Albright's sophisticated father, Josef Korbel, in failing to prepare his daughter for the likelihood that the family's past—its Jewish past in Czechoslovakia—might well resurface as her career in government service took off? Or, for that matter, the behavior of Albright herself, who finally acknowledged her Jewish parentage only after she learned that *The Washington Post* was about to publish an article tracing the history of the Korbels in Czechoslovakia and revealing that most of the family had perished in the Holocaust?

My uncle Ozzie, also a sophisticated and well-traveled man, was just as convinced that no one was likely to suspect the Jewish origins of the Jacoby family. He insisted that I absolutely *must* be wrong when I told him that Jacoby/*Yakobi* was instantly recognizable as a Jewish name everywhere in Russia and Eastern Europe. Both my uncle and my father subscribed to their father's credo—"At myself I will begin and end." And they were both surprised to be confronted with the evidence, in the form of my increasingly insistent questions about the past, that their father had been mistaken.

Whether a Jewish parent converts to Christianity openly or tries to "pass" by denying his or her origins altogether, the need to know why a father or mother took such a radical step often becomes a life-long preoccupation for the next generation. The writings of Mary Gordon, who offered no hint in her early work of a background that was anything but Catholic, provide a window into the emotional conflict—engendered by parental withholding or outright lying—that prevents so many half-Jews from fully owning up to and owning their heritage.

Gordon's first novel, *Final Payments*, was widely praised in 1978 as a Catholic coming-of-age story. The narrator, Isabel Moore, has devoted the first decade of her adulthood to caring for her invalid father, a devout Catholic intellectual in a working-class community where no one but his daughter truly understands him. Physically released but not spiritually freed by her father's death, Isabel describes his passion for the Catholic faith as being "clear as that of a child who dies before the age of reason. . . . He loved the sense of his own orthodoxy, of holding out for the purest and the finest and the most refined sense of truth against the slick hucksters who promised happiness on earth and the supremacy of human reason." Nowhere in this novel, or in Gordon's other early work, is there even a hint of what my sixth-grade nun called "certain influences." I was utterly surprised to learn, many years later, that the author's real father, like mine, had been a Jewish convert to Catholicism. Nearly two decades after the publication of *Final Payments*, Gordon finally attempted to come to terms with her father's tangled legacy in her memoir, *The Shadow Man*.

It is a terrible story. David Gordon, who died of a heart attack when his daughter was seven, had lied about nearly everything *except* his Jewish birth. He told his family that he was born in America and a graduate of Harvard. His real first name was Israel; he was born in Vilna; and he dropped out of high school to go to work. That is not the terrible part. As Gordon delved further—she knew her father had written for Catholic publications after his conversion in the 1930s—she learned that he had found a spiritual home among the most reactionary, anti-Semitic elements in the American Catholic Church. He became a follower of Father Coughlin's home-grown fascism and wrote letters and articles declaring his support for Mussolini and Franco. Later on, he made it clear that he was more concerned about the Nazis' treatment of Catholics than the deaths of Jews in concentration camps. In a 1943 article titled "Can Christianity Survive Hollywood?" he wrote that "we do not allow Jews, even of the highest caliber, to control our schools, but we allow the worst class of them to control the mind-molding amusement of old and young, boy and maiden, indiscriminately." And on and on. This devoted father, who taught his daughter to read and left her with an indelible love of language before she was seven, was also a fascist fellow traveler who reviled Jews—as he had rejected the Jew in himself.

It is hard for me to imagine how Gordon found the courage to read, much less write about, the true history of a father whose memory could only have been more precious to her because he died when she was so young. I don't know how I could have borne the discovery of such poison in my father's life. I knew my father as a man who had lied to protect his own children (and himself) from the painful slights he had endured as a child, a man whose parents did not give him enough pride in himself, or in his heritage, to sustain him into adulthood. But my father's internal sense of shame never metamorphosed, as David Gordon's did, into an emotional alliance with bigots and persecutors. My dad possessed a basic sanity, and a congenital indisposition to extremism, that protected him from the wilder ideological possibilities his upbringing might have nurtured.

Even though Gordon's father took one of the most twisted paths available to a man wishing to escape his Jewishness, he could no more avoid passing on a sense of an unarticulated past to his daughter than my father could. The one thing Gordon's father and mine had in common was that their stories didn't add up; no child can begin to make sense of her upbringing until the true background of the parent is known. The labyrinthine nature of the search for long-concealed truth, with its inevitable false starts and dead ends, may explain why half-Jews have not yet established an imaginative voice in American literature—why a writer as talented as Gordon spoke for so long only in the voice of a Catholic (or a lapsed Catholic). As a young writer and a young woman, she was neither ready nor able to speak in the voice of a daughter whose father had denied the Jew in him, of a girl who, whenever she displeased her maternal relatives, had been told, "That's the *Jew* in you."

Gordon's story is no more "typical" than my own, and (as my brother's attitude demonstrates) there are half-Jews, especially those in which the Jewish parent's Jewishness was always known, who have not been strongly affected for good or ill by their mixed upbringing.

When I asked my brother to rethink his assertion that he was never bothered by the huge gaps in our father's account of his childhood, he insisted—and I believe him—that the contradictions never entered his mind when he was growing up. "I was in my senior year of high school when you told me Dad was Jewish," he recalled, "and I was mildly interested—but only mildly. I felt bad that Dad thought this was something he had to keep from us, but that was about it. Of course, I was at the age when all you're thinking about is yourself— but the truth is I'd never given much thought to our father's family at all, because we were so much closer to Mom's parents. If I thought about the Jacobys, it was just in terms of 'Granny Jacoby is mean and Aunt Edith is crazy and Ozzie's a great cardplayer.' When I got a little older, the thing that fascinated me wasn't so much that the Jacobys were Jewish but that they had all married Catholics and converted. What are the odds against that, three siblings, living in different places when they're adults, all finding an Irish Catholic to marry?"

I don't know. It was certainly no coincidence that my father, uncle, and aunt all married gentiles: they were set up by their upbringing to regard other Jews as undesirable marriage partners. Aunt Edith was the only one of the siblings who fell in love with the Church itself; I have a feeling that she would somehow have found her way to Catholicism with or without Ted. Neither Uncle Ozzie nor my father showed any particular enthusiasm for the Catholic faith at the outset of their marriages; my father waited eight years to convert, and it took a near-fatal auto accident to draw the recalcitrant Ozzie into the embrace of the Church. One factor—Granny Jacoby's view that Catholics (American-Irish Catholics, at any rate) were beneath her sons—may, subconsciously or consciously, have pushed Dad and Ozzie in the direction of those very women. What a great way to get back at overbearing Mother! Granny Jacoby would, I suspect, have been quite pleased if either of her sons had made a match with the daughter of an old-line New England WASP family. And the family's desire to distance itself from Jews could have been served just as well by conversion to some Protestant denomination. But if there was one common theme in each sibling's conversion to Catholicism, it was the need for an ethical and a practical structure that their upbringing did not provide. And there was nothing like the pre–Vatican II Catholic Church, as my father pointed out, for supplying a structure. "So, what are you now?" was a question no member of my father's generation would be asked or would have to answer again—not, at least, in the narrow religious sense. But questions of loyalty and belonging—the questions one asks oneself— cannot be laid to rest so easily. Many years before the rabbi asked me where I stood, the issue of loyalty, as distinct from that of religion, had surfaced for me in an unsettling and surprising way when my brother married Eve Moscicki, a daughter of Polish (not Jewish) immigrants who were concentration camp survivors. And what, I wonder, were the odds that my brother, having dated a wide assortment of all-American girls, would fall in love with and marry a daughter of anyone who had survived Hitler's camps?

IN 1998, I took my niece, sixteen-year-old Alex, to a screening of a documentary film, *My Knees Were Jumping*, about Jewish children who were rescued from Nazi Germany, Austria, and Czechoslovakia by the Kindertransport movement just before the war. Thousands of desperate Jewish parents, with the aid of a Quaker organization, were able to send their children to safety in England. Most of these parents, unable to get out themselves, perished in the camps—so that what was intended to be a temporary separation turned into a permanent one. The film was made by thirty-eight-year-old Melissa Hacker, herself a daughter of one of the Kindertransport children. I thought Alex would be interested because the Kindertransport survivors, now in their sixties and seventies, were talking about what they had experienced when they were Alex's age. And she was riveted—but not for the reasons I expected. My niece was much less interested in what the actual Kindertransport survivors had to say than in how *their* children, now in their thirties, felt about the way their parents communicated, and did not communicate, the true nature of their experience. The grown children of the Kindertransport children spoke of having been raised with the knowledge that their parents went through something painful and terrible—but the precise nature of the pain and terror was off-limits. These American-born children had nightmares about Nazis, but they kept quiet because they knew, without being told, how disturbed their parents would be to hear of these dreams. They grew up knowing that any form of separation was almost unbearable to their parents, but the "why" was rarely, if ever, explored. The parents, in turn, were surprised to hear how deeply the children had been affected by the half-discussed past; they had tried so hard, one said, to blend in and to behave exactly like other Americans.

As we left the movie theater, Alex told me she identified strongly with the second generation in the documentary. Like those adult children of survivors (and like me so many years ago), Alex has had her own nightmares starring Hitler. "I'm the grandchild, not the child, of people who were in the camps," she said, "but I have a lot of the same feelings as the grown children in that movie. I was stunned to hear them talk about it—the feeling of growing up with something that's known, but only half known. It's there, but something you're not supposed to get too close to."

ALEX'S GRANDPARENTS, Alexander and Maria Moscicki, were waiting for their U.S. entry visas in Sweden when their first daughter, Eve, was born in 1948. Both of Eve's parents had been in the Polish resistance against the Nazis. Her mother was imprisoned at Auschwitz, her father in a smaller camp. It is one of the ironies of my family history that my two nieces, Alexandra Sara and Anna Sofia Broderick Jacoby, the grandchildren of immigrants who took great pride in their Polish heritage, are also the first Jacobys in this century for whom their Jewish ancestry is a source of pride rather than shame. But in the early 1970s, when my brother and Eve announced that they were getting married, I was not at all happy to learn that her family was Polish (a sentiment I kept to myself because I was, rightfully, ashamed of it).

I had only recently returned from Russia, which had also been my jumping-off point for reporting trips to Poland, Czechoslovakia, and Hungary. The Polish Jews (and Polish-born Soviet Jews) among my acquaintances had drawn vivid portraits of the intense hostility they had been subjected to by Poles before the war. I spoke with survivors who had attempted to return to their native villages after the war, in the hope that other surviving relatives would also return, only to find a local Polish population filled with hate for the few Jews who had come back alive. Ironically, my negative picture of the treatment of Jews by the majority of Poles was reinforced by my acquaintance with a small number of Jews who had survived only because decent Polish neighbors and friends had risked their lives to hide them and to bring them food. As far as I was concerned, those Poles were the proverbial exceptions that proved the rule. To save a Jew from the Nazis in Poland required even more courage than it did in occupied Western Europe—not only because the German occupation of Poland was far more brutal, in view of the Nazi categorization of Slavs as subhumans, but precisely because of the enthusiasm for the Final Solution on the part of a significant proportion of the Polish population. Polish rescuers were as frightened of being turned in to the Germans by their Polish neighbors as they were of being discovered by the Nazis themselves. Because they thought it wise to keep quiet long after the war about what they had done to save Jews during the occupation, many of these heroic Polish men and women were among the last rescuers to be honored as "Righteous Persons" by Israel. Even in the late 1960s and early 1970s, having helped Jews three decades earlier was nothing to broadcast to one's neighbors. As a young reporter, I was appalled to find that such Poles still feared being identified by their countrymen as Jew-lovers. In the nineties, the rescuers, as well as the Jews they helped survive, are dying off, but anti-Semitism continues to flourish in a Poland virtually without Jews. (Even more disturbingly, some right-wing Catholic organizations, inside and outside Poland, still promote the historically false proposition that Catholics and Jews suffered equally under the Nazis. In April 1999, the U.S. Catholic League for Religious and Civil Rights ran a quarter-page advertisement, in a prominent spot on the op-ed page of the *Times*, drawing a parallel between Nazi persecution of Jews and Catholics. The ad equated the deaths of three million Polish Catholics during the war with the deaths of three million Polish Jews. No mention was made of the fact that the three million dead Jews represented more than 90 percent of the prewar Jewish population of Poland, while the three million dead Poles, who included soldiers as well as civilians, represented only 10 percent of the prewar gentile Polish population. No distinction was made between the systematic genocide intended by the Nazis for all Jews and the selective murders of Polish gentiles, including intellectuals and participants in the resistance, who posed a particular threat to the Nazi occupiers. The authors of this misleading advertisement would have done well to speak with the Polish rescuers I interviewed about the attitude of their countrymen toward those who did try to save Jews. It is nothing less than an insult to the memory of those noble Polish souls, who risked everything in aid of Jews who were being hunted down like animals in the forests or gassed in extermination camps, for any organization of American Catholics to suggest today that the behavior of the rescuers was supported by the majority of their fellow Polish Catholics during the war.)

When my brother and Eve were married in 1973, I brought all of my still-fresh experiences in Russia and Eastern Europe, and the attendant emotional turmoil, to the wedding. I wanted to pack up my baby brother, take him home with me to New York, and find a nice Jewish girl for him to marry. I simply could not still the voice inside me whispering "Holocaust"—though collective guilt was as loathsome an idea to me then as it is today. In 1973, I could still hear Katya's gentle voice talking about her good German soldier and her disagreement with Russians who hated all Germans. Yet I imagined myself interrogating Eve's father: "So, Mr. Moscicki, exactly what did you do in the Polish resistance? Were you the kind of partisan who tried to help Jews escape to the woods, or the kind of partisan who turned them in? Did you care when the Warsaw ghetto was burning, or did you only care about what happened to Poles?"

Fortunately, my husband was able to persuade me that it wasn't my place to ask such questions or to appoint myself as a spokesperson for murdered Polish Jewry. In 1973, I had known that my father was a Jew for only seven years, and I was searching for a way to identify myself indisputably with the heritage the Jacoby family had cast off. Like many American Jews who had always known they were Jews but who were, nevertheless, grappling with similar questions of identity and memory, I seized upon the Holocaust (with particular eagerness in view of my childhood preoccupation with the destruction of European Jewry) as my only real Jewish legacy. The term *Holocaust* was not yet widely used outside Jewish intellectual circles, and the event itself had yet to become *the* institutionalized touchstone of collective identity for American Jews, but the ovens of Auschwitz—before which I had recently stood—were my link to my Jewish "half." Had my great-grandfather not left Breslau in 1849, I might have been turned to ash in one of those ovens. I saw nothing sad or ironic in my desire to create a Jewish identity for myself by embracing victim status at a three-generation remove. It was a blessing for my relationship with my father that he had not yet delivered his memorable pronouncement on the misguidedness of declaring myself a Jew solely on the basis of my preoccupation with "Holocaust, Holocaust, Holocaust." At twenty-eight, I would not have been able to recognize either the intellectual or the emotional acuity of his observation.

My unease about my new Polish in-laws persisted throughout the marriage ceremony, performed by a Polish-American priest on the shore of Lake Huron, and the celebratory luncheon afterward. (Eastern Michigan, from Detroit to the piece of land, jutting into the lake, known as the Thumb, has had a large Polish immigrant population for more than a century. After the war, the older Polish community was swelled by new immigrants fleeing Communist rule.) The Catholic wedding was a given, since Eve's parents were devout Catholics—and my brother, in any case, had no objection whatsoever to being married in the Church. I realized that Eve's parents must know perfectly well, though my family was Catholic, that my father had been born a Jew. There is no possibility that anyone born and raised in Poland, whatever his attitude toward Jews, could fail to identify "Jacoby" as a Jewish name or my father as a Jew from his appearance. I remembered Eastern European Jewish friends telling me that Poles and Ukrainians prided themselves on always being able to spot a Jew even if the Jew had blond hair and blue eyes.

Then I began talking to Eve's father, a slender, gentle-appearing, and obviously perceptive man whom I had never met. I liked him immediately and had the uneasy feeling that he was probably reading my mind—and my prejudices. At some point, he took my husband and me aside and said, in formal, lightly accented English, "You know, I am sure Eva has told you something about our background. I must say candidly to you, that before the war I had certain thoughts about the Jewish people [like my dad, Mr. Moscicki did not say *Jew*] that were in some ways typical of those around me in Poland. It was not until the camps, the deportation of Jewish people from their homes, that I realized fully how wrong these attitudes were, so that after the war I could understand fully—*fully*—what the Jewish people in Poland, and throughout Europe, had suffered. There are no words to describe those who could go through this evil and not see where beliefs in national and racial superiority end—where they end for all people. I am proud of being Polish, and a large part of the reason I decided to leave was that I did not want to live under a Communist government. However, I also wanted to begin a family, to raise my future children, free of the prejudices and sorrows of that part of the world. I shall be proud, as I hope your parents will, to have grandchildren—I hope there will be grandchildren—who are part of and take pride in the history of *all* of their ancestors."

This long and entirely unsolicited speech astonished me with its honesty and sensitivity, not least because it was addressed to my husband and me instead of to my father. These remarks were surely intended for my parents' ears, but Alexander Moscicki had chosen instead to speak to the sister and brother-in-law of the groom. I thought he had sought us out because he knew we had spent time in Russia and Eastern Europe and would understand what he meant without his having to spell it out. I did not repeat this conversation to my father until some years later, after Mr. Moscicki's death in 1978. My reasoning was that it might have upset my dad, in 1973, to know that his Jewish origins had been a subject of discussion on the part of his in-laws. Only now, looking back on everything I did and did not say to my father about his Jewishness over the years, have I come to understand how deeply I was torn between the need to find and speak the truth and the desire to protect him. I saw myself as a disturber of the peace, and was seen that way by my family, but as I grew older, I kept a great deal to myself because I did not want to upset my dad. I did not realize how much he himself had changed, as he demonstrated when I finally told him about my conversation with Eve's father. "It might have bothered me to hear that at the time," Dad acknowledged. "But it might have upset Mr. Moscicki too if he'd said those things directly to me. He was a very fine man, and it would probably have been uncomfortable for him to come right out and say, 'I know you're Jewish,' when these things aren't supposed to matter in America today. What he said was honest—not, 'I've never been prejudiced,' the way some people say that about blacks and you just know there's a 'but' coming up. He was saying he grew up with the prejudices of his time and place, and he's tried to overcome them. I could say that about myself. Except who I was prejudiced against was myself."

My nieces know much more about both sides of their family than I did when I was growing up. That is due, in considerable measure, to my sister-in-law, who is bilingual and was raised with an emphasis on cultural heritage far more characteristic of European than of Ameri-

can families. She was astonished by my brother's lack of interest in
our family's past, and she has transmitted her sense of the importance of history to her daughters. Anna has just turned ten, but Alex
was old enough when I began writing this book to be interested in
what I had learned about our family. It was one of the proudest
moments of my life when she read the first chapter in manuscript
and became caught up in my father's story. Almost as proud as the
moment when my brother phoned to tell me that Alex had been
selected to represent her school at the 1993 opening of the Holocaust Memorial Museum in Washington. If only both of her grandfathers had been alive! For my father, having a granddaughter who
did not regard him as a skeleton in the closet but as a precious part
of her heritage would have closed the circle. The man who feared to
tell his children that he was a Jew because they might blame him if
they didn't get everything they wanted in life has a granddaughter
who, as her Polish grandfather (for whom she was named) hoped, is
able to take pride in her entire ancestry.

MY JOURNEY would surely have been more complicated if I had had
my own children. While Jewishness is something else, and something
more, than a religion, the Jewish fundamentalists are right on one
point: the history of the Jews cannot be separated from the history
of Judaism as a faith. To understand what it means to be a Jew
today—or, in my case, to honor the Jewish part of me—it is impossible simply to ignore Judaism. And yet I would no more want a child
of mine to believe what is taught in Jewish day schools (or even in
the Sunday schools where the stern God of Israel becomes the cozy
figure in the song "There Is No God Like Our God") than I would
want them to believe in the Virgin Birth. Alex tells me I'm making
this all too complicated: kids have to be taught something, she
reminds me, and they can make up their own minds about what
they've been told as they learn to think for themselves. And she has
a point: I do not regret my Catholic education for a moment, because
it exposed me to a history and a theology I would not otherwise have

encountered. When I decided I did not believe in that system of thought, I abandoned the religion and kept the education. As a parent, though, I could hardly subject my children to indoctrination in what I believe to be falsehood. Yet if I had had children with a Jewish husband, I would have been strongly tempted to swallow my atheist principles and see that they received some sort of Jewish education. Oh yes, I can just hear myself explaining that Mommy doesn't really believe it was very nice of God to strike down the Egyptian first-born, and, to be perfectly honest, Mommy doesn't really believe that God exists, but darling, Mommy wants you to know where you come from. . . . The whole relationship between religion and cultural identity is so much more complicated for a Jew than for a Christian. One may be an ex-Catholic but never an ex-Jew; to be a Catholic or a Christian is purely a matter of belief, whether one is born to the faith or not. But it is impossible, as I believe my father came to realize, to abandon Jewishness along with the Jewish God.

That is why conversions to Christianity are generally perceived as a form of betrayal by secular as well as religious Jews. For a Jew, conversion is not simply a rejection of religion but a rejection of history that bears more of a resemblance to an African-American's passing for white than it does to any conversion from one Christian sect to another. I doubt that even my grandfather, so attuned to the slights he had experienced as a Jew and to the social advantages of being a Christian, would have sent "congratulations on your conversion" cards to his children. I have no doubt that the Christian parents of a child who converts to Judaism also feel a sense of loss, but betrayal may be experienced in its fullest sense only by those whose very existence is at stake (or who believe their existence to be at stake). The Jews for Jesus are wrong, and so was my aunt. You cannot be both a Christian and a Jew.

When I recently read the English translation of Victor Klemperer's diaries—he was one of a minuscule number of Jews who managed to survive the entire Nazi era within Germany—I bristled at his account of the polite treatment he received during a brief incarceration for violating blackout regulations in Dresden. The local jailers, who were not Gestapo but ordinary prison workers, treated Klemperer in kindly and respectful fashion, lending him a pair of glasses because his had been taken away. "Religion Mosaic?" they asked, preparing a document for the prisoner's signature. Klemperer, a convert whose father had been a rabbi, replied, "Protestant." Because Klemperer's identity card was stamped with the "J" required of all Jews, the workers were surprised at his declaration that he was a Christian. Their prisoner then explained that he was Jewish not by religion but "by [Nazi] law, by descent." In his diary, Klemperer notes that his jailers reacted with "even greater politeness than before."

Why does this passage bother me so much? It is not because Klemperer is reporting decent behavior on the part of some Germans during the Nazi era; it is well known that the few German Jews who escaped deportation to the death camps after 1942 (like the Jews who survived in Poland) did so because they were helped by gentiles. What is so unnerving, what makes the passage so insufferable to me, is the undertone of pride in Klemperer's description of having confounded his jailers by identifying himself as a Protestant. *That'll show 'em how idiotic those Nuremberg Laws are. I'm a Protestant, and still they stamp me with a J.*

I find that I cannot think about Jewish conversions to Christianity without being aware of an echo—an echo that seems to come simultaneously from a distant place and from deep within—of what my ancestors (those legendary rabbis) would surely have regarded as betrayal. Which is not to say that I wouldn't have converted, at various points in Jewish history, in an effort to save my own skin. But there is a difference between converting to preserve life (even if the lifesaving property turns out, as it so often has, to be illusory) and converting for social advantage—as Klemperer surely did long before the Nazi era, as many members of my father's family did for several generations. As my father himself did. That such conversions may involve a mixture of spiritual and temporal motives only means that the convert, like my father, has already been deprived of the spiritual sustenance offered both by religious Judaism and cultural Jewishness.

My problem with Victor Klemperer is the problem I had with my dad. Conversion could no more erase the "J" from my father's image of himself than it could render Klemperer impervious to the externally imposed "J" of the Nazis. I am no longer angry at my father—how could I be, with everything I now know about his upbringing?—but his story still engenders a deep sadness in me. I cannot see the family's determined abandonment of its Jewish past as anything but a loss, intertwined as it was with generations of shame and lies.

At the same time, I no longer experience the legacy of my ancestors' choices, the "special condition" of half-Jewishness, as a burden. While I will never know the consolations or the confinement of belonging to one tribe in which everyone knows who he is and what God expects him to do, I derive a sense of pleasure, excitement, and purpose from being both an outsider and an insider in not one but two cultures. America has allowed Jews unprecedented freedom to be simultaneously outsiders and insiders; to be an American half-Jew is to experience this condition twice over. Yes, if we are talking about Diaspora Jews, I insist on being included. The Jacoby family was mistaken not in its reach for a more expansive future but in its failure to honestly acknowledge the importance of the past. What does a half-Jew believe? "Anything she wants," I would now tell everyone who was aggravated by my *Present Tense* essay. There are worse, and certainly much less interesting, fates.

Yet I live with the certainty that something precious was lost along the way—lost by my father's family, lost to him, and lost to me. For much of his life, my dad lacked what the writer Adam Hochschild (also a half-Jew with a father who was extremely ambivalent about his origins) aptly describes, in his memoir *Half the Way Home*, as a sense of "possession as you possess your own past, which belongs to no one else, and whose power over you must be admitted, felt, accepted, before you can leave it behind and live the life before you."

Nevertheless, the older I become, the more I realize how right Katya was to tell her children that they couldn't write themselves out of Jewish history. My niece's interest in the Jewish part of her heritage is proof enough of the surprising ways in which the past makes itself felt in each generation. As the old Yiddish saying goes, "The heart is half a prophet." I have felt a deep obligation, as a half-Jew and my father's daughter, to reconstruct what could be reconstructed of the fragments the Jacoby family left behind, to leave a record for my nieces of how and why we came to be who we are. That has been my way of fulfilling Dad's wish that my identification with Jewishness amount to something more than "Holocaust, Holocaust, Holocaust."

XIII

Elegy

The place where I have not been
I never shall be.
The place where I have been
is as though I have never been there. People stray
far from the places where they were born
and far from the words which were spoken
as if by their mouths
and still wide of the promise
which they were promised.

And they eat standing and die sitting
and lying down they remember.
And what I shall never in the world return to
And look at, I am to love forever.
Only a stranger will return to my place. But I will set down
all these things once more, as Moses did,

after he smashed the first tablets.

—YEHUDA AMICHAI
"The Place Where I Have Not Been"
(Translated by Ted Hughes and Assia Gutmann)

I DO NOT HAVE TO look at my copy of this poem when I read it at my father's funeral in 1986, for I know the lines by heart. Many years ago, when I came across "The Place Where I Have Not Been" in a magazine, it instantly spoke to me not only of what had been lost but of what remained in the heart of a man who wanted to protect his children from the cries of "baby Jew-boy." I hope these lines, translated from the Hebrew, will honor the Jewishness in my father and his effort to come to terms, late in life, with all that caused him such unnecessary shame. For this funeral, I have my mother, and her increasingly antireligious tendencies, to thank. A priest presides—appropriately enough, since my father died a Catholic—but there is no Mass, and the service is held in a funeral home instead of a church. This infuriates Aunt Edith, but her meddlesome outrage is familiar and somehow comforting. I am relieved beyond measure at the nonecclesiastical tone of the proceedings. My brother and I do most of the talking, which is what Mom says our dad wanted. Rob is very funny; he describes our father's indifference to and ineptitude at the usual Michigan father-and-son activities—hunting, fishing, and camping. The people who knew Dad best laugh out loud at the image of him trying to stake down a tent in the woods. The interment takes place, thankfully, in an indoor mausoleum: two feet of snow have fallen on Lansing during the three days since my father's death. My mother, who hates nothing more than the Michigan winter, looks out the limousine window at the falling snow and whispers, "Fairyland." That does it. Here come the tears I did not shed while I was eulogizing Dad. He loved snow. When snow had fallen during the night, he would rush to the living room picture window, gaze with the wonder of a child at the white coating on the bare branches of our maple trees, and wake us up with the cry of "Fairyland." Lines from another Amichai poem flash through my mind: "Since then I love him even more. / And because of this / let him be woken up / gently and with love / on the Day of Resurrection."

The process of burial has become much more sanitized than it was only twenty years ago, when we buried Granny Jacoby. Then we stood by an actual hole in the ground, as people have for millennia, and saw the coffin being lowered. I have a sudden, mirth-filled memory of my father standing too close to the edge, losing his footing, and being rescued by Uncle Ozzie, who said, "Bobbie, Mother's being gone doesn't mean you have to plant one foot in the grave yourself." Now my father and my uncle are both gone. That expression, "he's gone," once sounded in my ears as a euphemism for death, like "passed away." Now it resonates within me as a literal description of both the physical and metaphysical realities. My dad is gone. Not here. He won't see his three-year-old granddaughter grow up. She'll never see him dancing by the light of the moon as he recites "The Owl and the Pussycat."

At the luncheon after the interment, I find out how much Dad was loved and cherished by his friends. It is no surprise to hear about his many small kindnesses—the jar of homemade (by him) gazpacho left for a neighbor whose wife was in the hospital; the sympathetic ear offered to an old friend whose husband had dumped her after thirty-five years of marriage; the breakfast visits, bringing doughnuts or muffins, to my aging Granny Broderick, who moved from Chicago after my grandfather's death to a small apartment near my parents. What does surprise me is that people valued my father most for the quality I respected most in him—his utter lack of hypocrisy. "You always knew where you stood with Bob," says our former next-door neighbor, who has driven hundreds of miles in a blizzard in order to attend the funeral. Then he surprises me by adding, "I think your father would have liked that poem you recited. You know, your dad told me you were looking into the Jewish side of your family, and that he was proud of you for doing that." I didn't know that my father had revealed his background to anyone outside the family, but now I realize that it has been many years since he last urged me to drop "this Jewish business." I hope this means that, by the end of Dad's life, at least one of the wounds of his upbringing had truly healed—insofar as healing is possible for any child raised to be ashamed of his lineage, his heritage, his flesh and blood.

. . .

I HOPE SO, but I do not know, for I was not truly present during the time of his dying. It all happened with such suddenness for a man who, at seventy-one, had looked and acted like a man in his fifties. I saw him healthy for the last time in the summer of 1985, on one of my regular trips to Michigan. He was swimming with his customary vigor in the pool of the apartment complex where he and my mother had lived since they sold their home—my childhood home—on Greenwood Drive. In October, I flew off to England on a rather cushy magazine assignment that enabled me to visit Disraeli's and Churchill's homes. In London, I made a point of stopping at Fortnum & Mason to order a special Christmas present for Dad—a package that included some of his favorite foods, including Scotch shortbread and canned clam chowder. Fresh clams, like most of the seafood Dad loved, were unavailable in Michigan, so he was always on the lookout for high-quality canned chowder. Since Dad was something of an Anglophile, I anticipated his delight at opening a package with a label from Fortnum & Mason, purveyors to Her Majesty. I did not know that by Christmas, my father would be so nauseated from chemotherapy that he would scarcely be able to stand the sight of food.

In November, Dad was diagnosed with lung cancer that had already metastasized to the bone. All those years of unfiltered Camels had caught up with him; he had managed to quit—too late—only in his mid-sixties. Surgery was pointless: Dad went into the hospital for a round of chemotherapy and then went home to die. He tried hard to put on a cheerful face at first, to insist that he was going to "beat this thing" in spite of the grim prognosis, but the family knew better. At the time, we were stunned and numbed by the suddenness of his decline—one day poised on the diving board, the next day gasping for breath. Coming from a family whose members generally lived active and healthy lives well into their eighties, I was unprepared at forty to face the death of a parent.

During those awful two months, my mother didn't seem to want any help from her children. I held this against her. My brother and I both flew home for brief visits, during which we felt like intruders, mere witnesses to our parents' last collaboration. Mom didn't even want us to come home for Christmas, because she said it would be too much of a burden, for her and my father, to celebrate a holiday when he had so little time left. *She wants him all to herself,* I thought resentfully. In an era when most people die in hospitals—regardless of their true desires—Mom enabled my father to die on his own terms, in his own bed. That he wasn't hooked up to machines or IV tubes was mostly her doing, with the help of a sympathetic family doctor who saw that Dad had all the morphine he needed to keep him comfortable. Now I think if my mother did want her husband all to herself, she was surely entitled. There aren't many people who have the fortitude to witness a partner's suffering and death, twenty-four hours a day, in their own home instead of at a sterile institutional remove. One of the last things my father said to my mother before he died was, "I could never have made it without you." Now I see clearly what I did not want to see then—that when a husband and wife are sharing the end of a long and complicated journey through life, children really *are* outsiders. Including Daddy's Little Girl.

In truth, nothing important was unsaid between my father and me by the end of his life. He still reproached himself for having spent too much time at work when Rob and I were growing up, and I assured him, when I saw him in January for the last time, that he had always been the most emotionally *present* father I knew. In my last image of him, he is sitting in the den, trying, crumb by crumb, to please me by forcing down a piece of shortbread.

IN 1972, during one of my summer visits, Dad asked if I would go with him to see the film version of *Fiddler on the Roof* at a local movie theater. I was touched by this suggestion, coming as it did only six years after I had brusquely pushed my father—forced him, really—

to admit that he was a Jew. He was trying to tell me that even if he was not entirely comfortable with his origins, or with my knowledge of those origins, he was not as uncomfortable as he had once been.

In spite of my father's propensity for weeping over everything from TV episodes of *Lassie* to Arthur Miller's *Death of a Salesman*, I was not prepared for his reaction to the immensely popular adaptation of Sholom Aleichem's tales of shtetl life. He cried through the wedding scene (all right, *everyone* gets misty over "Sunrise, Sunset"). He cried when the locals ruined Tevye's eldest daughter's wedding feast with a mini-pogrom; when Tevye's middle daughter went off to join her anticzarist revolutionary boyfriend in exile in Siberia; when the youngest daughter ran off and married a goy. He was crying, he whispered to the urgent shushes of the other moviegoers, because the scene reminded him of my first wedding, when I had been just nineteen years old. Did I remember? *Shush.* Oh yes, I certainly did remember that wedding. Dad, understandably unenthusiastic about his daughter's decision to marry before she finished college, had begged me to reconsider. He had initially assumed that I was pregnant, but he eventually decided, when my flat stomach throughout a six-month engagement attested to my nonpregnant state, that I was merely out of my mind. He had even tried to talk me out of going through with the wedding as we were about to walk down the aisle. In the movie theater, I responded to my father as I had years before in church—with the "Oh, *Daddy*" of an exasperated teenager.

After this detour down miserable memory lane, Dad refocused his attention on Tevye's travails and cried hardest of all at the ending, in which all of the Jews are expelled from their shtetl by edict of Czar Nicholas II. "There's nothing to cry about," I said reasonably as we left the movie house. "It's a happy ending. Tevye is going to America. He's not going to be around for World War I, and his family isn't going to be around to be killed by the Nazis during World War II." Wiping his eyes, Dad replied, "I'm crying because those are my roots, and I don't know anything about them." In 1972, people did not go around talking about their "roots." For my father, who had never expressed even a casual interest in his family's past, the reference was extraordinary. "What do you mean, your roots?" I asked. At that point, I was under the mistaken impression that both the Sondheim and Jacoby families had lived in Germany for generations before emigrating in 1849. Dad told me he was sure the Jacobys had originally come from Poland, or even farther east, because his mother—whose family *was* established in Frankfurt by the middle of the eighteenth century—had always made a point of disparaging his father's Polish origins. This was one of my first clues to the Jacoby family's real history.

On one level, my father's reaction to *Fiddler* was no more than the characteristically sentimental response of a sentimental man. In this, he was no different from the millions of unashamedly Jewish Jews who flocked to the play and the movie in order to enjoy a prettied-up glimpse of the past that preceded the American Jewish success story—or, for that matter, from the gentiles who also laughed, cried, and went away with the same message—"Boy, are we all lucky to be here and not there."

But my father's tears had a deeper meaning, revealing a yearning for the full self-acceptance that he could never attain as long as he was still ashamed of being a Jew. By the end of his life, my dad did succeed in transcending the legacy of parents who, in different ways, had failed to give him a sense of his true worth. A significant part of that parental legacy was Dad's denial of the Jew in him. He—and we—had come a long way since the day when he cried in the kitchen out of fear that his daughter might blame him for having been born a Jew.

I am a half-Jew, American born.

My Jewish father is gone.

INDEX

SUSAN JACOBY began her writing career as a reporter for *The Washington Post*. She is the author of numerous articles and books on such diverse subjects as the civil rights movement, women's health, Russian society, aging in America, and the relationship between justice and revenge in Western culture. *Wild Justice: The Evolution of Revenge* was a *New York Times* Notable Book of the Year and a finalist for the Pulitzer Prize in nonfiction. Ms. Jacoby is also the author of a collection of essays on women entitled *The Possible She*, many of which have been reprinted in anthologies. The author's articles, essays, and reviews have appeared in *The New York Times*, *The Washington Post*, *Newsday*, *Harper's*, *Glamour*, and *The New Republic*. Susan Jacoby lives in New York City.